LANGUAGE AS HERMENEUTIC

More Walter J. Ong titles available from Cornell University Press:

Interfaces of the Word: Studies in the Evolution of Consciousness and Culture
$32.95 paperback | ISBN 978-0-8014-9240-2

Fighting for Life: Contest, Sexuality, and Consciousness
$26.95 paperback | ISBN 978-0-8014-7845-1

Rhetoric, Romance, and Technology: Studies in the Interaction of Expression and Culture
$29.95 paperback | ISBN 978-0-8014-7847-5

Receive 30 percent off the retail price when you enter code 09ONG on orders placed at cornellpress.cornell.edu.

Available wherever fine books are sold.
Prices subject to change without notice.

LANGUAGE AS HERMENEUTIC

A Primer on the Word and Digitization

WALTER J. ONG

EDITED AND WITH COMMENTARIES
BY THOMAS D. ZLATIC AND
SARA VAN DEN BERG

CORNELL UNIVERSITY PRESS
ITHACA AND LONDON

First published 2017 by Cornell University Press

Printed in the United States of America

Library of Congress Cataloging-in-Publication Data

Names: Ong, Walter J., author. | Zlatic, Thomas D., editor, writer of added commentary. | Van den Berg, Sara J., editor, writer of introduction.
Title: Language as hermeneutic : a primer on the word and digitization / Walter J. Ong ; edited and with commentaries by Thomas D. Zlatic and Sara van den Berg.
Description: Ithaca : Cornell University Press, 2017. | Includes bibliographical references and index.
Identifiers: LCCN 2017027640 (print) | LCCN 2017032360 (ebook) | ISBN 9781501714498 (epub/mobi) | ISBN 9781501714504 (pdf) | ISBN 9781501714481 | ISBN 9781501714481 (cloth : alk. paper) | ISBN 9781501712043 (pbk. : alk. paper)
Subjects: LCSH: Communication and technology. | Language and languages—Technological innovations. | Writing—Technological innovations. | Digital communications. | Hermeneutics.
Classification: LCC P96.T42 (ebook) | LCC P96.T42 O54 2017 (print) | DDC 401—dc23
LC record available at https://lccn.loc.gov/2017027640

CONTENTS

PREFACE

Upon his death in 2003, Walter J. Ong S.J. left unpublished a mostly completed manuscript that he had worked on from 1987 to 1994: *Language as Hermeneutic: A Primer on the Word and Digitization*. This manuscript was his last book-length project. We offer it here in the hope that it will serve both the general reader and the scholar already familiar with Ong's work. To this end, we have provided a context that includes explanatory materials on the life and work of Walter Ong. Our goal is to show the continuing relevance of his multidisciplinary studies in language and culture for further research along these lines.

In the introduction, Sara van den Berg provides an overview and assessment of Ong's thought in relation to *Language as Hermeneutic*. The editors then present the reconstructed text of the manuscript, which consists of a prologue, eleven chapters, and an epilogue. The next two parts of the volume describe the reconstruction of the text and contextualize its themes in relation to other works by Walter Ong. In "*Language as Hermeneutic*: The Evolution of the Idea and the Text," Thomas Zlatic traces the decade-long development of the manuscript, and describes the editorial principles and methods used to shape the text for publication here. In the second explanatory chapter, "*Language as Hermeneutic*: An Unresolved Chord," Zlatic demonstrates that the book is a synthesis of sixty years of Ong's publications.

Language as Hermeneutic was not Ong's last important piece of writing. In the final years of his life, he wrote a number of significant articles, some of which were derived from this manuscript. One paragraph in the tenth chapter of *Language as Hermeneutic* generated a substantial unpublished essay, "Time, Digitization, and Dalí's Memory," which was found among Fr. Ong's papers. This essay expands on the dialectic between digitization and hermeneutic, and is included in this volume as an appendix. That essay is accompanied by a previously published article by Thomas Zlatic explaining the circumstances of Ong's Dalí essay and suggesting its resonance for *Language as Hermeneutic*.

Walter J. Ong's archives, including the four iterations of *Language as Hermeneutic*, are housed in the Archives at the Pius XII Memorial Library of Saint Louis University. The reconstruction of the text for publication was possible only because Ong kept complete, detailed, and carefully organized (though somewhat idiosyncratic) records of his scholarship, teaching, and correspondence. The librarians at Saint Louis University have described him as "an archivist's dream." We came to regard him as an editor's dream as well.

The Archives at the Saint Louis University Library will continue to be of great help to future scholars. The manuscripts of *Language as Hermeneutic*, Fr. Ong's notes and papers, and his extensive correspondence are readily available. Much of this material is now online as the Walter Ong Digital Collection, but researchers are also invited to consult the original materials in the Walter J. Ong Manuscript Collection.

We thank Douglas Mercouillier, S.J., former provincial of the US Jesuits Missouri Province, for initial permission to undertake this project; Ronald Mercier, S.J., provincial of the US Jesuits Central and Southern Province, for reaffirming permission; and David Cassen, director of the Saint Louis University Libraries, for permission to publish these texts from the Walter J. Ong Archive. We are grateful to John Padberg, S.J., for arranging the deposit of the archive in Pius XII Memorial Library Special Collections. Gregory Pass, head of Special Collections, and Jonathan Sawday, Ong

Chair in the Humanities at Saint Louis University, gave helpful advice at the beginning of this project. John Walter, as a graduate fellow of the Walter J. Ong Center, did much of the early work to survey and catalog materials in the archive. Former archivist John Waide has been a faithful steward and expert advocate. He and his successor, Timothy Achee, gave us extraordinary help in identifying and locating documents. Paul Soukup, S.J., granted Thomas Zlatic permission to republish "The Persistence of Memory: Picturing Ong's Oral Hermeneutics," *Communication Research Trends* 33.1 (2014): 10–15. Thomas Zlatic thanks James Braun for his tireless service and technological expertise in helping to organize archival materials electronically. Sara van den Berg also thanks Paul Soukup for granting permission to include portions of "Current Opportunities in Ong Scholarship," which was originally published in *Communication Research Trends* 33.2 (2014): 4–9.

The editors dedicate this book to the late Thomas M. Walsh, who was a student and colleague of Fr. Ong for many years, and who would have wanted to include this volume in his definitive bibliography of Fr. Ong's publications.

LANGUAGE AS HERMENEUTIC

Introduction

Sara van den Berg

Language in all its modes—oral, written, print, electronic—claims the central role in Walter J. Ong's speculations on human culture. His provocative work was honored by his scholarly peers, by the American and French governments, and by readers who came to know his writings not only in English but also through translations into many languages, including Polish and Japanese. He spent his career in St. Louis, and traveled throughout the world to lecture, to conduct research, and to meet with other leading intellectuals (Farrell, *Walter Ong's Contributions*). In the final years of his life, Ong paid special attention to the new electronic culture that now dominates the globe. He himself deserves special attention for his prescient comments and the challenges he saw for our future.

After his death, his archives were found to contain four versions of a book manuscript, *Language as Hermeneutic: A Primer on the Digitization of the Word*. The last version was dated 1994. The edition presented here consolidates all four versions into a single text. Ong had envisioned his book as an overview of his work, but *Language as Hermeneutic* developed a new argument of its own, centered on issues of cognition, interpretation, and language in our era of new electronic media. Digitization and language had existed since ancient times, but their relationship changed in the age of new media. Digitization, the dichotomous organization of knowledge and thought, "matured" into computerization; language could interpret the resultant cultural changes. Ong set forth several principles basic to his understanding of interpretation: all meaning is negotiated between people; all language is hermeneutic; and digital technologies evoke interpretation as a corrective to the apparent totalizing of information that the dichotomous structure of digitization conveys. Digitization, he argues, is a closed system; language is an open system. That open system of reflection and interpretation can destabilize digital formulations and thereby make change possible.

Walter Ong offered his first noteworthy comments on electronic communication and culture in his widely read book, *Orality and Literacy* (1982), in which he traced the changes in consciousness that characterize shifts from oral to chirographic to print to electronic culture. Each of these stages enabled and sustained a distinctive habit of mind. During the next twenty-five years, he often returned to his ideas about electronic culture and interpretation, especially the interpretive mode he called *hermeneutic*. Although digital thinking precedes electronic media, these media depend on digital structure and form. At first, Ong did not make much distinction between the different forms of media from radio and television to new media, regarding them as products of "electronic" culture. In *The Presence of the Word* (1967), he commented on "the shape which electronics and sound give to social organization and to human life generally" (89).

Twenty-eight years later, in "Hermeneutic Forever: Voice, Text, Digitization, and the 'I,'" Ong concisely stated the argument in *Language as Hermeneutic*. Walter Ong was especially concerned with the impact of the computer on interpretation:

> With electronics, and particularly the computer, hermeneutics entered a more intensely reflective stage than ever before, as greater and greater stores of information can be dealt with by means of more and more potent technological aids to interpretation. (Ong 1995, 12)

Ong defined *hermeneutics* as "systematized or methodized interpretation, felt as different from the text on which it operates, even if the hermeneutic emerges as itself a text." He regarded hermeneutics as "explicit reflection about the interpretive process itself." In short, "Hermeneutics is interpretation grown self-conscious" (Ong 1995, 13). In order to cope with the new dominance of digitization, Ong argued, the traditional use of textual models in hermeneutics should be supplemented with models based on oral-aural discourse. He suggested that an "oral hermeneutic" was needed to interpret language in its fullness, beyond what could be captured in text.

Ong developed his new hermeneutic out of his formulation of "secondary orality," not as a return to the first form of oral communication but as a later stage that relied on literacy to craft orality in electronic communication. In a lecture at the Aquinas Institute in St. Louis, he made the following observation: "Secondary orality (radio and television): floods the world with sounded words. . . . But it is the product of a writing and print culture" (Ong 1994). "Secondary orality" has proved to be one of Walter Ong's most provocative ideas. He coined the term to name the transmission of speech in electronic media; this moreover, secondary version of orality depends on the underlying resources of literacy. For example, a person watching television or YouTube may see and hear someone "speaking," but that speech is an electronic equivalent of speech. Someone who is barely literate may constantly and comfortably use a cellphone for "oral" communication—or a "smartphone" for many other purposes—but that communication is made possible only by the literate culture that developed the telephonic system.

Ong's formulation reflected his appreciation for the complexity of culture. He was not a primitivist who celebrated oral cultures or idealized the "residual orality" in literate culture, nor did he posit a linear idea of cultural "progress." Instead, he sought to understand how different modes of language coexist in the palimpsest of modern culture. Ong neither privileged orality nor rejected electronic media, but sought to explain the multiple consequences of cultural change. He regarded different modes of transmitting thought as the key to change in consciousness as well as in culture. For that reason, he sought to articulate the difference between language and digitization, even as he often framed his own language in the dichotomous mode of digitization. If digital formulations set up a closed system, mapping a totality by identifying its divisions, language challenges and undoes what would seem to be definitive divisions: "As hermeneutic, language seeks ultimately not to divide but to integrate." He offers this bedrock principle of language as hermeneutic: "Everything is related to everything else" (16).

Fr. Ong's reflections on electronic culture will be of special importance to those who are familiar with his earlier cultural analyses and to anyone interested in language and digitization as competing modes of organizing expression and knowledge. The argument of his book also suggests the continuing relevance of his work, not only for those interested in the history of communication, culture, and consciousness, but also for those exploring current and future problems and possibilities for the interpersonal and ethical uses of new technologies.

Fr. Ong first gained prominence with the publication of *Ramus, Method, and the Decay of Dialogue* (1958) and its companion volume, the *Ramus Talon Inventory*. Peter Ramus, a sixteenth-century French pedagogue, challenged the Thomistic logic that dominated educational practice. That logic rested on the resources of language. The new logic of Ramus emphasized dichotomous formulations based on mathematics rather than language. According to Ramus and his followers, all thought could be formulated using this new method. Ong was critical of Ramus, but acknowledged the profound intellectual influence of Ramism and linked it to the new technology of print. Print enhanced the spread of literacy and introduced a new mode of cultural thought that was less dependent on oral formula, repetition, and community. Moreover, it enabled singularity, interiority, and multiple modes of presenting an argument in the visual space of the printed page. Despite these important psychic and cultural gains, the Ramist valorization of visualist and spatial paradigms for knowledge led to a reduction of being to idea; meaning was considered only in terms of the concept, not the existential reality in which the utterance was made. Ong's lifelong project was to correct what he regarded as a fundamental error.

Paradoxically, that reduction led to an expansion as well. Ong's first meditation on modern technology emphasized the transmission of speech and writing by the telephone and the telegraph. One of the final essays in *Rhetoric, Romance, and Technology* (1971) evaluates the way new technologies erase the constraints that time and space traditionally placed on communication. Knowledge, moreover, would no longer be stored and retrieved by personal memory but by machines. As Ong remarks, "Our most sophisticated knowledge storing and retrieving tool is the computer, essentially a visual device" (296).

Orality and Literacy (1982) put forward Ong's comments on electronic culture. Writing restructures consciousness, as the title of the fourth chapter famously declared, and he argued that new mode of communication also altered the way people think and live. In the preface to the 1983 edition of *Ramus, Method, and the Decay of Dialogue*, Ong explicitly linked the dichotomizing method of Ramus to computer technology:

> Were I to do this again, I know there are many things that would need reconsideration and revised assessment. One connection that would have to be brought out would be the resemblance of Ramus' binary dichotomized charts . . . to digital computer programs. Like computer programs, the Ramist dichotomies were designed to be heuristic. . . . The quantifying drives inherited from medieval logic were producing computer programs in Ramus' active mind some four hundred years before the computer itself came into being. (viii.n)

The computer may have altered consciousness, but the continuous presence of binary thought and of language as the opposite mode of interpretation dates back to Ramus and even earlier. The relative cultural force of each term and the awareness of new possibilities for digitization provide opportunities to create an integrative foundation for cultural change. Ong argued that hermeneutic, the language of interpretation, made change possible by integrating elements that digitization divided and by bringing together old and new modes of cultural communication.

The computer revolution has transformed culture worldwide since the 1980s, changing both public and private life. Ong's work coincided with the appearance of personal computers, some of them almost forgotten: the Commodore, the Compaq, the Kaypro, and the Apple. The Apple II was distributed to schools, and applications were soon developed to take advantage of digital computing. Business and the professions were not far behind. Virtually every business and many individual people, now called "users," have their own websites. We have access to massive amounts of information, and interpretation in the digital humanities has shifted away from the singular person, object, or event in favor of analyzing "big data." This shift paradoxically coexists with the apparent power of the individual user. People use personal computers for social exchange, personal expression, information storage, shopping, and access to information.

Walter Ong's comments emphasize the individual person in relationship with others. At the same time that a single person's "voice" can go viral and have an enormous impact, the anonymity and scale of big data can absorb and override the voice of the single interpreter. Because we are awash in information, Ong asserts, we need a corresponding hermeneutic language to unify it for ourselves, to turn data into knowledge, and to maintain the centrality of the individual voice.

The cultural changes observed by Walter Ong go beyond the efficiencies and social transformations of electronic culture. Distance, time, memory, privacy, and truth are only a few of the assumptions that have been challenged or transformed by the immediacy and scope of electronic technology. As Philip Leith observes, following Ong, digital programming alters consciousness: "we will not look too closely at 'information' since it will seem unproblematic to us. Indeed, we do see information as unproblematic, due in large part, to the way that computers have changed our perspective" (1990, 162).

Although Walter Ong wrote before the advent of big data, his work offers an important alternative to its dominance. The role of big data has grown to mean far more than increased storage of information. Big data can absorb individual voices, so much so that the self, the interpreter, may seem vulnerable, even lost. Big data compilers gather information an individual user seeks or provides, and can bundle together groups of users to discover commercial or even ideological patterns. The compilation of big data makes possible new kinds of interpretation and research on a vast scale, but we recognize the need to debate the challenges to privacy, ethics, and security posed by surveillance over space and time.

Those challenges often seem to be outweighed by our hunger for information. The memory stored in the machine relieves us of the need to use our own memories as our primary repository of information. We seek computers that have more and more "memory," an ever greater capacity to store information not only on a "hard drive" but also beyond material structures in "the cloud." Unlike human memory, that storage is flat, without affect or nuance. Researchers at the MIT Media Lab, led by Rosalind Picard, seek ways to incorporate affect into computing, to balance emotion and cognition, and to develop technologies that can recognize, generate, or respond to emotion (Picard,1997). Other scholars have turned to affect as a major element of language (Besnier), most recently in relation to the neuroscience of the brain (Leys). As a vehicle for expression, language permits affect, nuance, and interpretation. The resources of language (including rhythm, qualitative and quantitative emphasis, tonal registers, linguistic differences, grammar and syntax, punctuation) and its social context can also be considered restraints. Language provides a way not only to categorize but also to interpret information, to develop novel ideas, and to critique established concepts.

Two years after the fourth draft of *Language as Hermeneutic*, Walter Ong published "Information and/or Communication: Interactions" (Ong 1996). That essay presents hermeneutics and digitization not merely as oppositional but as interrelated modes of expression. He also moved beyond a discussion of the electronic age to introduce speculations on our new age of genetics. He understood the genetic code as "information" without language; that is to say, that code does not transmit thoughts or symbols. Since then, we have come to realize that the genetic code expresses and forms the living body of the person, who has the capacity to develop and use language; and language is the vehicle for "much more than simple diffusion of units of information" (1996, 507). Ong believed that contemporary information systems, whether electronic or genetic, have "overwhelmed our human lifeworld" (514). Although "big data" lay in the future, he asserted the importance of the individual person, the interpreter, and the need for "intimacy" (515). He called for a new rhetoric, a new language of interpretation, to meet that need. He anticipated the current resurgence of ideas about language and its effects, and the theoretical turn away from the impersonal mode of knowing that digitization seems to assume in favor of affect as the response to information and as the driving force for interpretation, intimacy, and relationship. Although scientists struggle to develop computers that can reflect and interpret, the human interpreter continues to be crucial as we seek to understand what we do, how we feel, and who we are.

Language as Hermeneutic does not reject or condemn digital technology. Ong valued that technology, but regarded hermeneutic as its necessary complement. This book, and his final essays, document Ong's intellectual engagement with the problem of language as a vehicle for interpretation in our electronic and genetic postdigital age. He calls for a balance and interaction of hermeneutic and digitization, and he insists that both require examination. For Ong, the dichotomous formulations of the digital mode are the beginning, not the end, of inquiry. Even the nonverbal digital dichotomies of computer language and DNA require the hermeneutic of verbal or alphabetic language. As computing grows ever greater in speed and scale, as the chip is replaced by the quark and even by the human cell, and as the human body itself comes to be regarded as the expression of genetic information, we have an ever greater need for interpretation and for language. "Everything is related to everything else" was, for Walter Ong, the principle of hermeneutics. Digitization endures, most obviously in the very structure of DNA, yet it is through language that we comprehend relationships. That need for relationship, and relationship itself, Walter Ong honored as a mystery. In 1998, he questioned any rigid dichotomization of hermeneutic language and digitization in his extended review of Denise Schmandt-Besserat's *Before Writing* (Ong 1998). He suggested that a commonality binds together all forms of information: "The way into writing remains, psychologically and sociologically, somewhat mysterious. At the heart of the mystery is the role that digitation, now matured in the computer, played in the ways human beings stumbled into writing in the first place" (548). Late in his life, Ong remained eager to engage new information about "information," to speculate on what was changing in culture and what remained constant. That engagement permeates *Language as Hermeneutic*. His intellectual commitment to the interpreting self, more than to specific insights and ideas, is the continuing legacy of Walter Ong.

PART I

Language as Hermeneutic

A Primer on the Word and Digitization

Walter J. Ong

Prologue

Total verbal explicitness is impossible.

Language, Hermeneutics, and Digitization

A thesis of these reflections is that there are two encompassing and complementary movements significantly dominating the development of world culture today, digitization and hermeneutics—which is to say (as will be explained more fully throughout the work)—a fractioning movement and a holistic movement, and that these movements explain something of what has been going on in the development of human beings' intellectual relationship and concomitant relationships to the world around them, chiefly in highly technologized societies but indirectly through all the world.

Everyone is aware of how deeply digitization influences modes of thought and action in our electronic world, most pervasively through the use of the digital computer. Digitization refers to division into numerically distinct units and to operations carried on by means of such units. Digitization proceeds always by division into distinct units, and thus is based on fractioning, although the digital units can be made so exquisitely tiny that results appear not fractioned at all but virtually continuous, and are indeed capable of reproducing what is continuous more accurately than nondigitized reproduction can manage. No matter what wonderful unities digitization can effect, it effects unity only by making division so minuscule that, humanly speaking, it leaves in effect no trace of its divisiveness.

But in our present culture, there is another development, less widely known and very little reflected on, that relates to digitization, namely hermeneutics (or hermeneutic—the plural and the singular can often be used interchangeably). "Hermeneutics" is the Greek-based English word corresponding pretty closely to the Latin-based English word "interpretation." Both words refer to explanation. But "hermeneutics" (or "hermeneutic") usually refers to intensive, scholarly, more or less systematized verbal interpretation (as against dramatic or other interpretation) of textual material. Hermeneutics is interpretation grown self-conscious. In its intensified form, it can become a hermeneutic of suspicion, based on the presumption that the text is saying something other than, or even contradictory to, what it seems at first blush to be saying. As will be seen, the growth of hermeneutics or interpretation is a function of the growth of information in world cultures—most spectacularly in high-technology cultures, but to some extent in all the cultures of the world.

In the past couple of centuries—roughly, since the Enlightenment—hermeneutics, labeled as such and thought of as learned and more or less systematic explanation, first made its way into Western thought as referring to the interpretation of biblical texts. But today it is growing beyond all bounds, enveloping innumerable subjects in academia (as it will, more and more, in the rest of the world). In a university library with only one-third of its holdings thus far in its computerized catalog, in this computerized catalogue under the subject heading of "hermeneutics" I find listings of "literary hermeneutics," "hermeneutics and analysis," "science, hermeneutics and praxis," "Buddhist hermeneutics," "hermeneutics as method, philosophy, and critique," "context and hermeneutics," "hermeneutics, tradition, and reason," "hermeneutics and deconstruction," "hermeneutics and social science," "hermeneutics as politics," "hermeneutics of postmodernity," "hermeneutics of postmodernism," "hermeneutics of intimacy," "hermeneutics versus science" (sometimes hermeneutics is opposed to science, sometimes allied with science, sometimes used to explain science), "the hermeneutics of the subject," "postmodern literary hermeneutics," "religions, literature, and hermeneutics," "feminist hermeneutics," "phenomenological hermeneutics," "philosophical hermeneutics" (is hermeneutics allied with philosophy, opposed to philosophy, interwoven with philosophy?), "transcendence and hermeneutics," "T. S. Eliot and hermeneutics," "Yeats's autobiography and hermeneutics," "energetics and hermeneutics," "hermeneutics and critical theory," "Jung's challenge to biblical hermeneutics," "hermeneutics and personal structure of language," "hermeneutics and poetizing," and so on.

Let us forget hermeneutics for the moment and turn to the more commonplace concept of interpretation. There is no end to interpretation. In its quite ordinary and simple sense, to interpret means to bring out what is concealed in a given manifestation, that is, in a given phenomenon or state of affairs providing information. We can interpret not only verbalized expression, but anything that provides information: a sunset, a roll of thunder, a gesture, a person's attitude shown in various ways, an utterance. We do not interpret what is unconcealed or evident in a manifestation, only what is concealed. And something is always concealed. For no manifestation reveals everything, and interpretation, no matter how carefully formulated, can never be total in its verbal formulation. In context, verbalization can achieve truth, but the context is never totally verbalized (see Tyler, *The Said and the Unsaid*) so that it thus both reveals and conceals, as we shall see, and hence calls for further interpretation. Heidegger's *aletheia* or "disclosure" is never complete in words alone, as is clear in the ongoing discussion of what Heidegger's full meaning of *aletheia* was—one can always ask one more question to disclose more. Interpretation itself is a manifestation, and interpretation both reveals and conceals, and hence calls for further interpretation as occasion demands. The definition and discussion of interpretation just provided here itself calls for interpretation.

Interpretation floods present-day consciousness, most notably in high-technology cultures but to a degree everywhere. The vast float of printed and electronically processed and delivered information that chokes our mailboxes, our radios and television sets, and our minds has provided more than good reason to style world culture today an information culture. In our electronic age, information thrusts itself upon us all day long via radio and television as well as telephone and print and other communication devices in such quantity that we cannot absorb any but a tiny fraction of what we are wallowing in. Speaking recently to a person with a position in one of our largest copying machine companies, I ventured to estimate that not one tenth of the photocopied pages in the United States was ever even glanced over by any human being. The copying machine company representative did not need to stop for any reflection at all but shot back immediately and with utter confidence, "That is far too high an estimate." But we need the choking float of information, he maintained: "The question is whether you want to do something or nothing." We all know that the more efficient systems often if not always operate with a huge amount of waste: of the millions or billions of acorns dropped from the oaks in Missouri, how many grow into trees? Very few do or ever did. But there are still a lot of oaks in Missouri.

Much of what we think of at first blush as "information" contains a lot of interpretation or explanation. Not only the editorial pages of our newspapers but also the news columns deliver an interpretation of the news, not only by evaluating one item as newsworthy and publishable and another not so, but also by the tone or slant they give to the information they deliver. This slant is not necessarily despicable, for one or another slant is inevitable—there has never been an ahistorical reporter without an inevitably historical point of view, although the slant given can be despicable or outright dishonest and false. Newspapers are more interpretive today than they used to be. A strange memory here haunts me. When I was in college in the early 1930s, I recall distinctly an observation of one of the speakers at the annual Missouri College Newspaper Association meeting at the University of Missouri at Columbia (where the first course in the world in journalism had been given in 1879–84). This speaker stated that in the future news stories as such in United States newspapers would become more interpretive than they were at the time (the early 1930s). How the speaker was able to make this prophecy still puzzles me and fills me with awe. But you have only to compare newspapers from his day with those of our day now to see how right he was. The increase of information has made us not more interested in simple "facts" (more about "facts" later) but in understanding the "facts"—which means interpretation. By the same token that it is an information age, our age is an interpretation age.

Language as Hermeneutic

Interpretation can apply to any sort of thing and it can be realized in all sorts of ways, verbal or nonverbal—raised eyebrows, a gesture, a refusal of a proffered gift, a knowing grin. One can interpret a nonverbal situation or a verbal remark by a wordless mime. Yet words have special relevance to interpretation. Verbal interpretation always involves more than words, as thinking and words themselves always do, yet, like much human communication activity, interpretation reaches a certain special focus in verbal explanation, in words formulated either externally for others or internally for oneself.

As infants, our first appropriation of language as language is an encounter with language as interpretation. The acquisition of a first word or clusters of words interprets, brings out what was previously concealed—but not concealed in words the infant has possession of, for being an infant means precisely being without words (*infant* is the anglicization of the Latin *infans*, from *in-*, *not*, and *fans*, *fantis*, present participle of *fari*, *to speak*). *Infant* thus means precisely a nonspeaker, someone not yet familiar with any words. The first word or words of an infant must thus be an interpretation of the nonverbal context, in William James's well-known description, "the big, blooming, buzzing confusion" in which the infant is embedded. An infant's acquisition of language comes about in a context of all kinds of other activities and awarenesses. First words are overburdened with context, out of which their meanings have to be carved. And context is never fully escaped from. Another way to note this is to say that total verbal explicitness is impossible. Words always exist in a context which at some point or points includes the nonverbalized.

Interpretation not only is implemented by verbalization, verbal explanation, but also tends to be called for by verbal utterance more readily than by other matters. Paradoxically, verbal utterance often cries for interpretation more than do other phenomena because verbalization is fundamentally interaction between persons who can constantly look for verbal or other explanation or clarification from one another and because the interpretation provided from either side is never totally conclusive in every way. For practical purposes, persons can and do bring explanation to an end and arrive at a truth adequate for the current situation, but there always remains more that could be asked and responded to if one wanted to go further. In this sense, verbalization is always a kind of unfinished business. The meeting of minds, the understanding, in a given situation involves not only words but also the nonverbal existential context, which could be subject to further verbalization.

The reflections in the present work, however, focus basically on verbal interpretation and often, though not exclusively, on verbal interpretation of verbal utterance—which does, of course, always have a nonverbal context, with which we may at times be concerned. But, unless otherwise specified, these reflections focus primarily, then, on verbalized interpretation of verbalized expression.

The Greek-based term "hermeneutics" or "hermeneutic" commonly means much the same as "interpretation," namely explanation, the bringing out of what is concealed in a given state of affairs. But it more commonly refers more explicitly to verbalized interpretation of verbal texts rather than of oral utterance or other phenomena. And hermeneutics commonly refers to such verbalized interpretation which proceeds on more or less formalized methodological principles, as in interpreting the Bible. Hermeneutics is interpretation (in the sense of verbalized explanation) grown self-conscious. But, as Gadamer has so thoroughly shown in his *Truth and Method* (see also Neil Gilbert, *Renaissance Concepts of Method*), the concept of formalized methodology is not entirely clear-cut. The terms "interpretation" and "hermeneutics" can never be totally "scientific." Moreover, other extensions of hermeneutics to nonverbal aesthetic material, such as Gadamer discusses, are not to be denied. But they are not our chief focus here. As with interpretation, our chief concern here with hermeneutic or hermeneutics focuses on verbalized explanation of verbal expression, often, but not always, verbal expression in textual form.

However, with allowance, where called for, of the tendency of "hermeneutic" or "hermeneutics" to refer to interpretation of texts, the terms will often be used here in the more general sense as synonymous with "interpretation," in a way in which they are commonly used today and a way which context should make clear.

All sorts of special hermeneutics, or more or less methodical interpretive procedures and theories, have been developed for different sorts of texts—literary, poetic, political, religious, philosophical, scientific, and so on. Elaborate, often deeply insightful procedures for textual hermeneutics have been devised, notably by theologians such as Friedrich Schleier-macher, Rudolph Bultmann, and Jürgen Moltmann, by philosophers such as Wilhelm Dilthey, Ludwig Wittgenstein, Edmund Husserl, Martin Heidegger, Hans-Georg Gadamer, and Paul Ricoeur, and by hosts of literary commentators, from the Formalists and the New Critics through the Deconstructionists.

A literature is developing that shows how radically the recent growth of hermeneutics as a special verbal activity separate from other verbal activities depends on writing. Gadamer views formal study of hermeneutics as having been first rooted in the study of texts (*Truth and Method*, 353). The reason for this, to be discussed in detail later, is that writing provides a visually (and tactilely) fixed set of words to which one can address other words as though the textualized words were somehow things, coming out of the past and set off from the movement of living discourse. Such a scenario is quite impossible to imagine in primary oral cultures (cultures with no acquaintanceship with writing at all or of its possibility).

The text as such seems to be constituted as separate from oral discourse, is given a special status, by the introduction of a technology, writing, which produces a seemingly separate and totally fixed, controllable "object," visual and tactile. On this object, the activity of hermeneutics or interpretation seemingly can be carried on more effectively than on spoken words. However, in ancient Greece of Socrates' day and later, literate but with a high degree of residual orality, *hermeneia* did not yet have this explicit textual focus but applied equally to spoken words. Paradoxically, of course, interpretation, too, can be and often is ultimately put down—in several senses of this expression—in a text.

This work consists of reflections on interpretation or hermeneutics rather than of exhaustive analyses. It concerns matters treated in various other ways by persons in many active, and indeed often very fashionable, fields today, literary, linguistic, philosophical, and other. These reflections in many ways cross through works on intellectual and cultural history and the history of consciousness, through phenomenology, structuralism, deconstructionism and anti-deconstructionism, speech-act theory, reader-response criticism, through a bit of existentialism, and through the vast hermeneutic tradition in philosophy (and sometimes theology) stemming from Schleiermacher, Dilthey, Husserl, Heidegger, and others into Gadamer's masterful *Truth and Method*, as well as through Ricoeur's work and that of others which focuses many philosophical questions quite explicitly around questions of language.

However, the present reflections do not derive primarily from any of these traditions. Rather, they have been generated more specifically out of concern, spanning the past thirty-five years and more, with the evolution of verbal communication and the gradual but inexorable transformation of verbal expression and of thought from the original spoken word through the technologies of writing, print, and electronics. Hermeneutics or interpretation will differ of course from culture to culture. These reflections are centered on the cultures of the West.

The reflections here presented are, I hope, in many ways closer to readily accessible common experience and common knowledge than are the lengthy formal philosophical traditions concerned with hermeneutics or interpretation and the many other formal and complex linguistic and literary and philosophical traditions mentioned above with which the reflections intersect and interweave and to which they are obviously indebted. Some of the reflections may be commonplace, but in settings, one can hope, which make them less so than they would otherwise be. Some connections with other lines of thought will of course be made explicit, but not all, if only because, as these reflections often bring out, although we should normally strive for all the explicitness a given situation calls for, total explicitness is impossible.

The overall thesis of these reflections is that all use of language from the very beginning is interpretation or hermeneutic. A subsidiary, but still central thesis is that each successive application of a new technology—writing, print, electronics—to language moves language toward greater and greater digitization (reduction of everything to numerically distinct units), creating a greater and greater need for a complementary, integrative interpretation or hermeneutic which is counter-fractioning in its drive to relate everything to everything else, to put all together again, to resituate all in the unbroken web of history, to ambition not fractioning but unitive truth. Moreover, digitization, while it moves in the opposite direction from the holistic drive of hermeneutic, can, paradoxically, be used by hermeneutic to assist hermeneutic's own work, and, conversely, hermeneutic can be applied to explain digitization, as digitization itself can never do but as this work undertakes to do within its own obvious limits. Advanced digitization and advanced hermeneutic are both marks of our age.

Hermeneutics and Phenomenology of the Sensorium

Something needs to be said about the sensory phenomenology at work in the statement earlier in this prologue that "to interpret means to bring out what is concealed in a given manifestation." The terms "concealed" and "manifestation" as well as "bring out," in the fashion common at least since Plato, takes the sense of vision as the analogue for intellectual knowledge. Intellectual knowledge, which we are doomed to think of as analogous to sensory knowledge, for Plato, is like seeing, not like hearing or smelling or tasting or touching. In fact, it is like all these sensory activities, although it is true, as many philosophers have been aware, that sight is the *sensus maxime cognoscitivus*, the sense that gives most "information" (and thus the sense most closely allied to computerized "knowledge" in our day).

But it is not exhaustive to think of interpretation or hermeneutics simply in visualist terms of concealment and information. It is possible to consider explanation or hermeneutics as making was is said or what is in a text "more resonant" (sense analogue for intellectual knowledge, hearing), or "more pungent" or "more odoriferous" (sense analogue, smell), or providing "fuller savor" (sense analogue, taste), or "more palpable" (sense analogue, touch—which would include hotter or colder, or rougher or smoother, or softer or harder, etc.). Touch is so minimally abstract that no one knows exactly how many individual senses it encompasses—Geldard has calculated 27 (see Ong, *The Presence*, 165, 170).

Nevertheless, despite the relevance of these other sense analogues and the greater richness they can bring to our sense of interpretation or hermeneutics, the distancing and dissecting power of vision gives it peculiar power as an analogue of intellectual knowledge in interpretive and hermeneutic operations. For, whatever else they are, these operations are dominantly abstracting and fractioning, which means both advantaged and constrained. Hermeneutics or interpretation is of itself not without built-in deficiencies.

1

ORALITY, WRITING, PRESENCE

The historical origins of hermeneutics as a self-conscious discipline from the study of texts together with our typographical fixation on texts have occluded general awareness, even among scholars, that all use of language, not just textual use, is hermeneutic. This is the center point of this work. Hermeneutics, in the sense earlier described, the making clear to a given audience or milieu something in a manifestation that is not evident to this audience or milieu, was being practiced tens or even hundreds of thousands of years before writing was even thought of as a possibility. Speech, oral or textual, is always a hermeneutic event in the sense of an interpretive event. The ancient Greek cognates and sources of our vernacular term "hermeneutics" refer indiscriminately to explication of oral speech or texts—more often to the former.

Words and thoughts were devised initially, we need to remind ourselves, to explain nonverbalized, nonconceptualized context. The nonverbal universe is the context that antedates all verbalization by billions of years. *Homo sapiens* has been on earth some 150,000 years, to take the most likely date according to our present knowledge. And, as Stephen A. Tyler has detailed (*The Said and the Unsaid* 461–65), it is the initial nonverbal context to which words undertake to give meaning that itself gives meaning to words—to the first words initially and to all later words reductively. Here we have one of the limitless examples of the hermeneutic circle: words are defined by the nonverbal when they are uttered to explain the nonverbal. The nonverbal to which the words relate is not presented to us but represented to us and defined by the use of the verbal. Words are not a substitute for the nonverbal (simply making the nonverbal "present"), but an interaction with the nonverbal. In a recent study, Roger Seamon has convincingly shown how all scientific poetics, including structuralist and deconstructionist poetics, ultimately fail to be fully "scientific" because the "subversive secret" in all poetics, "scientific" and other, is the need for hermeneutics or interpretation in comprehending the poetics. This always means involving the poetics with something else which includes the nonverbal and with which the poetics is interacting.

The matter of style is curiously relevant here and calls for brief mention. In one way or another, all verbal expression exhibits style. The more attention to verbal style as style is foregrounded, the more interpretation of verbalization can be called for, insofar as style is precisely the nonexplicit in which the verbalization involves itself, the "way" in which verbalization is carried on. Interpretation of style speaks about style and thus moves the nonexplicit elements of style into the realm of the verbally explicit, toward which, as has been seen, interpretation or hermeneutic gravitates. Oral style of course commonly lends itself more openly to interpretation than does written style, for oral delivery involves nonverbal elements—gestures, eye movements, other bodily movements, volume of voice, and so on—quite patently or obtrusively, whereas written style, although it involves the nonverbal in the way it employs the verbal, does so much more unobtrusively or even guardedly or cryptically.

Gadamer's survey of the history of textual hermeneutics and speculation about the hermeneutics of the past two centuries makes clear how much of present-day discussion (textuality as such, readers' roles, intertextuality and intersubjectivity, etc.) lay embedded in earlier discussion, sometimes close to the surface. Schleiermacher and others treated by Gadamer (167–73) work with the relationship between verbal expression and context, nontextual and textual, and with the relationship between the context in which a text is written and the context in which it is read, where Schleiermacher sees "the act of understanding as the reconstructive completion of the production" (Gadamer 169). Gadamer's survey also makes clear that the interaction of verbal utterance and context has hitherto been considered mostly in discussion of texts. One purpose of the present treatment is to introduce into the study of hermeneutics more reference to the oral. Of all languages in human history, only a relatively tiny number have ever had any textual existence at all, as will be noted further below.

Gadamer makes beautifully evident how Plato's Socratic dialogues are themselves a form of hermeneutic and how in them the hermeneutic function of oral exchange is quite clear, so that one can legitimately "describe the work of hermeneutics as a conversation with the text" (*Truth and Method* 331). That is to say, all hermeneutics resembles Socrates's conversation or dialogue. One must interact with a text in a way resembling that in which Socrates and his interlocutors are represented as interacting orally.

But oral-textual relations are even more introverted than Gadamer allows for. Gadamer's work was too early to take cognizance of what we now know through the work of Eric Havelock (*Preface to Plato*) and others, namely, that the Socratic dialogues themselves, although presented (in writing) as oral, employ even in their oral format mental procedures which are themselves the heritage of writing in that, although they are presented as though oral, they in fact are organized in ways impossible to the mind not formed by the technology of writing. The purely oral mind does not objectify in the way Socrates and his interlocutors do. Plato wanted to exclude poets from his Republic precisely because, as representatives of a basically oral culture, they did not use the objectifying procedures which his dialogues used. At the center of earlier Greek verbalization was not *logos* but the basically oral aim of imitation. Hearers of the *Iliad* and the *Odyssey* were to identify with Achilles and Odysseus, not to analyze them or their values. Knower and the known were to be merged. Writing implemented the fuller separation of the knower from the known, even in the oral speech of those who had interiorized writing. Thus, although in real life (not just in Plato's text) Socrates and his interlocutors may have dialogued in the way Plato presents them as talking, such dialogue is not in fact fully oral (Ong, "Writing"). The present work intends to consider hermeneutic as extended back beyond the formal dialogic discourse of Plato, which depends on a literate mind-set, into language generally, including that of primary oral cultures, cultures with no knowledge of writing at all.

Starting hermeneutics from texts can well favor the so-called Adamic view of language, in which words are supposed to have started with a clear-cut "proper" meaning, more or less associated with textual representation of words, from which later meanings deviate. Linguists know that, generally speaking, the opposite is true: varying contexts often at first define words vaguely, and the words often acquire greater precision through use. At a crucial point in textual history, Samuel Johnson had to work against the quite common Adamic view in getting up his *Dictionary* (Kernan 187, 190, 193). Even today, it is not uncommon for users of dictionaries to regard a dictionary as proceeding from Adamic principles: dictionaries are often popularly thought to be usable as showing how words start in good clear-cut shape with clear-cut meanings and then are "corrupted." Textual presentation of words favors a feeling that the normal or original or "real" senses of words are intrinsically neat and clear, as visually apprehended texts are—visually.

It might be well here also to advert to one problem involving context that is particularly relevant today. Present-day literary criticism and philosophy are filled with discussion about words as making "present" what they refer to. This view of words, presumed to be the common view, deconstructionists and others decry, because words, we are told, cannot make anything "present." But ordinary parlance, at least in English and many other languages, has never commonly treated of words or of thoughts as "presenting" or making present what they treat, but as "*re*presenting" what they *re*fer to. "*Re*presenting" is a complicated concept, although it may appear innocent and straightforward enough at first blush. By being put into words and thought, what we are attending to somehow nonverbally is brought back *again* verbally and mentally (cf. Derrida's *différance*) and thus inevitably in a somehow new way (once more, cf. Derrida's *différance*). The *re-* in "represent" suggests some kind of sense of presence antecedent to verbalization. The word for chair and the thought for chair are neither of them the same sort of thing as the sensorily present phenomenon they represent. A post-Kantian awareness appears to be embedded in this quite ordinary and longstanding way of thinking and speaking in terms of *re*presentation, although the awareness has been muted until recently.

The impression that words "present" things, make things present—rather than *re*presenting things—is encouraged by addiction to working programmatically with textualized words. Text is "present" in a way spoken words cannot be: you can see and even feel the text. Text is durably present to the senses. Being "present" suggests a certain duration, and the visual (and tactile) element of text thus fits text well into our sense of "presence." Oral words are never "present" in this durable way: they are sound events in time, existing only as they are going out of existence. You cannot "hold" a word in position as you can a moving picture frame: stopping sound yields not sound, only silence. Thinking of words as "signs" tends to assimilate them to the visual field, whereas, as basically oral, they are calls or utterances.

The paradigmatic sense of presence is the presence of one conscious human being to another. If I am in a room with an object—say, a chair—it is meaningful to say that the chair is present to me. If the object is a potted living plant, some would feel that the plant is present in a fuller sense than the inorganic object, the chair. If the other being in the room with me is a living subhuman animal, particularly one felt as close to the human lifeworld—for example, a dog—most would feel that the dog is present in a fuller sense than the chair or plant. If the other in the room is another human person, the full sense of presence can be realized. The other beings are "present" only by some kind of analogy with human presence. For presence is fully realized when it is reciprocal (Ong, *The Presence*, passim). I can feel another human person's presence because he or she feels mine. The chair or the plant is present to me, but I am not present to it. I can be present in a certain way to a living subhuman animal, but not as the animal is to me. There is no full reciprocity. Someone has noted the terrible emptiness that stares out from an animal's eye. In deconstructionist and other literary theory and philosophy, the "presence" with which the use of textualized (or oral) words are associated or dissociated is not quite presence in its fullest human sense, but only an analogue of such presence derivative from presence in its fullest sense, the presence of person to person. We have taken a term which in its deepest being comes from Martin Buber's "I-thou" world and transposed it without notice into Buber's "I-it" world, where it functions well enough, but quite differently. Some effects can be psychedelic.

2

HERMENEUTICS, TEXTUAL AND OTHER

I

Language, Gadamer observes in *Truth and Method* (354), is essentially writable and gains by being written. This observation is incontestable, although, as earlier noted, Gadamer's work was too early to take note of the now vast studies (e.g., Havelock, Goody, Ong) concerning what language and thought were like in primary oral cultures (cultures with no knowledge of writing or even of its possibility—which is to say almost all human cultures over the ages, from some tens of hundreds of thousands of years ago until only some 5,000 years ago, when the first writing appears). Paul Ricoeur states that "writing is the full manifestation of discourse" (*Interpretation* 25–26). In its inattention to letterpress print (related to writing but differing from it technologically) and print's vast new social effects, and in its inattention to computer-generated work as a possibly fuller manifestation of discourse, Ricoeur's statement might be contested as being another example of the textual bias that had characterized most thinking about language until recent times and that only now is being adverted to and seen for what it is. Writing does entail certain losses for discourse. We know, for example from Lord's and Havelock's work, that writing culture can no longer produce an *Iliad* or a *Beowulf* or a *Mwindo Epic* (Ong, *Orality* 78–116), but in a qualified sense Ricoeur's statement is certainly true.

As a time-obviating and space-obviating mechanism, writing effects massive gains which are impossible without writing and which are retained and strengthened as well as transformed almost beyond measure in print and in computer-generated text. Moreover, writing is connected with and often brings about fundamental reorganization of society in countless ways, however gradually, varying from culture to culture, as Jack Goody has shown with worldwide detail in *The Logic of Writing and the Organization of Society* and as the studies collected by Harvey J. Graff instance. Writing even produces societies with far greater output of spoken words than do societies without writing. Print and now electronics produce what I have styled the secondary orality of radio and television, which produce far more decibels of sounded words than could be achieved in a primary oral culture and which are secondary in that their orality depends not just on the human organism, as oral speech does, but also on writing and print, without which the *mechanism* they constitute could neither be devised nor effectively used.

However, if it is true that language gains by being written, it is also true that language did not begin by being written. By far most languages in the world have never been written and never will be. Of the tens of thousands of languages which have doubtless existed since *Homo sapiens* first appeared on earth, it has been estimated that only 106 have a literature, and of the some 3,000 to 4,000 languages still more or less in existence today (many are dying very fast) only some 78 have a literature (Edmonson 323, 332). The total variety of human language activity has thus, almost all of it, never been affected in the least by writing, which we recall first appeared in the basically pictorial cuneiform script of Mesopotamia only around 3500 B.C.E. (Ong, *Orality* 85).

II

The Semitic alphabet, first of all alphabets and source, directly or indirectly, of all other alphabets across the world (but not of all writing systems) appeared only around 1500 B.C.E. The Semitic alphabet was basically consonantal. Semitic languages, such as Hebrew, to this day do not normally write vowels, except for schoolchildren in the early grades, for whom the consonantal texts are supplied with special vowel "points" that are not part of the alphabet but special aids for the not-yet-competent learner. In ordinary Hebrew texts the unwritten vowels are supplied by the reader, who must be reasonably familiar with the vocabulary and grammar of the language to manage the requisite guesswork for supplying the unwritten vowels. Vowelless alphabets are feasible in Semitic languages because in Semitic languages consonants are more important than vowels in determining the lexical content of words, vowels largely determining grammar and construction (Coulmas 144)—as, for example, the different vowels in the English words *man* and *men* distinguish singular and plural, and in *run* and *ran*, present and past tenses. But vowels do not do these things regularly in Indo-European languages, so that Indo-European languages are virtually unmanageable in an alphabet of consonants only. Faced with this fact, the ancient Greeks devised the first alphabet with letters for vowels as well as consonants, often called the vowelized or vocalized alphabet, or simply the alphabet (Ong, *Orality* 85–89). We might say that the Greeks lucked out.

Since the vowelized alphabet in various forms (alphabetic letters can be variously shaped and/or variously arranged to make words) is so commonly used and becoming more and more common across the world, it is well to note here why the vowelized alphabet (an alphabet of consonants and vowels) is paramount in writing systems and, it would appear, unimprovable in its general principle. (This is not to say that it has every advantage any script can have—Chinese character writing, for example, has special advantages as well as great disadvantages of its own—in a computer age particularly urgent disadvantages.)

No other kind of script is so democratic (easy for anyone to learn), as sparse, and as abstract as is the vowelized or vocalized alphabet—hereafter often referred to simply as the alphabet when the context is clear. Although it can be incidentally improved by such measures as the addition of letters or diacritical marks fitting it better to the phonemic system of one or another language, the alphabet appears essentially unimprovable as a match for oral utterance because of the fact that its visual patterning system in principle is based quite exactly on the sound patterning system used not in one or another spoken language but in every spoken language.

More than other scripts, the alphabet provides the visual equivalent of oral speech. (This does not mean that those who first devised the alphabet were able to explain the nature of the match they had achieved or, in the absence of a science of phonetics, could have been aware of it.)

This match of the visual alphabet with the oral patterning system of *all* human speech is achieved by using the meaningless to construct meaning. All spoken language exhibits what has been called duality of patterning (see Pyles and Algeo, *Origins* 4): (1) meaningful sound units, or, better, morphemes (words and word parts), such as the separately meaningful sound units *Mary, like-, -d* (signals past tense), *peach-*, and *-es* (signals past tense), in the sentence "Mary liked peaches") and (2) sound units in themselves essentially devoid of meaning which are used to make up the meaningful units (the sounds or, better, phonemes) represented by the symbols *M, a, r,* and *y* in *Mary* are in themselves meaningless—in a given context, of course, the symbol *a* may represent a complete word, but this is because of the context not because of simply the letter as such. All the characters in the alphabet are of this sort, in themselves meaningless—in principle although not of course historically, for it appears that the letters of the alphabet derive, in ways we have not completely puzzled out, from meaningful signs, generally pictures. In sum, one can say that to invent the alphabet one had ultimately to isolate the *meaningless* units in the sounded, spoken language and encode *them* only. Since Saussure, spoken language itself has been recognized as a system of structured relations of otherwise meaningful sound elements. But the alphabet is a similar phenomenon in the *visual* world: it provides meaning by the way it structures into visual (and/or tactile) units, each in itself otherwise meaningless. It could hardly be a coincidence that the discovery of the primacy of structure in speech grew up in an alphabet-using milieu.

The consonantal alphabet, such as the Semitic alphabet, also uses meaningless units to construct meaning, but it does not do so to the full as the vowelized alphabet does. To read a text written in a consonantal Semitic alphabet, one has to understand the language and know the general context of a given word in order to determine from the general context of meaning what the missing vowels are. The missing vowels are thus not entirely free of meaning in the sense that they are generated out of the meaning that the consonants suggest. The reader must have laid hold of some meaning in order to supply to the word the proper vowels the consonants suggest. In context, the Hebrew letters *dbr* can be gathered to stand for "word" and thus, because one knows how "word" is pronounced, the vowel sound *a* can be generated in the two proper places between the consonants to produce the pronunciation *dabar*. Thus the writing symbols of the consonantal alphabet are, in an indirect, operational way, not quite so free of meaning as the symbols of an alphabet which includes also vowels, and thus uses them in themselves as distinguishable visual units.

III

Faur has discussed the well-known propensity of the Hebrew tradition (see also Boman 68–69 passim) to link writing and vocal speech where the ancient Greeks tended to separate the two, as Plato does quite vigorously. This propensity is doubtless connected in various ways with the differences between the consonantal and the vowelized alphabets. But the propensity of the Hebrew culture to link writing and oral speech and the propensity of the Greek to separate the two are also related to the varying etymologies of the Hebrew word for "word," *dabar* (original root meaning "drive forward"), and of the Greek word for "word" *logos* (a cognate of the verb *legein*—original root meaning "gather, collect, arrange"—see Boman, 68–69 passim). The Hebrew *dabar* means "word," but it also means deed (an action, the use of muscular power, just as a spoken word is an action involving power). The Greek *logos* does not mean "deed" but suggests, rather, arrangement (orderly, more or less static, spatial, visualizable arrangement).

More will be said later on the contrast between the Hebrew and the Greek concepts of "word." But here we should note that the tendency of the Greeks to dissociate writing and speech is evident in the *Phaedrus* and elsewhere, where Plato's Socrates explicitly separates writing from speech and rates oral dialogue well above writing, above even written dialogue (Havelock, *Preface;* Ong, *Orality*). It is significant that the Greek gods were illiterate, although quite vocal. Divinity for the Greeks entailed the power of speech, but it did not involve knowledge of writing, a quite separate matter. Literacy was not particularly godlike. But "the God of the Hebrews is eminently literate" and the Torah "was written before the creation of the world" (Faur 33). It appears that a literate God implies a ranking of writing (suggesting a deed or act of power) at least on a level with oral speech, whereas for Plato writing is far beneath the oral.

Writing systems that, unlike the alphabet, are pictographic or phonographic build permanently on symbols which are in themselves meaningful, although original meanings of symbols may eventually be varied, adjusted adroitly to new meanings. Thus in Chinese character writing the written character for "good" [pronounced approximately *hau*] is formed by joining the character for "woman" [pronounced approximately as the French *nu*] and the character for "child" [pronounced approximately *dzuh*]. The visual etymology of the written words here is clearly not the same as the oral-aural etymology of the spoken words. Chinese speakers unable to write in standard Chinese characters do not have the explicit association woman-child-good that writers of Chinese all have.

The combinations adduced here are very simple ones: other ways of combining and adjusting meaningful Chinese written characters to produce other meaningful written characters can and do become fantastically complex (DeFrancis). There are meaningless elements, of course, in the Chinese characters, namely, the relatively small number of standardized individual strokes of brush or pen used in constructing the characters, but these are not set up to correspond, each one, to individual meaningless units of which sounded words are composed. They are simply standardized ways of using the writing instrument (brush, etc.). Thus they do not function as an alphabet.

Written words made out of meaningful components, as in Chinese, can be and often are tremendously rich in associative signification. Chinese character writing is far more charged with meaning and far richer than spoken Chinese, and knowing the characters means knowing in greater depth a whole culture, but a writing system thus grounded in meaningful units is also very difficult to learn compared to the alphabet. The K'anghsi dictionary of Chinese in AD 1716 lists 40,545 *different* individual characters (Ong, *Orality* 87)—compare the twenty-six different characters of our English alphabet, which are all the parts that have to be integrated in our English alphabet! So long as the units in a script retain in themselves vestiges of meaning, the writing system simply cannot match the abstract economy of the vowelized (vocalized) alphabet. One needs to know individually around 2,000 of the 40,545 different characters in order to be functionally literate in Chinese. As Chinese friends have mentioned to me, not reading Chinese for a good many years makes reading it difficult: you forget the meaning of many individual characters.

We can recall that the twenty-six marks which we call the letters of the alphabet are in themselves completely neutral so far as meaning goes: their use in principle depends not directly on what they mean but only on what is constructed out of them, on how they are combined. By contrast with Chinese, one can appreciate more, it would seem, what was here noted earlier, namely, that Ferdinand de Saussure's seminal view of language, as consisting of structure rather than of meaning, is a specialized view, true indeed, but more immediately accessible to users of the alphabet than to those using other writing systems.

Since hermeneutics deals with meaning, various ways of mixing meaning and meaninglessness in various writing systems will encourage various kinds of hermeneutics when one is working with texts or, among literates, when one is working with texts and with oral expression as well. These present reflections treat textual hermeneutics basically in a Western, alphabetic setting, and generally, though not always, in a vowelized or vocalized alphabetic setting.

IV

The formal study of hermeneutics or exegesis or interpretation, as such study is known as a more or less formalized subject in Western learned circles today, began by centering on texts. With reference to the hermeneutical tradition as it had developed from Western antiquity, Gadamer summarily states, as has already been seen, "The classical discipline concerned with the art of understanding texts is hermeneutics" (146). He goes on immediately to explain how the concept of hermeneutics must be enlarged to include aesthetics, "the whole sphere of art and its complex of questions," and later notes that hermeneutics extends also to oral utterance. But aesthetics and oral utterance are presented in Gadamer's perspectives as "extensions" of the narrower original focus of what has long been styled hermeneutics, the Western textual focus, which Gadamer generally retains as a centering point. He insists "that the task of hermeneutics was originally and chiefly the understanding of texts" (353). This observation appears to have applied historically from the start not only in the Greek-based and Latin-based classical tradition but also in the rabbin-ical tradition, even in the light of the interplay of text and orality in this tradition described by Susan Handelman in *The Slayer of Moses.*

Gadamer has noted how the study of hermeneutics that began thus by focusing on texts and then extended itself to provide interpretations of nontextual art—and oral utterance—has extended its range more and more to embrace all the human sciences (146–47). It has moved on more recently, we might note, to include explicitly such matters as the scientific study of gesture and other "kinesics," a term dating from around 1952 and referring to the use of nonlinguistic bodily movements, such as shrugs, eye movements, manual gestures, and so on to communicate meaning.

Eventually, hermeneutics or interpretation has been extended even more widely, coming to include any human action that conveys "mean-ing" (Tyler, *The Said* 12–14). Interpretation or hermeneutics has here a much wider sense than when these terms refer directly to intentionally programmed words. As already noted, we can even speak of interpreting nonhuman phenomena, as a sunset. For, in its widest sense, as has been suggested earlier, hermeneutics or interpretation eventually means making evident to a given audience or milieu something in any manifestation that is not evident to this audience or milieu. "Evident" is here, of course, a relational term: it means evident enough for present purposes, in a given, concrete, existential setting. One can go on to explain further and further without end, though eventually not without inducing boredom.

V

Here, as elsewhere, rather than the term "relative," I use the term "relational"—related to other, often unspecified items, items which are simply assumed or are often lodged in the senses or in the subconscious or unconscious—rather than the term "relative." "Relative" and its cognate "relativism" suggest a certain exclusiveness: the entirety of knowledge is relative only to the knower, so that knowledge in two or more persons can in no sense be the same. "Relational" as I have just defined it, and its cog-nate "relationalism" suggest not exclusion but inclusion: everything is re-lated to everything else, and not simply but complexly. This view makes for great, but involved, specificity, including both articulate and inarticu-late elements.

VI

"Relationism" enters into all in-depth explanation (interpretation, hermeneutics). As Basil Willey has observed, "One cannot . . . define 'explanation' absolutely: one can only say that it is a statement which satisfies the demands of a particular time or place" (13). Put another way, this is to say that all explanation—even the most abstractly scientific—is in its deepest roots a rhetorical operation. It is rhetorical in the sense that, immediately or remotely, expressly or by implication, all explanation is situated in a real, existential dialogic setting, a setting not fully reducible to abstract logical articulation. By dialogic here, I refer to a live verbal exchange between two (or more) persons at a given time and place and in a given setting, where the speaker knows, at least for practical but not totally articulable purposes, what his or her hearers can be counted on to be aware of and what they cannot. In the case of texts, the given existentialist setting of the writer and that of the reader are different, but they are both existentialist settings. As there are no time-free words, so there are no time-free explanations. There never has been and never will be any abstract, ahistorical audience to whom an explanation can be tailored.

Again, this is not to say that false explanations are indistinguishable from true explanations or false conclusions or statements from true conclusions or statements. It is simply to say that you cannot judge what is true or false outside a real historical context, never fully verbalized, with which you are in contact, reflectively or unreflectively, immediately or, perhaps by dint of exhaustive research, mediately. It also means that nothing can ever be *totally* explained—related to the potentially infinite everything else. This state of affairs is covered by the earliest observation that total verbal explicitness is impossible.

Dealing with words alone cannot reveal their truth or falsity. Rhetoric, in the sense of expression addressed in a real historical context from one person to another or others in a context always more than verbal, with an intent to affect the addressee(s) here and now, is more inclusive than any logic. Rhetoric is the most inclusive of what medieval Latin-speaking academics called the *artes sermocinales*, the verbal arts, which they summed up under grammar, rhetoric, and logic. Or, we may say, pragmatics is the context of semantics (see Tyler, *The Said* 461–65)—what words mean depends on how you are using them.

Paradoxically, all philosophic and/or scientific explanation necessarily in a certain sense moves away from the level at which understanding takes place. Human verbalization moves into, reinforces, actuality, but also moves in certain ways away from actuality. This does not mean that verbal explanation is unnecessary or undesirable. It means that verbal explanation is also incidental to something more. Understanding, knowledge, truth are realized in the total, existential human lifeworld. In the *Seventh Letter* Plato says that truth, such as the philosopher desires, is "not something that can be put into words like other branches of learning: only after long partnership in a common life devoted to this very thing does truth flash upon the soul like a flame kindled by a leaping spark, and once it is born there it nourishes itself thereafter" (341). Plato put this in his own way, but many persons in academia and many others today generally have enough existential continuity with Plato's own world to be able to understand him here without any particular further explanation. Although far from perfectly, thanks to massive scholarship, they can reconstruct the fuller historical context, which is a social, interpersonal context not limited to words, in which Plato was writing.

VII

In Western classical antiquity rhetoric was at first thought of as basically applying to oral speech, although it later took over written expression as well (without anyone's noticing, for the most part, this extension of its meaning—Ong, *Interfaces* 53–54). However, since the ascendancy of writing, even when interpreting the nontextual, there can still remain the tendency to take interpretation of texts, not of oral discourse, as the model for other interpretive activity. This has been especially true since the ascendancy of print and is being reinforced by the growth of electronic textual communication.

In "The Model of the Text: Meaningful Action Considered as a Text," Paul Ricoeur proposes that the human sciences (*sciences humaines*, such as history, sociology) develop by interpreting human action itself by analogy with textual interpretation (529). One might expect that what we interpret might better be regarded by analogy with oral speech—anything that is interpreted "speaks" to us and we try to understand by interpreting what is "said." Interestingly, Ricoeur's referral of interpretation to textual expression rather than to live oral expression means that today's typical model for interpretation is to be found not simply in live oral human expression as such, but in human expression involving a technological component, writing. Unlike oral speech, writing is a technological artifact (Ong, "Writing Is a Technology"; see also Ong, *Orality*). Ricoeur does not advert to this state of affairs. Why this adamant association of interpretation of all human action not simply with discourse but with technologically aided discourse? This question will be returned to later.

Jacques Derrida of course goes much further than Ricoeur:

> Text, as I use the word, is not the book. No more than writing or trace, it is not limited to the paper which you cover with your graphics. It is precisely for strategic reasons that I found it necessary to recast the concept of the text by generalizing it almost without limit, in any case without present or perceptible limit, without any limit that is. That's why South Africa and apartheid are, like you and me, part of this general text, which is not to say that it can be read the way one reads a book. That's why the text is always a field of forces: heterogeneous, differentiated, open, and so on. ("Critical Response" 167–68)

The most sweeping gesture in this statement is the inclusion of "you and me" in the concept of text, a technological construct. Am I a technological construct? What about the persons before c. 3500 BCE, when there were no texts at all? Are you? Ricoeur (*Interpretation Theory* 26) objects rightly to Derrida's draconian separation of writing from speech and exaltation of writing and does so on the grounds that all discourse, written as well as spoken, is in the last analysis dialogically generated and constructed.

In *Oral Poetry: An Introduction* (141–52), Paul Zumthor moves even farther into sound. For Zumthor, language has not fully realized itself until it has expressed itself in song (voice, noninstrumental, hence nontechnological), thereby moving more deeply into sound rather than simply into the technological empowering conferred by textuality—which, through tools, invests language in the visual and tactile.

3

AFFILIATIONS OF HERMENEUTICS
WITH TEXT

Words, both oral and textual, as has been seen, can call for interpretation with a certain special urgency. For words themselves are always efforts at explanation, yet insofar as words, spoken or written or printed or processed electronically, never provide total explanation, they invite further interpretation, the completion of the business they have left unfinished. Utterance of any sort is always in some sense un-finished business. One can conclude verbal exchange quite satisfactorily and arrive at truth when what is at stake in a given situation is cleared up. But one could also always ask one more question. This is sometimes why disputes are facilely dismissed as "merely verbal," for "merely verbal" differences can be the most profound of all differences and it is comforting to sweep them under the rug.

A basic reason why text can call urgently for interpretation or hermeneutics is that text comes always out of the past. Spoken words come into being always in the real, existent, holistic present. Writing does not. Taken up by different readers at different times, always after its creation, the text constantly emerges in always new contexts, to which much of the original world out of which it emerged may well be quite strange. Thus Gadamer notes the need for the reader's "conversation with the text" and for an "effective-historical consciousness" (*Truth and Method* 310, 325, 331).

Further, as suggested earlier in the Prologue to the present work, this is because a text, produced by a technology (writing, print, electronics), is a kind of thing, a given visual object, lying there passively, able to be operated on as spoken words are not, for they are moving events in time.

The thing-like quality of a text is enhanced by the often subtle ways in which text involves the tactile. Touch figures in the act of writing or printing a text, and the computer calls for "hands on" training. The concept of "digitization," which will be discussed in detail later, suggests "fingering" (*digitus* is the Latin term for finger). Even reading texts involves the tactile, if often inadvertently, as in side-to-side and up-and-down eye movements, in muscular adjustment of the eyes for parallax, and other ways (apart from reading braille, where the involvement of touch is of course more direct and crucial). Texts have a kind of "feel" of a sort that spoken words do not have: the full meaning of "text" can at times depend on the "texture" of the paper or other material on which it appears. And the kind of organization that results from textuality—word spacing, paragraphing, punctuation, the use of capitals, italics, boldface, and the like—has a tactile component. All this reinforces the thing-like quality of texts as texts. Since they are, for all their thing-like quality, involved in verbal communication, we can feel a need to make this involvement more evident by using additional words to interpret texts.

Spoken words are in great part further given meaning, further explained, interpreted as they are being uttered, not merely verbally but often in other ways such as subtle personal interaction with the other party or parties to the discourse as well as by nonverbal elements in the fuller context or situation in which they are spoken—who is speaking to whom, on what occasion, with what sort of force, in what sort of social structure, with what unarticulated presuppositions involved in the situation or its background, with what facial expressions, gestures, and so on. Such nonverbal elements are missing in a text and need somehow to be made up for. Interpretation or hermeneutics makes up for such missing elements, the absences with which all text presents us, as deconstructionists have liked to insist.

Texts themselves of course are not context-free in the sense that they exist in various sets of conventions established for reading and that they all connect with our experiences of reading other texts. But the context is normally more remote than the immediate context of oral utterance. Our sense of intertextuality has made us aware that all texts, even when they are not explicitly citing other texts, are interwoven with other texts often in the most complex and elusive ways. Thus we find Michel Leiris's "reflections on the associations of the name 'Persephone' alongside Derrida's discussion of the limits of philosophy or, perhaps at the greatest extreme, Derrida's *Glas* which presents in parallel the text of Hegel's analysis of the concept of the family and a text of Jean Genet, interfacing and correlating the seemingly incommensurate two" (see Culler, *On Deconstruction* 136). In a given text, intertextualist critics look for the most unexpected traced of other texts, each text being a "set of relations with other texts" (Leitch 59) cued in by various methods, conscious or subconscious or unconscious, such as allusion, metaphor, synecdoche, and so on. There is no end to this game. One can produce always one more study, or a hundred more studies carrying the interrelationships of texts into new innings, if not always into new thoughts.

The Western focus of hermeneutics on text has been determined also until very recent generations by the special relationship of Latin to learning, a relationship all too little adverted to in intellectual and cultural history. After Latin ceased to be a vernacular around AD 700 (the exact time varied from place to place), it became a sex-linked, male, chirographically controlled language (Ong, *Fighting*). Spoken as well as written by hundreds of thousands of males, though only by the small percentage of the male population who were schooled (and by some females, too, though so few as to be negligible by comparison with the number of males), Latin became a language completely controlled by the text, normally learned not in the family (there was no Latin baby-talk) but outside the family from male teachers in schools. It was the first language of none of its users, spoken only by those who could also write it, with no direct feed-in from purely oral developments, such as is normal with languages. After around AD 700, new words were made up from textual sources, not from the way people spoke. Since such Learned Latin was the language of academia and of formal intellectual life in the West (including the early American colonies) for a thousand years or more, and since it was, as a foreign tongue, the language most subject to hermeneutic activity, its widespread academic and other use bound hermeneutics to textuality in a special way.

In another way, hermeneutics is curiously, and indeed paradoxically, involved with texts. Hermeneutics is commonly thought of as a methodized, more or less "scientific" explanation of verbalization. But for such linear, scientific organization of thought, including orally verbalized scientific thought, the mind has to have its processes structured by writing (Havelock, *Preface*). Hermeneutics, in this sense of scientific or quasi-scientific explanation by literate persons, approaches texts on a textual basis, even if done orally.

Of course, their being in a full, more-than-verbal present context does not of itself exempt spoken, oral words themselves from the need for interpretation. The nonverbal context itself—the physical, psychological, and cultural setting of spoken words—normally itself is not fully clear and calls for explanation in further words if we are to understand the words spoken in this context. The fact that a fixed, existent, physical, and/or psychological context provides a setting for spoken words does not contravene the principle that total verbal explicitness is impossible. We can never disengage utterance fully from the never fully explained nonutterance in which it is set. As Paolo Valesio's book title engagingly indicates, in dealing with words we must "listen to the silence" (*Ascoltare il silenzio*).

In the light of what has been said thus far, it should be evident that, with regard to their total context, of course all speech acts, oral or textual, not only call for interpretation but, even before they are interpreted, are in themselves inevitably interpretive or hermeneutic, bringing out something that is concealed. This is true even of deliberate obfuscation or an outright lie, for these, too, in some way make evident something that was not evident before, although they do not clear things up in the way other more straightforward speech acts do. They themselves may conceal, and deliberately, far more than they reveal. But examination and interpretation of their deliberate obfuscation can be even more revealing in the long run than is the case with more straightforward verbalization.

4

THE INTERPERSONALISM OF
HERMENEUTICS, ORAL AND OTHER

I

In interpreting verbal utterance, as already noted, we can be called on to interpret oral speech or to interpret text. The two activities are different, but not entirely different. One paradigmatic form of interpretation in oral performance is that of reciprocal discourse or conversation between two (or more) persons in which an utterance of one interlocutor gives rise to another utterance by the other interlocutor, that to another by the first, and so on. This person-to-person dialogue Mikhail M. Bakhtin rightly maintains lies at the ultimate base of all utterance, written as well as oral, scientific as well as casually conversational or formally literary (*Dialogic Imagination,* see editor's Introduction xx). In such dialogue the speakers are always necessarily engaged in hermeneutics, in interpreting one another. Not only for the hearer, but also for the speaker meaning is being negotiated in the discursive process. The speaker by addressing this person here and now in these given circumstances learns more fully what he or she, as speaker, is trying to say, what he or she means.

In fact, in oral utterance the negotiation begins even before the oral utterance itself. The first speaker needs to anticipate some conjectural feedback from an interlocutor before he or she can devise something to say or even to think. Only if we are to some degree in the mind of another can we formulate our own thought, for what I say (and articulately think) depends on my conjectures, before I begin to speak, about your state of mind and about the possible range of your responses. Without conjectural feedback from at least an imagined interlocutor, there is nothing for me to say (or think, even to myself). Speaking of a given matter to a child, I will say something quite different from what I say in speaking about the same matter to an adult. The audience whose state of mind I feel as enabling me to shape my own words and thoughts may be vague and only subconsciously attended to, but it will be there. When I am writing a text or even when I am mulling over something silently to myself, I imagine myself or someone else, more or less distinctly, as an interlocutor.

Your actual response to what I say may or may not fit my earlier conjecture about your state of mind on the subject. In either event, your response enables me to clarify my own thought. Your actual response makes it possible for me to find out for myself and to make clear in my counter-response what my fuller meaning was or is or can be. Your response, whether it is a question or some other type of utterance, forces me to apply hermeneutics or interpretation to my own thinking. Even if you say simply, "Yes," I have to interpret this "yes" in terms of the whole situation, calculating whether the "yes" refers to what I was trying to say or whether it came so easily that I know I was not clear. (Normally we do this type of interpretation automatically and swiftly, not reflectively, and are thus mostly unaware of it.) But I need an interlocutor, real or imagined, in order to carry on thought: my own thought constantly calls for interpretation, even to myself, or especially to myself, as well as to my hearer, whom I have to conjure up in my own consciousness or subconscious when I am alone.

Thus reciprocal oral discourse commonly interprets itself bilaterally (or multilaterally if more than two are engaged in it) as it proceeds. It negotiates meaning out of meaning. Dialogue is thus itself a form of hermeneutic, indeed the ultimate model of hermeneutic. Dialogue (or also multilateral conversation) is hermeneutic in hermeneutic's natural habitat. The person I am speaking to often makes clearer to me what I myself mean, by questioning me, or just by looking puzzled, calling attention to what was not clear (often I was half aware of exactly this unclarity in speaking, but I left my utterance unclear, perhaps advertently, perhaps inadvertently). Oral conversation advertises the intersubjectivity of all human thought and its tie-in with the intersubjectivity of expression.

The etymologies of the terms "hermeneutic" and "interpretation" advertise their grounding in the world of interpersonal exchange or intersubjectivity. Let us look at "interpretation" first. The third syllable (*-pres*) of *interpres*, the Latin word lying back of the term "interpretation" and its cognates, comes from an Indo-European root, *per-*, meaning to traffic in, to sell, and, more remotely, to hand over, to distribute. This root of the *pre-* in "interpretation" belongs, with many other verbal roots, to a more generalized Indo-European root group, also *per-*, which forms the base of many prepositions and many preverbs with the fundamental meaning of "forward," "through," a meaning which becomes widely extended to senses such as "in front of," "before," "early," "around," etc. To this root, *per*, which in its "through" meaning bespeaks betweenness, the Latin form adds the preposition *inter* which itself also means "between" (Indo-European root *en*, in) and thus compounds the notion of exchange underlying intersubjectivity: between-between. The Latin term *interpres* thus refers initially to an agent who enters between two parties concerning something already at stake between the two parties, a between-the-between. From this tangle, *interpres* comes to mean interpreter pretty much in the English sense of the word, that is, an explainer. It will be noted how far all this is from any sense of language and/or thought as logocentric, that is, as a set of signs simply cued one-to-one to each other and purportedly to external reality outside consciousness. Rather, the whole situation is radically *inter*personal, an intensely human operation.

To sum up, in the world of interpretation or hermeneutics we are in a climate of interpersonal negotiation, in which meaning is sustained by the often complex interaction of two (or more) persons in discourse with one another. The issue, the meaning, lies somehow "between" the two discussants, and the interpreter inserts himself or herself into this betweenness to deal with it so as to bring out what may need being brought out, for utterance always both reveals and conceals, as Heidegger has made us insistently aware and has often been noted earlier here.

Moreover, an interpreter can be not only in between persons interacting with one another in conversation, but also between persons and phenomena not yet verbalized by them, as when an interpreter interprets something previously outside the verbal continuum itself, such as a band of red clouds at sunset or a gesture or an animal's cry. In such cases, the interpreter herself or himself introduces the subject into the interpersonal world.

The Greek term *hermeneus*, interpreter, which, with its cognates, provides the Greek-based English "hermeneutics," more or less the equivalent of the Latin-based English term "interpretation," is of obscure origin. Strangely enough, it may or may not be directly related etymologically to the name of the Greek god Hermes, a name seemingly derived from the Greek word *herma*, a heap of stones such as was commonly used to mark boundaries, and which was thus itself a kind of in-betweenness. Whatever the exact etymological connections here, Hermes was conceived of as a supreme negotiator, the god of commerce, eloquence, invention, travel, and theft—all involving some sort of in-betweenness. It thus appears evident that, whatever the etymological facts, the terms *hermeneus* and *Hermes* would doubtless be associated in the minds of Greek speakers. Thus "hermeneutics" is, even if not etymologically, at least in meaning very much of a piece with "interpretation." Both underscore interchange, although, as earlier noted, "hermeneutics" today tends to refer to a more studied, self-conscious, "scientific" operation than does "interpretation."

II

From what has just been said, it appears that, despite our tendency to think of interpretation as applying paradigmatically to texts, the world of interpretation historically (that is, here, etymologically—for real etymology is history) is in a deep, basic sense primarily an oral world, for oral communication is immediately and irremediably interactive and interpretive. In oral expression, real people must here and now really interact with real people, as all must interact with the environment, human and non-human, in which they are embedded, interpreting to one another and to themselves as they verbalize.

It is easy to believe that texts are not at all part of such open, ongoing interpretive negotiation. One of the most widespread and fundamental errors of the past few generations of literary critics (such as the Russian

Formalists or the American and British New Critics) has been the assumption, quite often not clearly articulated, that to put an utterance in writing is to remove it from this state of oral discourse and thus to "fix" it, to specify and totalize its meaning once and for all. Such assumptions have not been uncommon in philosophy and science and they lie back of the often mindless attempts to establish exactly what the totally explicit meaning of the United States Constitution or of other legal documents was when they were written. By dint of historical research, one can of course discover much about the original meaning of a text and the intent of its author or authors, but not with total explicitness, for the original intent and text could not be totally explicit, even to the authors themselves. As noted earlier, total verbal explicitness is impossible, in inscribed texts as much as in spoken words.

As a member of President Lyndon B. Johnson's 1966–67 Task Force on Education, which was engaged in, among other things, suggesting exact texts out of which to devise laws, I can testify personally to some of the problems here. After the Task Force had settled on a text for a proposed law, we would regularly have to call in expert educational consultants to help us discover more fully what our wording would actually mean in the real world of education to which we were addressing ourselves. We ourselves found that alone, we could not fully pin down our own intent. We did not know fully enough the situations we were talking into so that the edges of our thought even in our own minds were fuzzy. The law had to deal with and had to be given its meaning in terms of specific imaginable situations. No one of us could envision all the situations. But the expert consultants could envision more than we could and thus could enable us to understand better what we were trying to say and/or wrote.

As earlier suggested, because texts are totally fixed visually, because they have limited borders, they encourage us to think that the meanings they express are similarly bordered—all act and no residual potential. "A poem should not mean/But be," Archibald MacLeish wrote in his widely acclaimed "Ars Poetica," presumably having in mind a poem set down in writing or print, as his own poems were (106). But words cannot just "be." Words are living events, happenings, moving with the flow of time, not things, as texts make them appear.

III

A text certainly does separate an utterance from its author, who, once he or she has written down the text, may as well be dead. In this sense, writing creates anonymous discourse, as has often been pointed out. But removing an utterance from its author is not removing it from discourse. No utterance can exist outside discourse, outside a transactional setting. Putting an utterance into script can only interrupt discourse, string it out indefinitely in time and space. But not "fix" it, in the sense of endowing it with a totally determinate meaning apart from all other discourse. A closed system of any sort is always impossible, and texts are no exceptions to this rule. In fact, they are conspicuous nonexceptions since the meaning of every word in them has to be determined from outside the text itself and ultimately from nonverbal rather than verbal context. Putting an utterance into script, then, can only interrupt discourse, postpone its continuation, protract it indefinitely in time and space. But not "fix" it, not give it a totally determinate meaning all from within, apart from all other discourse. An utterance does not become clearer or more independent of context simply by being written down. It becomes simply retrievable—quite often with the original context largely lost.

When is a text most truly a text, an expression of words? When does an inscribed text "say" something? Insofar as a text is static, fixed, "out there," reified, it is not an utterance but a visual (and/or tactile) design, not a reproduction of sound, but a visual code for the code of spoken words, a code of a code. This is of course by no means to say that script is simply a substitute for writing. In one way or another, codes modify what they encode. Writing raises consciousness (Ong, *Orality*). Text, however, functions fully as a text (and thus in actuality raises consciousness) only when it reenters auditory discourse (or in the case of congenitally deaf persons, the equivalent of auditory discourse, closely related to tactual movement). Text can be made to reenter discourse, to function as utterance only by something nontextual, that is, by a code in a living person's mind for converting the visual into the auditory, the code that we learn in order to read. When a person possessing the appropriate reading code moves through the visual structure of an inscription and converts it into a temporal sequence of sound, aloud or in the imagination, directly or indirectly—that is, when a reader reads a text—only then does the text become what it was put down to be, that is, an utterance and only then does the suspended discourse continue, and with it verbalized meaning.

There is some evidence (Stubbs 12) that reading can be done without subvocal speech, that is, without muscular and nervous activity around the larynx, but even were this absolutely certain, lack of subvocal speech does not mean lack of imagined sound. Reading silently even without subvocal speech, a person reading a Korean text is imaginatively in a different sound world from that of a person reading an English text. Since they have to be read to function as texts, all texts have human meaning only insofar as they are converted into the extratextual, the auditory (or its equivalent), at least in the imagination.

IV

All text is pretext—in pretty well all the senses that can be assigned to this statement. This is why any text can be so readily deconstructed: despite appearances, it never was standing and never could stand on its own feet. (Neither, for that matter, can spoken words: for their function, they depend ultimately on the nonverbal, including silence.) Writing is a technology that restructures thought, which at its origins had been orally based. Writing has restructured thought marvelously and productively but also stressfully—the stressfulness must not be forgotten. (See Ong, *Orality;* "Writing Is a Technology.")

Since text separates utterance from its author, a distinctive feature of textual utterance as against oral utterance is that its author cannot absolutely predict or often even discover who all will continue the discourse he or she has engaged in by inscribing the text. To this extent the writer cannot discover by any means all that he or she has said in his or her written text, because it is in the interchange with interlocutors, as indicated above, that the fuller meaning of what is said in an utterance appears even to the utterer. Anyone might pick up and read a text once it has been set down and in doing so would have to interpret it, that is, fit it in one way or another into the ongoing thought and conversation of the milieu in which the reading is being done—which means develop its concealed implications, as speakers in a dialogue do with one another's utterances.

This is what hermeneutics does in explaining a text from antiquity: it makes the text intelligible by introducing it into living dialogue that must be carried on in present-day terms, not infrequently with great difficulty. When the reader reads the text, to understand it he or she has not only to recreate the lifeworld in which the text actually came into existence, insofar as this world can be recreated (and it never can be fully recreated), but also to introduce that world and with it the text from it in one way or another into the reader's own world—Gadamer's "conversation with the text" (*Truth and Method* 331).

That is to say, when the reader reads a text, the interrupted discourse is picked up—one can hardly say simply resumed, for the interlocutor who has had his or her say in the text is generally no longer at hand after the point at which his or her text ends. He or she cannot respond to the reader's response, which may actually be a query. (This is what Plato in the *Phaedrus* objects to about writing—it cannot respond to questions it unwittingly or inevitably creates, although Plato of course puts his objection into writing—see Ong, *Orality* 80.) With special skills and great effort the reader may be able to reconstruct conjectured responses of the absent writer which will fit the text somehow into the milieu in which the reading is being done. No matter what, this fit must somehow be made, for to understand the text the reader must relate it somehow to what he or she knows in the present living milieu. In doing so, of course, the reader may well have to enlarge the present milieu's purview—one way in which studying the past enriches the present. But if the reader cannot in any way at all relate what was said to the ongoing dialogue setting in which the reader really lives, the reading is utterly meaningless.

All this is to say that when the reader reads a text, the interrupted discourse resumes, often—or even most often—between persons who have never known one another, perhaps resumes with great effort, implemented by laborious, self-conscious, and one-sided interpretive work (fitting past into present-day living consciousness), without which the inscription may say very little, for the living interlocutor (the reader) must align the dialogue alone, that is, in the absence of the other interlocutor, the writer, who may have been dead for centuries. Hermeneutics isn't always easy. And the discommoding time-span need not be centuries. One can even have problems of this sort in interpreting a note made to oneself a month ago—or even yesterday. (Where was I, in what state of mind, when I wrote *that* down?) Human thought is thus all linked to discourse. Thought and discourse are always contoured by time. There is no time-free knowledge floating about somewhere outside specific, individual, time-bounded human beings. Again, this does not mean that thought cannot be "objective," but that objectivity can be known only subjectively, that is, only by the individual historical persons in objective historical settings—there is no objective human knowledge at large somewhere outside individual existing human consciousnesses.

Once again, this existence only inside human consciousnesses does not make the truth of human knowledge unverifiable. Quite the contrary, it makes the truth of human knowledge eminently verifiable, but historically and complexly and open-endedly so. To verify the truth, one has to take into consideration the knowers, too—speaker and hearer or writer and reader—and the density of the history in which the knowers are embedded. To verify human thought, one has to verify as well other matters in the total environment of the originator and of the receiver of the message. In other words, as earlier noted, human thought is marked not by "relativism" (indeterminacy, lack of fixity) but by relatedness (multiple and active engagement with other thought and with actuality in a variety of ways, always including the nonverbal as well as the verbal, the unsaid as well as the said—see Tyler, *The Said* and *The Unspeakable*).

All human thought and expression is complex. If it ties into the oral world, to be interpreted it must be related to all the density of the existential world in which the oral expression is embedded. If it ties into writing, it must be verified and interpreted by being related, so far as possible, to the world of the original text and to the other texts (and oral utterances) with which the original is interwoven explicitly or implicitly. It must be related as well as to readings that the text can be given over time as readers come to the text with more and more knowledge that will enable them, for example, to make more and more explicit what the writer, not only consciously, but also subconsciously or unconsciously and unwittingly, but really, was getting at.

Thus Freud verified and interpreted what Sophocles was presumably unconsciously dealing with in his *Oedipus Rex*—presumably, Sophocles would have agreed with what Freud made of his text had he been able to see into what he was saying as Freud's later age was able to do (however you interpret or evaluate Freud). Far from being relativistic and indeterminate, good hermeneutic is massively determinate, tying in with everything. Of course, this kind of multiplex determinacy troubles people who like to believe that all "true" meaning is monistically simple, as no meaning ever is. Among others, Piaget has made it clear how meaning is not monistically simple even among young children. No thought is ever free-floating abstraction or free-floating anything else. Thought interlocks everywhere with context. To interpret anything with absolute fullness, you would have to know everything.

All this is, or should be utterly commonplace in an age of reader-oriented criticism and related philosophy. But it is well to advert to it in the perspectives in which it is set here because of the need to attend to what is alike and what is different when we contrast interpretation of oral performance and interpretation of written work.

5

HERMENEUTICS, PRINT, AND "FACTS"

Our text-centered mentality, and especially our print-centered mentality, can and does create special illusions about the nature of "facts" which affects concepts of interpretation or hermeneutics. By habituating us to visually fixed representations of spoken words texts can lead us to overvalue fixity itself. We tend to think of a "fact" as in some sense something fixed. Yet its fixity is paradoxical, for a fact can only be identified by the use of words. And words are not fixed, for they are events in time. Moreover, there is no one thing to say about anything—a fact which seems to compromise the very concept of "facts."

In a highly informative essay, "Grammar and Meaning" (*American Heritage Dictionary* xxxi–iv), Richard Ohmann provides a hermeneutic for this statement (mine, not his) that "There is no one thing to say about anything." He considers what happens when one asks a number of speakers to describe a simple drawing representing a fact or set of facts. Even though each of, say, twenty speakers gives a factual description qualifying as true and exact, almost certainly none of them will describe the drawing in exactly the same words. Professor Ohmann instances these typically variant true and accurate descriptions of a given drawing: (1) "A bear is occupying a telephone booth, while a tourist impatiently waits in line." (2) "A man who was driving along the road has stopped and is waiting impatiently for a grizzly bear to finish using the public phone." (3) "A traveler waits impatiently as a bear chatters gaily in a highway telephone booth." Ohmann then reports that, using not all the words available in English but only the vocabulary and structures supplied by a given twenty-five typical sentences describing the drawing in question, he found by computer analysis that the vocabulary and structures of the twenty-five given sentences, permuted "in all possible ways (so long as the resulting sentences are grammatical)"—for example, one could say "stands" or "is standing"—will "yield the material for 19.8 billion sentences, all describing just one situation" (xxxi–ii), namely that in the bear-in-the-phone-booth drawing. He further points out that, since the number of seconds in a century is only 3.2 billion, no one could possibly become aware of all the ways which his calculations yield to describe the drawing in question.

Thus, if one says of any description, "that is the way it really is," one may be stating the truth but in a way that may be curiously picayune. Why is it that out of the 19.8 billion and more ways of doing a true description I pick this one? Most often, for reasons in me, not reasons "out there" where the "facts" are. These subjective reasons need not at all falsify the facts, but may merely determine which facts are attended to. I may specify "grizzly bear" rather than simply say "bear" because I can tell grizzlies from other bears and am temperamentally inclined to one-up other persons. But the bear is in fact identifiably a grizzly bear. And so on with the thousands of other ways one can be motivated, consciously or subconsciously or unconsciously, for one or another perfectly true and perfectly "objective" expression. My statement of the fact, though one hundred per cent true, still bears my own marking. In the nature of the case, when by verbal statement we isolate a "fact" or "facts" from the unbroken web of actuality around us, the total world in which facts are embedded we do so always under historical and/or personal circumstances. The German historian Leopold von Ranke (1795–1866), famous for his promise to write about history "the way it really happened," was not promising quite as much as he may have seemed to be.

The question of truth or falsity is not what is at stake here. This question can of course be raised and often answered. "There are eighty bears in a telephone booth" is certainly a false description of the drawing in question. So is "There is a man in a telephone booth and a bear outside." No limit to falsity. But no limit to true "facts" either, although there are constrictions on facts as there are not on falsity. The drawing just mentioned constricts the number of bears in the telephone booth, the number of men, the position of the man outside the telephone booth, etc., etc., without end.

Despite the constrictions, however, facts are not epistemologically simple matters. For a "fact" is involved not just in the reality one is dealing with "out there," but also in one's articulation of the reality. "Out there" in the drawing, there are more than 19.8 million and more "facts," the focusing of any one of which involves verbalization. And does so not only in ways involving the speaker's own conscious or unconscious reasons but also involving historical elements, since the speaker must use or build on words and concepts that have been formed over generations of human experience. For all words and concepts are historically formed, by interchange among historical peoples in one or another language group, as a comparison of the etymologies of comparable words in various languages makes abundantly clear. The existing words and concepts can be modified or adjusted, but only within certain limits.

Once again, what is at issue here is not a matter of relativity—in the common subjective sense that you and I may have completely different views as to whether a given figure is a rectangle or a circle and one can never determine who is right. This kind of belief is at best sophomoric: shocked that matters are not as simple as one thought, one decides that everything is totally confused and delights that now one knows of a confusion that ordinary uninformed adults are not aware of. Or, to put it another way, having become aware that knowledge exists always within one or another subject, one triumphantly proclaims that knowledge is entirely subjective, dependent only on the subject, so that objective truth and falsity are indistinguishable. But matters are not so simple. Again, what is involved here is not relativism in the subjective sense but rather relationism: one can indeed determine truth or falsity, but truth is ultimately verifiable in complex ways, not in any simple way.

Further, the verification of truth depends of course on dialogue (definition, it should be noted, is a form of dialogue), on the exchange of thought, on who actually is talking or writing or electronically communicating with whom, explicitly or implicitly.

Even a seemingly clear-cut term from mathematics such as "circle" is not an unambiguous term outside a given context. Outside an ultimately nonverbal context, no term is unambiguous. What a "circle" or anything else exactly means has to be determined by extraverbal contexts that we so fundamentally take for granted that we seldom attend to them. A mathematical circle, such as is referred to in formal mathematical discourse in Euclidean geometry, cannot be found anywhere in the physical world and how far a physical circle has to approximate such a mathematical circle to qualify as a circle can depend, for example, on whether you are addressing manufacturers of garbage-can lids, or precision-tool makers who measure habitually in fractions of millimeters. A circle for garbage-can lid manufacturers may not be sufficiently a circle for precision-tool makers. The two approximate differently a truly mathematical circle, which does not exist outside human consciousness. The audience is one of the determinants of the meaning of "circle" whenever the term is used.

Facts can be true and useful and good, but they are not things that pop out extraverbally, all alone, to found discourse and thought. The extramental world and language and thought go together, in a unique relationship. "The mind and the world jointly make up the mind and the world," as Brian Stock has put it (664), "but there *is* a world." In her book *Against Interpretation*, Susan Sontag (5) cites Nietzsche's observation, "There are no facts, only interpretations." This implies of course that Nietzsche's observation here itself is an interpretation, which of course can call for further interpretation as may be necessary. But it does not mean that the observation is not true or verifiable. I would interpret it to mean that facts cannot be dislodged as such without language or dislodged totally into language without nonverbal context. They have to be demarcated and dislodged verbally and thus mentally from and within the "big, blooming, buzzing confusion" which, in William James's words, is the total world around us.

Our present reflections suggest we can fail to note this state of affairs partly because our common textbound state of mind gives visual-tactile fixities a special paradigmatic appeal even when oral verbalization is involved. Facts caught in (textualized) words would be something laid to rest, like the "dead letter." True facts are more like something living, as is shown by their involvement with language, which is at root oral, produced here and now by the living, and by their involvement with the living thought that goes with language.

6

HERMENEUTICS AND THE UNSAID

If we begin with oral utterance in a primary oral culture (one with no knowledge of writing at all) as the initial field of hermeneutics, we can bring out more fully and cogently what the textbound state of mind tends to obscure, namely, that words are ultimately given their meaning by a nonverbal context. Imagine a person uttering the first word that was ever uttered. Any situation we imagine here is hypothetical, a bit unreal, but the construct can be informative nevertheless. Since no words exist to define or help define the meaning of the first word or words, the meaning can only be known by sizing up the situation in which the word is being uttered.

As Tyler has shown, both in *The Said and the Unsaid* and in *The Unspeakable*, such a situation involves intention. Somehow, the hearer of a sound used as a word, a linguistic sign, has to know that this sound refers to something other than itself. The utterer has to know that the hearer understands his intention that the sound be a linguistic sign, and the hearer has to know that the hearer understands that the utterer has such an intention. And all this before or by the time the first word is spoken. (We have noted earlier that the term "sign" is borrowed from the visual world, whereas words are fundamentally sounds, and we need to remain aware of this fact, even though we may not be able to forego the established use of the term "sign" as referring to words, even specifically to spoken words.)

The triadic definition of a linguistic or verbal sign function as found in Saussure, Ogden, Richards, and many others, stating that sign, speaker, and object account for meaning is quite inadequate. Tyler notes (*The Said* 385–87), and many persons cited by Gadamer note, that for anything to be taken as a linguistic sign, it must be intended to be a sign by the user and taken by the recipient as intended to be a linguistic sign. A mere noise is not a linguistic sign. "There are no signs without intentions, and no intentions without signs" (Tyler, *Said* 462). Moreover, there are no signs without convention, based on prior intersubjectivism and intersubjective means of evoking a consensus (Tyler, *Said* 19). Ultimately, meaning is not assigned but intersubjectively negotiated, and out of a holistic situation. It takes at least two persons, each intentionally dealing in verbal communication, for words to achieve significance in the first place (Tyler, *Said* 461–65).

Signs demand a dialogic context "which presumes a patterned alternation in the roles of speaker and hearer" (Tyler, *Said* 462). Signs cannot originate in monologue. The ultimate reason for this is that intentional signs are ultimately conventions, and the convention is initially established in the act of speaking (Tyler, *Said* 462 passim), not in advance of the act. There is no way for a person or persons with absolutely no language to set up in advance of use, and arbitrarily, a conventional association between an arbitrary sound and its referent. (We can put aside here the question of pure onomatopoeia, which need not constitute a true word but can simply be an imitation of nonverbal sound, although onomatopoeia can of course be made into a true word by communication of the intention to use it as a word.) In comparable fashion, if one falls back on gestures as indicating the meaning of words, it is in the intentional use of gestures that their referential character is established. Only in the act of communicating can such a convention be set up. In speech this involves always what is said and what is unsaid or supposed. From what is said and unsaid the meaning is formed (Tyler, Valesio). Thus human speakers must be linked intersubjectively even before they speak. Each can and does understand that the other can intend to communicate and that he or she intends to communicate here and now.

A frequently cited incident in Helen Keller's life (*Story* 34–37) shows how communication involves intention that engages and intermingles both intersubjective and objective issues. When Helen was seven years of age, on the day which she calls "the most important day I remember in all my life," her tutor, Anne Sullivan, hitherto unsuccessful in teaching the blind and deaf Helen the use of words, at one point held one of Helen's hands under the water coming from a pump and spelled onto Helen's other hand the word "water." Anne Sullivan had done this sort of thing before unsuccessfully with objects and words such as "doll" and "mug." But this time the procedure finally worked. "Suddenly," Helen writes, "I felt a misty consciousness as of something forgotten—a thrill of returning thought. . . . I knew that 'w-a-t-e-r' meant the wonderful cooling something that was flowing over my hand." From the rest of her account it is clear that it here suddenly came to Helen that (1) there was a present existent that could be *re*presented by the sign for "water" (not presented, for the water was already present), (2) that what she felt flowing over hand *was* water, (3) that Miss Sullivan knew that it was water, (4) that Miss Sullivan knew now she, Helen, knew it was water, and (5) that Miss Sullivan knew that Helen knew that she, Miss Sullivan knew it was water, and that other persons knew and knew that other persons knew that it was water, and so on *ad infinitum*. The intersubjective world had come into full bloom and, with it, the objective world. We can never fully possess the one world without the other.

In learning to speak, as Piaget has abundantly shown in *The Language and Thought of the Child* (see also John McShane, *Learning to Talk*), the child does not learn merely isolated words and/or isolated meaning but has to construct around himself or herself a whole world into which the meaning of words ultimately fits, from which the meaning is gathered. This beginning of language can hardly be construed as a simply logocentric undertaking. Language begins and develops out of hermeneutic, an attempt to make sense of a total world, nonverbal and verbal, not out of simply juxtaposing sounds and things. Meaning is negotiated in holistic situations, not assigned.

7

MEANING, HERMENEUTIC, AND INTERPERSONAL TRUST

Ultimately, meaning and hermeneutic are based on personal intersubjective trust. A few years ago, as I know directly from a participant, a national task force was set up to devise a sign or symbol to serve as a warning notice to mark a projected underground storage dump in the United States for dangerous nuclear waste. The sign or symbol was to be one that would render its warning of serious danger to all ages forever, independently of any languages that might be spoken from now until the end of time and independently of any divergencies in cultures. Of course—although it took the task force many months to arrive at this conclusion!—there was absolutely no way to make the sign or symbol work apart from living connections between living human beings, which is to say apart from some kind of diachronic and continuous dialogic setting.

Symbols must always be embedded in interpretation or hermeneutic to function as symbols. Anyone who saw the symbol would have to interpret it—there would be no other way for it to be a symbol, no other way for it to have meaning, to be understood. But any symbol, apart from a living context, was always open to all sorts of varying interpretations. Around an isolated symbol, all sorts of interpretive myths could and would spring up and grow. The most threatening sort of isolated symbol—say, a diagram of a massive explosion blowing an entire landscape to smithereens—could always, and very plausibly, be interpreted by the viewer as a ruse. The symbol might have as its real rationale, its deeper interpretation, not the actual threat of danger but the fact that gold and diamonds were stored in the spot marked. In a more fully understood context, it need not really mean, "Keep away, danger!" The symbol might always have as its real rationale, its deeper interpretation, not the actual threat of danger but the fact that gold and diamonds were stored in the spot marked. The symbol was intended to be misinterpreted to keep persons away not because of any real danger but because the originators of the symbol wanted to frighten viewers away from a hidden treasure. How could this possibility of duplicity or other confusion be avoided?

After many months of work, the task force decided that the only procedure that could make its inscription (illustration, lettering, logo, or whatever) work was to set up and permanently maintain a commission of living persons entrusted with knowledge of the real situation, persons who themselves could be trusted, who trusted one another, and who would be replaced gradually and continuously over the centuries by equally trustworthy persons to whom the real meaning of the symbol had been explained. The meaning of the symbol could be known by consulting this commission. Any discourse requires trust—what Gadamer (339–41) means by reciprocal relationship and commitment or what Plato implies in the *Seventh Letter* (341) when he speaks (writes) of the necessary "partnership in a common life devoted to this very thing" (the quest of truth). Trust overrides deceptive intent. Words alone can never do this—again, the meaning of words is determined by the nonverbal.

Meaning must come out of dialogue in the last analysis. All science is only arrested dialogue. Because the speaker and the interpreter (hearer, reader) are involved in words which have a history in which they have acquired their meaning by being used, the speaker and hearer are engaged in conversations which predate their own and will postdate it (Weinsheimer 211). In the course of the conversation, concepts are formed, refined, ratified, and mutually understood, provided that a certain honesty of purpose is somehow at work. Words will not work with other words alone. Paolo

Valesio puts it another way: "The word can be understood only—let us say, better, exists only—in our listening to silence" (425).

Gadamer's *Truth and Method* concludes that truth does not depend on method but on "discourse with others" (498), on something that happens in language and the exchange of thought that language involves. Plato says the same thing after disqualifying writing and then even spoken words, too, in the *Phaedrus* and in the *Seventh Letter* (341). Not any treatise by Plato or anyone else can of itself produce understanding of truth, nor can any number of spoken words either. "Only after long partnership in a common life devoted to this very thing does truth flash upon the soul." This is another way of saying that, to achieve truth, trusting dialogue is needed between individuals. A verbal statement alone can "contain" truth only when it is part of a human context of trusting interchange. Trust of course operates in a multitude of ways, such as those, for example, which George Dillon explores in his *Rhetoric as Social Imagination*, and which are far too complex to go into here.

In the area of biblical hermeneutics, which is the chief area in which the study of hermeneutics was first rooted in the West, what has just been noted here makes evident that Jesus's leaving what he had to say orally within a living community rather than by inscribing it himself in writing could work to assure both the accuracy and the durability of his message better than a simply written text could. Jesus did not write his teachings that are found in the Gospels. A text removed from any diachronic dialogic community (in this particular case, the community of Christians in living dialogue with one another over time) could too readily misrepresent his full message. The text-bound mind assumes the opposite: writing something down in isolation guarantees independently and absolutely the preservation of its truth. But it does not. Without denigrating spoken words and/or text (for he read in the synagogue—Luke 4:16–20), Jesus gives a personal context to the apprehension of truth (as Plato and Gadamer do): "I am the way and the truth and the life" (John 14:6). Full truth is not found in human words apart from the persons who utter and receive them. This sounds surprising in our computerized age, but it is still true. Of themselves, computers do not give us truth any more than texts do. They give information, which can at best be at the service of truth and can always be preempted by falsity.

8

HERMENEUTIC AND COMMUNICATION
IN ORAL CULTURES

A hermeneutic of speech in oral cultures demands that we do not assume total likeness between oral speech events in primary oral cultures and oral speech events of literates. We must remind ourselves that in oral cultures verbalization is always tied to performance. The use of language is in no way associated with dictionaries or any other sort of inscription. Verbalization is human action—indeed, human action at its peak.

The high esteem of oral peoples for the "man of words" or "woman of words," the one who can verbalize to the maximum, is well known, and sometimes is so marked as to strike literate persons as childish. It is hard for us today to imagine or even to believe the fascination of oral peoples with the performance of oral epic poetry or other oral genres and almost equally hard for us to imagine or believe the lingering fascination with oratory in residually oral writing cultures, from the times of Isocrates and Cicero through the Renaissance and on to the Age of Romanticism. We can remember even in our own days the speeches of Fidel Castro running to some six hours or so—without notes—in the residually oral Cuban culture still surviving. The development of the orator's powers in oral performance was the aim of the overarching training in rhetoric that dominated academic education in the West from classical antiquity until relatively recent times. The famous *McGuffey's Readers*, published in some 120 million copies in the United States between 1836 and 1920, were designed to remedy deficiencies not in reading comprehension as such but in declamatory, oratorical-style reading (Ong, *Orality* 115–16). Harvard University still has its Boylston Chair of Rhetoric and Oratory, although its incumbent has by now been transmuted into a de facto professor of creative writing.

We can forget the massive oral heritage in Western academia in the past (see Ong, *Fighting*) and assume too readily that speech in oral cultures typically moves toward oral dialogues like those model dialogues constructed by literate persons—perhaps toward something like Plato's Socratic dialogues or the questions and responses on a MacNeil-Lehrer television newscast. A great many studies about speech in oral cultures suggest that in such cultures use of speech can often be and remain something quite different from this sort of thing.

Articles in *Explorations in the Ethnography of Speaking*, edited by Bauman and Sherzer, although they do not rule out direct dialogue between two or more persons, suggest some of the other sorts of performances and social structures with which oral language can be much involved. Karl Reisman, for example, has studied "speech routines" in an Antiguan village. These are all "forms of expression having living ties with the people who use them" (111)—by contrast, it would seem, to the ancient Greeks' efforts to abstract, once they had interiorized the vowelized alphabet, as in Plato's quite literate oral dialogues, that is, the ancient Greeks' efforts to separate the knower from the known, to "objectify" thought and speech (see Havelock, *Preface*). Again, in different cultures the ratio of speech to intervals of silence varies greatly, but in Antiguan culture often there is little silence or none in some of Reisman's "speech routines" where two people regularly speak at once. The point is that to enter such a speech routine one must assert one's personal presence rather than participate in an ongoing exchange of more or less formalized or "objectified" material (115). But through it all, "positive attention to the feelings of others" is still in play—oral cultures generally being inclined to pay more attention to personal interchange and relatively less to "information" being passed on than are cultures dominated by literacy.

The performances Reisman reports may appear to literates to be confusion when they are in fact simply performances orchestrated in keys with which literates are relatively unfamiliar. Positive value is attached to repetition and indirection of expression (121). Boasting, cursing (a regular verbal dispute form), and argument (not formal argumentation but vociferous proclamations of differing opinions) are the predominant elements in this oral verbal exchange, in which, however, "a certain contrapuntal air" develops (124). But these kinds of speech routines hardly bear much resemblance to dialogue in the sense we commonly think of.

In another noteworthy pattern, ideal speakers among the Vaupes of Southeastern Colombia (Jean Jackson in Bauman and Sherzer) will be multilingual, even in an individual settlement of only two families. "Father languages" (cf. Ong, *Fighting* 36–37n2, concerning mother "tongues" and father "languages") establish group identities—including, for example, what woman can marry what man—but other languages are used for individual speech acts. Language signals and certifies an individual's social identity more than it conveys simple "information." Speakers of several languages keep them scrupulously separate, although a certain amount of mixing may be tolerated on occasion. In this case the context of language and meaning becomes curiously complex. Sherzer (in Bauman and Sherzer 263–82, 462–64, 489) reports that among the Cuna certain lengthy oral performances are incomprehensible to their hearers (as is true among Christian charismatics, who are given to "speaking in tongues" and who in other ways are conspicuously oral not simply in their speaking but also in their modes of behavior).

Shirley Brice Heath has reported on "literacy events" that involve the use of extended oral discourse in a highly oral, but by no means entirely illiterate Appalachian community when literate and less literate persons there are concerned with written material such as printed announcements or directives. Contrasting this community with a nearby but less highly oral community, she shows how the oral language patterns of the highly oral, but not illiterate, community relate closely to other cultural patterns, such as space and time orderings, problem-solving techniques, group loyalties, and the role of the individual in the community (344). Here, in an oral-literate situation, where groups are relating through oral discourse to printed announcements, directives, and the like, by "talking over" such things, extraverbal settings control and interact with the verbal in ways which may be analytically dizzying but are humanly quite manageable.

In oral exchange in any culture, body language is interwoven with spoken language, the two giving meaning to each other. "Words [alone] inadequately express intense feeling" (Newbold 229). Body language is more easily learned than words are. It is preverbal, and spoken words are embedded in and give meaning to it as it gives meaning to spoken words. This kind of context, as has earlier been noted, is completely missing in writing, which is to say that a great deal of the environment in which words have acquired and retain their meaning is missing from writing. Such matters are worth recalling when we get lost in thinking of "logocentrism" as an utterly controlling force in language or when we think of hermeneutic exclusively or predominantly in textual terms.

These accounts of oral cultures or residually oral cultures are quite incomplete samplings, but they show verbal exchange as developing in no neat setting resembling a formal dialogue between literates. Further relevant accounts of oral verbal exchange and its interpretive demands as compared to written texts can be found in the studies in Bauman and Sherzer and in Tannen (*Spoken and Written Language*). Oral exchange, which sets the ground for the first use of words, spoken words, and thus reductively for all words, develops in almost incredibly complex physical and social contexts. It would appear that the kind of dialogue we generally have in mind for discussion of hermeneutics is often historically and sociologically a bit unreal, an exchange of speech in which issues are being reflectively and directly defined and refined. Such exchange depends on the separation of speech and thought from the total human lifeworld, which is one of the undeniably advantageous effects of the technology of writing (and later, even more spectacularly, of the technologies of print and the computer) but which can give us a curiously denatured sense of where words and thoughts come into being and shape up. The carefully focused text of Plato's Socratic dialogues, as has been seen, are obviously not purely oral dialogue but inscribed dialogue which is presented as simply oral but which in fact has been shaped by resort to thought structures brought into being by deep interiorization of script (Havelock, *Preface to Plato*).

Words in oral cultures often interact with one another and with the environment so complexly that they register a lifeworld all but unassimilable by literates. Maurice Houis (ch. 3) has gone so far as to maintain that in oral cultures in Africa, nature is one of the interlocutors in speech.

This accords with Havelock's position in his *Preface to Plato* and later works that oral cultures typically identify knower and known—audiences attended to the *Iliad* and the *Odyssey*, for example, to identify themselves with Achilles and Odysseus and thus appropriate the Greek cultural and psychic heritage, not to understand these heroes analytically. Oral cultures typically make formal use of language to be "with it," to "get into the act," not to break up knowledge as an objective something "out there" in the way one might do in typical classroom discourse. One of the effects of writing is the classroom-type separation of the knower from the known, a separation which would seem to be at best only incipient when one dialogues with nature.

Classifications such as logocentric and phonocentric appear rather remote from the seemingly undifferentiated complexities of the actual primary oral world—which is the world language initially came from. Here everything is seemingly deconstructed from the start in the sense that one does not begin with a language or thought system so precisely consistent that its constructs appear self-supporting and so organized that, without external help, its use can come out utterly consistent with itself. There never has been nor can there be any such language or, for that matter, any such complete system of thought. In oral cultures this truth is not as obscured as it can be in writing, print, and electronic cultures.

The variant modes or forms of verbal communication in oral cultures across the world have only been sampled here. There are a great many other verbal modes or forms in oral cultures that have been studied or that remain to be studied. Those sampled here, and many of the others also, could well be dismissed as simply "barbarian" by those whose paradigms for discourse have been shaped basically by writing, as is the case with most readers in cultures across the world profoundly subject to writing, print, and computerized verbalization. In writing, print, and electronic cultures, occasional instances can doubtless be found more or less redolent of those oral performances here reported in Antiguan or Cuna oral cultures or in the residually oral cultures of Appalachia. But in our own more literate cultures, we are inclined to regard them as deviant from a more "normal" state of affairs. Nevertheless, they have long been regular, frequent, established human ways of verbalizing. They call for different hermeneutics from the hermeneutics we are used to, for the mixture here of the said and the unsaid is strange to us. But it is we who are the deviants, not those in the primary oral cultures, in the sense that it is we who have moved away from the foundational oral world.

It is true that the advances made possible by writing, print, and electronics are magnificent human achievements that can hardly be realized in cultures dominated by those modes of verbalizing which have just been sampled here. But oral modes of verbalizing such as those instanced here are also indisputably human and have been antecedents of those modes which are more familiar to us. They show what a distance was traversed when the mind was empowered by writing—empowered not just for the production of texts but for the production of new modes of oral speech and thought. Havelock contrasts the chirographically organized mind of Plato and his followers with that of ancient Greek oral culture as represented in Homer. But there were pre-Homeric Greeks, too, and still more remote ancestors as well. If we had the evidence, we might well find that the ancestors of the early Greeks may have manifested verbalization patterns not entirely different from those reported by Reisman for the Antiguan people or by Sherzer for the Cuna. These and similar reports situate language and thought in the real world, which is quite different from the textual world treated by deconstructionists but within which and out of which the use of language and the textual world itself eventually grows.

9

LOGOS AND DIGITIZATION

I

In this digitizing age of the computer, by a somewhat more than bimillennial hindsight, one can see something of the deep psychological history and prehistory of digitization reaching back to ancient Greek and its use of the term *logos*. What is noted here does not constitute the whole history of digitization, but it is a central and very human part of its history and prehistory.

Because the term *logos* is commonly translated today as "word," it is readily connected with the world of oral speech. But the history of the term is more complex than such translation suggests. The ancient Greek term *mythos*, which yields our English "myth," at its root means anything delivered by word of mouth and thus from the start was radically acoustic. From the start, it means word, speech, tale, story, and so on. The Indo-European root is *meudh* or *mudh*, and signifies to reflect, think over, consider—activities interior to the human being. The term *logos*, by contrast, comes from the Indo-European root *leg-*, which is based radically not in acoustics and oral speech at all, but rather founded on a spatialized, exteriorized, visual and/or tactile metaphor.

Leg- is the same root which gives us our English term "lay" as well as the Greek verb *legein*, of which *logos* is a cognate. In ancient Greek *legein* means basically to pick up, gather, choose, count, arrange, and thus involves manipulation of discrete units. From this meaning, *legein* develops as an extended meaning "to recount, tell, relate"—that is, to pick out and lay matters in order by use of words. A multitude of terms in English (and other languages) cognate to the Greek *legein* incorporate in various ways this idea of ordering things in space: for example, col*lect*, col*lect*ion, se*lect*, ec*lect*ic (selectively out of order), catalogue. The Latin word for wood or firewood, *lignum*, comes from this same root, for firewood is something collected. The cognate Greek verb *dialegein* similarly means initially to pick out, to select, to separate (cf. digitization), from which its meaning is also extended to refer secondarily to discourse. It gives us our English term "dialogue" and its cognates.

This sense of order (at root coming out of a spatial metaphor) remains operational when *logos*, the noun cognate to the verb *legein*, comes to be used, as it soon does, to signify also the spoken word: *logos* refers specifically, if often only by implication, to the ordering potential in the spoken word—as against the word's more simply manifesting potential. As applied to mental processes, the noun *logos* means initially not just the spoken word as such, but, rather, computation, reckoning, account of money handled, hence treatment of cognitive matters in terms of discrete units—which are the basis of digitization. On the other hand, *logos* also develops a very generalized sense connected with discourse, coming to mean story, reason, rationale, conception, conversation, thought. Hence its meaning of "word"—but a meaning with a deep and complex history.

In a recent book, *Human Communication as Narration* (5), Walter R. Fisher, drawing on Ijsseling as well as Versényi and others, has traced nicely some of the history of *logos* in pre-Platonic and post-Platonic Greek in a way that is helpful here. He points out that, as applied to human activity and human productions generally, by extension of its original sense of gathering or putting in order, *logos* developed not only the very generalized set of meanings referring to speech and thought—"story, reason, rationale, conception, discourse, thought," but an even more generalized sense so that "all forms of human expression and communication—from epic to architecture, from biblical narrative to statuary—came within its purview." These could all be exemplifications of *logos*. *Logos*, in this extended usage, carried with it its original sense of ordering (ultimately, as just noted, associated with a spatial metaphor) which all of these and many other consciously directed human activities enforce or imply. Thus such seemingly diverse phenomena as speech and architecture might both be considered instances of *logos* because both exhibited ordering activity—they show what we today might think of as "rationality" or as "structure."

As *logos* developed from its original spatial-tactile-ordering meaning to mean *word, speech, discourse*, it could be used more or less synonymously with *mythos*, which had started with such meanings rooted in the auditory world, not with the spatially grounded meanings that underlay *logos*. Fisher goes on to note that the pre-Socratic philosophers, and even more Plato and Aristotle, undertook programmatically to oppose this synonymous use of *mythos* and *logos* and to draw careful distinctions between the two terms. Plato's contrast between *mythos* and *logos* is discussed in detail by Havelock in *Preface to Plato* (91, 236, 304 passim; see also Boman 68).

If we consult Plato's *Gorgias*, we find there (449–50) that Socrates wants to use the term *logos* for speech but objects to Gorgias's use of *logos* to refer to speech generally rather than to speech precisely as a rational account. Much of the *Gorgias* is devoted to restricting *logos* to refer only to rational, carefully ordered—today we might say scientific—discourse and thought. Fisher continues:

> As a result of their [Plato's and Aristotle's] thinking, *logos* and *mythos*, which had been conjoined, were dissociated; *logos* was transformed from a generic term into a specific one, applying only to philosophical (later technical) discourse. Poetical and rhetorical discourse were relegated to a secondary or negative status respecting their connections with truth, knowledge, and reality. Poetic was given province over *mythos*; rhetoric was delegated to the realm where *logos* and *mythos* reign in dubious ambiguity. A historical hegemonic struggle ensued among proponents of each of these three forms, and it lasts to this day. (5)

Poetry and rhetoric were less rationalized: they belonged more with *mythos* in our sense of "myth" as a kind of nonscientific narrative. The struggle between logic or dialectic on the one hand (the two were not always clearly distinguished) and on the other hand rhetoric (to which poetic was commonly assimilated) rocked back and forth through the Middle Ages and the Renaissance (Ong, *Ramus, Method* passim). In the Renaissance it came to a kind of peak in Western culture when Francis I named Peter Ramus (Pierre de la Ramée, 1515–72) Regius Professor of Eloquence (i.e., rhetoric) and of Philosophy (i.e., knowledge regulated entirely by *logos*—such knowledge included the equivalent of our modern science). This academic appointment in Paris was to interrelate more effectively the two subjects of rhetoric and logic—that is, reductively, *mythos* and *logos*. The group of Regius Professors whom Francis I founded at Paris would after the French Revolution come to be known as the Collège de France (Ong, *Ramus, Method* 25–27 passim). Ramus's prestige was tremendous: he was the first Dean of the Regius Professors—and thus, by anticipation of the today still active and prestigious Collège de France.

The duration of the struggle between logic and rhetoric into the present day is attested by such things as the current fierce disputes in philosophy, linguistics, and language teaching regarding assignment of priority to scientific-type discourse or to rhetorically managed discourse. Such disputes have generated countless books and journals such as *Philosophy and Rhetoric*, where the issues are discussed with careful scholarly acumen at times agitated to white heat. Is the human intellectual world and/or lifeworld governed at root by logic, that is by purportedly clean-cut scientific thought, or by rhetoric, that is by less than clean-cut, argumentative discourse between existent human beings which is not fully or formally logical, although not anti-logical, discourse involving, beside logical elements, all sorts of nonarticulate elements, including the obscured, practical, operational elements?

We have hinted that *logos* in its root meaning is involved somehow in digitization—although all that Plato encompasses in *logos* cannot be reduced simply to digitization, as is amply evident from Kenneth Seeskin's *Dialogue and Discovery: A Study in Socratic Method*. By digitization is meant here the treatment of knowledge in terms of discrete units. This includes, for example, "treatment of natural language in mathematical-technological terms" (Heim, *Electric Language* 83), such as we find in computers. Digitization means reduction to separate, numerable, forms, to digits. Knowledge thought of as so reduced we commonly designate as "information" or "data" (that is, what is "given"). The term "data" or "what is given" suggests not an oral, auditory world of knowledge allied to spoken words (the original habitat of *mythos*), that is, a world allied to verbalization, but suggests rather more directly a tactile-visual world, a world in which items are somehow physically "given" or handed over to us, are somehow placed "in hand," a world where manipulation is possible (*manus*, at the root of "manipulation," is the Latin word for "hand," *manipulus* the Latin word for "handful"). To conceive of knowledge as "data," as digitizing conceptualization today commonly does (the Latin *digitus* means finger), is to conceive of it as something that can be "handed around," moved around, manipulated.

Ultimately, digitization today culminates in the computer, with its common binary digitization, the reduction of knowledge (data) to the most basic, most stark, most simple of numbers, binary digits, 0 and 1, which a computer "handles" not by conceptualization (as human beings typically do) but simply by local motion, such as spatially separable units allow. Today, by digitization we commonly imply the use of complex instruments or technological contrivances to process (move around) vast, oftentimes billions, of those most elemental units, counters, 0 and 1, or "no" and "yes." Each "bit" of information in a digital computer is always the result of a choice between two alternatives, 0 or 1, no or yes. Such "bits" of information a computer moves around with amazing speed and complexity (often in clusters, or "bytes"). But in the last analysis, moving around or manipulating such information—0 or 1, no or yes—is all a computer can do. The French term for computer makes the situation clear: in French, what English styles a "computer" is called an *ordinateur*, that is, an "arranger."

II

Now for an organic and psychological excursus. "Digit," "digital," "digitize" and their cognates derive from the Latin term *digitus*, "finger." This is no accident. The fingers are commonly, and cross-culturally the first instruments of human digitization, the first instruments used from infancy for counting, processing knowledge numerically. Fingers are of course not numbers, but can be made to "stand for" numbers, as modifications of computer chips, which are not numbers, can be taken to "stand for" numbers. The concepts and/or words "one," "two," "three," and so on are not visual-tactile existents. Fingers are. They are things which can be used to deal with other things numerically, as separate units, data, givens—chickens, cows, ships, or what have you, or even, more indirectly, with distinctly conceived abstractions such as "whiteness," "democracy," and so on—in terms of something else, namely fingers, which can be used conveniently to "stand for" all these other things that they are not, including abstract numbers.

Here, in our fingers, we have a kind of archaic antecedent of the computer. The computer is a thing and the fingers are things. But the fingers are more: they are also a part of ourselves, not simply instruments or technological contrivances. If someone is hurting your finger, you can say, "You are hurting me." As parts of ourselves, these archaic antecedents of the computer are familiar, not strange or foreign. And they are distinct from one another only toward their tips: at their bottom ends, they form a part of a larger whole in that they are somehow one, united in my hand, and united to *me.*

Digitizing items with the fingers thus does not merely separate the items at one end but somehow also domesticates and humanizes them at the other, making them easy to live with and deal with, hooking them up with ourselves. What a wonderful arrangement for a child learning to count, to digitize! Here we have estrangement (*Fremdheit* or *Entfremdung*) on which all method depends, as Gadamer, following Dilthey, explains at length (146ff., 349ff.), but not entire, terrifying, estrangement, because the fingers as counters function as separate from me but not entirely separate from me. Our fingers make a big difference: the decimal numeric system, the dominant system across the world, appears to be based on the ten fingers.

To arrive at a more sophisticated digitization, the reduction of all counting to combinations of 0 and 1, as we do for computerized digitization today, more than fingers were needed. What was needed ultimately was a technology, something outside the human body, as the fingers are not, something admitting of limitless sophistication, so that it could deal (indirectly) even with words themselves. What was needed was first writing, next print, and ultimately an *ordinateur,* an electronic "arranger" or computer.

III

From what appears here, the concept of order, arrangement, seems to be tied ineluctably to a spatial metaphor. The Latin-derived English "order," Latin *ordo*, connects with the Indo-European root *ar-*, meaning to fit together. When the spatially grounded root *leg-* appears in terms referring to intellectual activity, the idea of spatialized order is generally involved, as has been seen: dial*ect*, *elect*, col*lect*, and so on. Order is often a very desirable good and can be indispensable to intelligence and understanding, but to reduce intelligence simply to order is to trivialize intelligence. When we say we understand a matter in depth, we mean more than that we can break it into ordered parts. Computers are not themselves intelligent, yet provide the ultimate in ordering. We often say that we understand another person. Personal relations are a deep human need and good, and they themselves can and do generate all sorts of order. But to try to reduce personal relations simply to order annihilates such relations. Persons are not things. To say that I have a personal relationship with you means more than saying that I am ordered to or by you, or that I can dissect myself and you into neat pieces.

With these reflections on the root meaning of *logos* and of the polarization of *logos* and *mythos* effected after the pre-Socratics by Plato and carried forward by Aristotle, it is possible to state a general theorem about digitization which connects our present computer culture in a deeply significant way, it appears, to the ancient Greek world. We start with the original spoken word, which is nontechnological, produced by the unaided human body alone.

The theorem is this: each application of a new technology to the original, nontechnological spoken word has clearly moved toward greater and greater digitization, radically binary, from the time of the ancient Greeks to the present time in three readily discernible stages. That is to say, the computer is the third stage in binary digitization development beginning with vowelized alphabetic writing and moving through print to the computer itself. Binary digitization of language and thought has been growing toward the computer for over two millennia.

Needless to say, the foregoing theorem is not proposed to explain everything regarding the development of binary digitization. Other forces beyond those considered here are at work variously in various parts of Western culture (which is our basic concern here), not to mention other cultures of the world. Sociological, political, philosophical, religious, and many other kinds of developments are in play. The theorem here regarding the application of technology to the originally vocal (nontechnologized) word is offered for whatever it is worth in connection with other considerations. It does appear important and what it refers to would seem to interact with many other developments and to make the whole more intelligible. The theorem might be considered as a partial hermeneutic of the history of verbalization and of other communication as well as of thought itself.

After counting on the fingers, the first great move toward digitization to which we are attending here followed on the development of the technology of writing, and in particular on the development by the ancient Greeks of the first fully vowelized or vocalized alphabet and on the effect, described by Havelock (*Preface*) on Socratic-Platonic-Aristotelian thought. The second great move toward digitization, more intensive than the first, followed on the development of the technology of printing, and its consequences are evidenced most strikingly—though far from uniquely—in the work of Peter Ramus and his thousands of followers (Ong, *Ramus, Method*). The third great move toward digitization, far more intensive and spectacular, but no more real, than the previous two, has followed on the development of the electronic technology of the computer.

This theorem is proposed first as assisting our understanding of the development of communication and thought, especially in its scientized form, in the West. Application of digitizing technology to the word has not been the only factor affecting this development (see especially Seeskin). Social structures, economic patterns, politics, religion, and many other factors have had their effects. But, it appears that the application of the technologies of writing, print, and electronics to the word is intertwined with many, if not most, of the other forces of mutation in the Western human lifeworld. (See, e.g., Goody, *Logic of Writing*; Graff; Eisenstein, *Printing Press*; Ong, *Ramus, Method*; *Presence*; *Orality*.)

Secondly, the theorem is not proposed as alarmist: the pattern it adverts to should not be taken as threatening or unacceptable but simply as indicating a state of affairs which deserves to be studied further—much further than is possible here.

Thirdly, assigning Plato a major role in the movement toward digitization of the word is certainly not to minimize all of Plato's countless other accomplishments, much less to reduce them all to forms of digitization—although it may variously relate them to digitization. The dialectic in Plato's Socratic dialogues involves much more than a move toward digitization.

Finally, needless to say, the effects of the shift from orality to writing to print to electronics have not been exactly the same in all cultures, although they have not been entirely different either. Here we are attending chiefly to a central line of development in the West.

IV

Of course, it is patent that the over-all thrust of Plato's thought was toward some kind of total synthesis of truth. Yet, in the perspectives in use here, the new technology of writing marked Plato's thought and constituted the first of three definitive steps toward digitization. As has been seen, Havelock's *Preface to Plato* and subsequent works by others (see Ong, *Orality*; "Writing") have made it clear how Plato's insistence on excluding the poets from his republic and on replacing their mode of thinking with the dialectic (binary) mode was a consequence of changes in thought conditioned by the greater and greater interiorization of alphabetic writing, and in particular of the vocalic alphabet which the Greeks had developed out of the initial Semitic consonantal alphabet. The use of the vocalic alphabet for writing promoted analytic thinking as against the more holistic thinking of oral cultures (Ong, *Orality*, 31–77; "Writing"). As earlier noted, Havelock has pointed out how in Homer, and to a lesser degree in Hesiod, the drive of Greek thought was toward identification of the knower and the known: the hearer of the *Iliad* and the *Odyssey* acquired the old-style, pre-Socratic Greek education by identifying with Achilles and Ulysses and others and thus absorbing the culture they represented. This identification was the deep message which the most highly developed oral verbalization, the epic, conveyed, the common public education that the earlier Greek culture provided itself in its use of language and thought.

Plato's approach was different from that of the oral poets, whom he regarded as retrograde sponsor of *mythos* as against *logos*. Plato's approach employed a divide-and-conquer technique, not only in separating the knower from the known but also in arriving at abstract conclusions concerning the known by a dialectical yes-or-no binary procedure, as in his carefully contrived Socratic dialogues. As has just been noted, Plato of course aimed ultimately at a grand synthesis of truth, and so did Socrates, who passionately believed in the use of careful discussion between human beings and, with this discussion, fostered constant concern with the ethical (Seeskin). Such concern with the ethical as such differentiates Socratic dialogue from simple digitization. Yet Socrates's thrust in the dialogues was to isolate issues and decide each item so far as possible in terms of binary yes or no, often by showing that the view opposed to his was wrong and by thus revealing the truth. Socrates (and Plato) wanted explanation: When you say what you say, precisely what do you mean? As Havelock (*Preface*) has shown, even though Plato's text represents the Socratic dialogues as oral discourse, this is a kind of discussion directed by a mind formed in a writing culture. Socratic-type dialogue is not a feature of a primary oral culture. *Logos* calls for yes-no responses, as *mythos* does not, and as computers later would. The strength of the Greek drive toward yes-no responses is confirmed by G. E. R. Lloyd, who, in his *Polarity and Analogy*, has shown how, by circumstantial comparison with a large number of other cultures across the world, ancient Greek thought from the pre-Socratics on specialized markedly in differentiation ("polarity").

V

The relationship of print to the formation and propagation of dichotomized patterns of thought has been worked out in detail in connection with the printed works of Peter Ramus (Pierre de la Ramée, 1515–72), the French educational reformer and philosopher (Ong, *Ramus, Method*). Until our computer age, Ramus was perhaps the most avid promoter of dichotomization (binary digitation) for all human thought whom the world has seen. As compared to ancient Greek logic, medieval logic had moved toward greater and greater quantification (Ong, *Ramus, Method* 54–91) but, aided by the new invention of print, Ramus in his own way went spectacularly further. He promoted digitization through printed dichotomized tables consisting of spatially ordered printed words.

In earlier schematizations at logic in the early days of print, before this new technology of print had been fully interiorized so as to affect thought in depth, iconographic models of thought processes, including iconographic models of logic itself, survived. Thus in his *Logica memorativa* (Strasbourg 1509), Thomas Murner (1475–37) explained the structure and function of logic in pictorial symbols (see Ong, *Ramus, Method* 84–89). Murner used such iconographic symbols as human and animal figures, bells (to denote enunciations—made with sounded words), weights (representing affirmative propositions), ropes (which stopped movement of the weights and thereby symbolized negative propositions), birds of different species to represent propositions with no common term, a schoolmaster with his switches (to extract logical answers from the pupils), and so on. (See figure 1.) All these designs were related to one another in illustrations accompanied by a text to explain what logic was and how it worked.

Some forty years later, when the effect of print had sunk more deeply into the psyche, Ramus and his followers replaced such mind-boggling diagrams of his predecessors simply with printed dichotomized outlines of words displayed in space, producing what were in effect precocious computer flow-charts (Ong, *Ramus, Method* [1983 edition], viii, 86, 87, 202, 317) explaining the organization of the logic of science by splitting it up into various "parts," all binary, these into further binary parts, and so on. (See figure 2.)

Dichotomized outlines are not entirely new with print. They occur occasionally in manuscripts before printing. But, as compared to ordinary continuous text, which can be multiplied by dictation to any number of scribes for simultaneous copying, elaborate dichotomized outlines or other diagrams demand individual visual access for copying and are subject to many copying errors. They are hard to reproduce manually. With print, however, once an outline, however complicated, is set up in print-controlled space, it can be multiplied on a press as readily as continuous text. The almost incredibly widespread use of dichotomized outline charts by Ramus and his followers is thus a consequence of the new print technology (see Ong, *Ramus, Method* 79).

Ramus's outlines, made up simply of printed words connected by lines in flow-chart form, divided logic itself into two parts, "invention" and "judgment," then each of these into two, then each of the resulting divisions into two, each of these into two more, and so on until the entire science had purportedly been entirely outlined in binary divisions. The digitization he applied to logic, Ramus insisted, also should apply to all organized human thinking on any and all subjects (Ong, *Ramus, Method* 225–69). Ramists printed dichotomized outlines of everything imaginable, from the Hebrew alphabet to the life of Cicero and even the bubonic plague (Ong, *Ramus, Method* 300–301). Ramus's mind-set was recognized by his contemporaries as what we today would style digitized. The Duke of Guise in Kit Marlowe's play *The Massacre of Paris* gives voice to a widespread perception when he characterizes Ramus as a "flat dichotomist" (Ong, *Ramus, Method* 199). As Frances Yates (234–35) has so well put it, Ramus practiced "inner iconoclasm," substituting for Murner's kind of elaborate and elusive iconographic imagery mere printed words arranged spatially in pairs, which were subdivided into further pairs, until the subject was exhausted.

The use of such printed charts by Ramus and his epigone was intellectually block-busting in its implications. Ramus's followers were numbered in the tens of thousands and the massive effects of his work, direct and indirect, in Western Europe and the American colonies, have not yet been traced entirely. His followers were, if anything, more rabid binary digitizers than Ramus himself. In 1618 Marcus Rutimeier published in Bern his *Idea methodica,* subtitled *Analysis logica,* in which not only the subject headings but every single sentence and/or word of the text of Ramus's *Dialectica* (the term was used synonymously with *Logica*) is spitted on dichotomized tables (Figure 2; Ong, *Ramus, Method* 317). Ramism leads directly to the linguistics of Cartesianism (Ong, *Ramus, Method* 307) and of John Locke.

VI

With the advent of electronic processing, the computer of course has carried to points previously inconceivable the digitization patterns adumbrated by Plato and his followers and institutionalized more spectacularly by Ramus and his followers with the aid of print. Today, the seemingly unlimited possibilities of computerized digitization are being worked out still further, *ad infinitum.*

Recognition of the pattern in evidence now for well over two millennia, since ancient Greece, should make the digitization process endemic to the computer perhaps a bit less threatening than it may appear to many. The computer is not an utterly new development. It represents the most recent stage in the technologizing of the word which began with writing, and most notably with vocalic alphabetic writing, and which was intensified by print. Each new technology applied to the originally spoken word restructures thought. As Havelock and others have done in the case of writing and as I and others have done in the case of print, so, in his *Electric Language* Michael Heim has undertaken to work out some of the noetic restructuring brought on by the advent of the computer. But it could be argued that this latest restructuring is no more drastic than that entailed when vocalic alphabetic writing separated *logos* definitively from *mythos* and took the first definitive steps into the modern scientific world by dislodging the word from sound and committing it programmatically—though never entirely—to space (see Havelock, *The Muse Learns to Write*). It will be recalled that the concept itself of *logos* has deep roots in spatial order, from which it was extended to verbalization and thought.

VII

A few more reflections are in order concerning what digitization entails. Treating of the ultimate (thus far) digitization found in the computer, Heim states that "When something is digitized, it is interpreted as a sequence of numbers, numbers that have a precision that cannot be experienced directly in the original phenomenon, though the original phenomenon may have a precision that cannot be reduced to quantities or numerical relationships" (84). Earlier computers were analog computers, which dealt with materials not entirely reducible to quantities or numerical relationships, but analog computers have by now been replaced almost entirely by digital computers (Hogrebe). With electronics, digitization is carrying the day in most areas of communication, from ordinary word-processing through three-dimensional computer simulations back into the world of sound itself, with digitized sound recordings and sound-production, and even digitized television.

A thermometer can perhaps serve as a useful example of what has been going on here. A column of mercury in a vacuum tube can be compared to an analog computer. The mercury moves up and down in a way comparable to, analogous to the outside temperature. If the outside temperature is never fixed but always in flow, changing, the column of mercury is behaving the same way. If we impose a numerical scale on the mercury column, we convert it into a digital computer. Now the movement of the mercury is measured in discrete digits. It is calculated as moving from 40 degrees to 41 degrees, or to 41.5 degrees, or to 41.52 degrees, or to 41.528741 degrees, depending on how finely one wishes to divide the numerical units. Imposition of these units makes the instrument more useful. But the units also leave out something, or entail a certain falsification. For the mercury in the tube can be constantly in motion, never stopping at any of the digits at which we consider it to be fixed. High technology seeks to solve the problem here by digitizing into smaller and smaller units, down, let us say, to millionths of a degree. The effect is that, to all intents and purposes, the difference between truly continuous motion and digitized motion can ultimately be disregarded. A few millionths of a degree makes ultimately no great difference to the human sensibility.

Strangely, despite the neglect of the truly continuous motion and the resort to utterly minuscule falsification, extremely fine digitization can in fact make for greater human accuracy. Dealing directly with the column of mercury without digitization, dealing with it as a true analog of the real temperature presumably never fixed at any point, could not possibly be managed very exactly at all. Treating the continuous as noncontinuous can be managed so as to provide tremendous advantages. (We will have to bypass the complex and at this point unrealistic questions about the possible constitution of matter in exact digital particles moving in exact digital patterns.)

To sense what is at stake here, it may be well to take the instance of the clock or watch. Timepieces of this sort represent an early example of digitization which remains perhaps the most spectacular example of all. For in the human lifeworld the least digitizable phenomenon would appear to be time itself. The time through which we move in our living experience simply has no clean-cut divisions in itself as time at all. *Tempus fugit*, time runs away, you cannot stop it. There are of course successions of days and seasons, but the break from one day to the next is not the kind of thing a clock makes it out to be. No one can find *precisely* the motionless instant at which yesterday clicked into today at what we consider to be midnight. You can get closer and closer to the hypothetical exact digitized instant, but the closer you get, the clearer it is that it cannot be found. For there was no motionless instant. Time was flowing without interruption. The interruptions we use—changes of light, of seasonal temperatures, and so on—are not time itself. They are occurrences in time. Time itself simply marches on.

Now a clock or watch pretends that matters are otherwise, that somehow there are separable units into which time can be divided—hours, minutes, seconds, tenths of seconds, and so on. A clock or watch is useful and indeed indispensable today in high-technology cultures, but most cultures have never used clocks or watches and many still do not. In high-technology cultures we have made clocks and watches so much a part of ourselves, so interiorized them in our psychic life that only with gargantuan effort can we distance ourselves from them to sense what they really are and what time really is independently of their measurements.

The deep effects within the psyche of the digitization of time make themselves felt overwhelmingly in the limp watches of Salvador Dalí's famous painting, *The Persistence of Memory*. Here the faces of watches, regulatory instruments which digitize time, the unmanageable, the essentially undigitizable, are disturbingly deprived of their prim flatness and neat precision by being draped misshapenly and listlessly over furniture and other objects. In these distorted, limp watches, which cannot possibly work, a deep symbol of the precision that marks the age of science based so heavily on interpreting reality in sequences of rigidly fixed numbers (on the faces of watches involved further with geometrical figures, circularity, and so on) has collapsed. The shock to the psyche is profound, and it is no accident that this is one of Dalí's most famous paintings in our digitizing age. On the occasion of his recent death, it was the painting that a great many, if not most, of the media accounts called attention to, without, so far as I know, any of the analysis just stated here. Perhaps this painting lies at the very heart of Dalí's significance for his era. The retrospective title of the painting itself is informative: *The Persistence of Memory*. Human memory dwells in time and is more than just recall: it is, strictly speaking, nondigitizable, as is the case with time itself. When we remember something, the memory has always a context, and a variable context, not the same today as yesterday. Human memory belongs with thought as such: it is not computerized recall.

VIII

What does the movement toward greater and greater digitization in our culture imply in that restructuring of the human lifeworld that we all sense is well under way across the globe? One of the results of the tremendous power of digitization in aiding verbalization and thought has been inevitably the dream of producing "artificial intelligence," the dream that the computer will eventually be able to do everything that the human mind can do. There is a literature on this subject simply too vast to be engaged here. Some of the literature has been reviewed by J. David Bolter in his *Turing's Man: Western Culture in the Computer Age* (see also Dreyfus, *Mind over Machine*), although the literature continues to grow by leaps and bounds year by year.

The present perspectives, however, suggest several specific reasons why the computer cannot match human language and thought. First, as has been seen, human language and thought are embedded in the nonverbal, the total human, historical, existential environment of utterance, with which they interact dialectically to produce meaning. This total environment cannot be entered into the computer. To digitize it would require infinite digitization. Second, language and thought are grounded not only in what is said but also in what is not said, in silence. This, again, cannot be digitized for computer processing. Thirdly, neither can the computer of itself enter into the personal dialogical relationship which involves both consciousness and the unconscious, the total human environment.

Artificial intelligence assumes that human intellectual processes reduce to the sort of thing that computers do so well. But the reduction is radically incomplete. Language and thought are only partly and superficially assimilable to digitization for reasons with which these reflections here have been dealing throughout. The totality of intellectual and verbal processes escapes computerization insofar as the totality is more than merely rational, beyond even the fuzziest "fuzzy logic." Bolter argues well (238) that "synthetic intelligence" would be a better term than "artificial intelligence" for the ventures being undertaken under this latter name. The computer can aid intelligence virtually without limit. But it is not intelligent and cannot be.

IX

The near obsession with hermeneutics in the academic world today appears to be a countervalent to the computerization, the digitation that affects us all, directly and indirectly. For the digitization drive that makes high-technology cultures today and is spreading across the world as all cultures come more and more into the ambit of high technology has been accompanied by the intense concern with hermeneutics and related subjects of which we have been treating here. Digitization is a fractioning movement. It sections actuality and thought and language into smaller and smaller pieces—pieces finally so small that humanly we can no longer keep track of them, so that what we seem to have in hand is not pieces but continuity, integrity, wholes—but these are always fractioned wholes, however insensibly minute the fractioned wholes, however insensibly minute the fractions are. Hermeneutics or interpretation follows a dialectically complementary pattern. It aims at defractioning, at merging at holistic apprehension of truth. As has frequently been noted here earlier, to interpret anything totally requires knowledge of everything, since everything relates ultimately to everything else, not digitally but existentially.

As has been seen, a closed system of any kind is impossible. When you conclude an explanation, for practical purposes in the given situation you may be finished, but, on further grounds—grounds not worth traversing at the time but still there—further questions are still possible. Total explanation, which no one realistically envisions or aims at, could conclude only when all is related to all. Hermeneutics in some way ambitions ultimately to embed everything in the seamless web of history.

It is arguable that both an intense commitment to digitization, fractioning, and an intense commitment to hermeneutics, holistics, are equally marks of our age. Moreover, digital computers are being used to expedite hermeneutics (although of themselves they necessarily fall short of being truly hermeneutical) and hermeneutics is being used (as here) to deal (imperfectly) with digitization, to try to relate digitation nondigitally or transdigitally to everything else. Perhaps nothing hints more directly how dialectically human thought is structured than this dual allegiance here. Allied to the totalizing effect of hermeneutics is the totalizing concern with the universe manifest in the ecological mentality that marks our age. Perhaps a final personal reflection would be in place here. The late Professor William K. Wimsatt and I were dear friends. I dedicated one of my books, *Interfaces of the Word*, to him, noting in the dedication that he had once told me, "I am a space man, you are a time man." As a space man, William Wimsatt was passionately committed to logic, and to collecting (putting together in spatial order—remember that the root of *logos* refers to gathering, collecting) many sorts of things: Native American Indian artifacts, postage stamps, rock specimens (all duly polished in a polishing drum and then displayed), portraits of Alexander Pope. His last book was an inventory of portraits of Pope, all arranged in order of their relationship to one another. I, too, am in favor of logic, but I like to remind myself that logic is an afterthought. And I feel sure that Wimsatt would agree: he and I both believed in both time and space, although we might tend to specialize differently.

In many senses, logic, as formally conceived structure, is an afterthought. Human beings had to do a lot of thinking, hundreds of thousands of years of thinking, before they discovered, following on the development of the fully vocalized alphabet some 2700 years ago, what we now call formal logic. Logic applies to what has already been thought, in the sense which Gadamer has hammered down: there is no completely logical method for setting up a way to get into full truth. We can keep our thinking and experiments as logical as possible, but the truth has to be worked out to some degree at random and then tested for logicality after we have stumbled on it by ways which may well involve some logic but involve much more besides (Tyler, *The Said*).

10

HERMENEUTICS IN CHILDREN'S LEARNING TO SPEAK

It is possible to discuss the learning of languages by children in terms of hermeneutic or interpretive processes involved, and indeed to view learning to speak as an exercise in interpretation—bringing out what is concealed in a given manifestation. For a child just learning to speak, in a special way words at first conceal much more than they reveal. Here we shall make an effort to discuss language learning very briefly as an interpretive or hermeneutic project.

A common, relatively unreflective, view of language considers it as a naming system. In this view, children learn language by simply learning to put names on things and actions and, ultimately, on all sorts of quite abstract concepts. They learn this naming process simply by imitating adults. We may even be inclined to think of naming as "labeling." But "label" is a script-based concept. Oral cultures have no way of conceiving of a word in this fashion, as something seen. A friend of mine who has done rather massive field work in the islands of southeast Asia has told me of oral peoples there who feel that a word names something because the thing in question "calls out" its name.

As John McShane's review and critique of recent literature in his *Learning to Talk* shows, a child does not acquire language by learning first simply individual words applied to things and then putting the words together grammatically to form sentences. Children work first not with words that they feel as words in the way adults do, but rather with utterances—sounded, vocal creations which first are more or less of a piece with other events and things in which a child finds himself or herself embedded. The context of language learning is communal and social. McShane (2–10) instances the use of "mummy" by a very young child not to label mother but to secure certain results, such as an adult might, for example, secure by means of a word such as "help." "Mummy" triggers responses: it can secure food, drink, mere attention. "Mummy" does something. It is a functional utterances rather than a designative name. Reflecting on observations such as these, a friend of mine recently remarked to me that her infant daughter uses "mummy" quite indifferently for her mother herself and for her baby-sitter or other persons to get results.

Children have to learn from interactions with others how sounds they make function in intentional settings (Fletcher and Garman). McShane notes that "Words, qua words, do not have salience for the child initially. . . . Language development is best studied as the development of intentional communication" (1). As Tyler puts it (*The Said* 26), a baby lives "in an environment predestined to interpret his cries as meaningful messages." As caretakers systematically respond "to the child's utterances as if these utterance are intentional . . . the child will thus come to learn that there are contingent relations between his or her own utterances and the behavior of other people" (McShane 146).

It should be noted that what "intentional" refers to here is not the notion that a speaker has an always explicitly definable intention in a given utterance. What the intention is will be a matter not merely of words but of the total existential situation, which includes uttered words but which cannot, as we have seen earlier, be made totally explicit verbally. The child needs to pick up simply the notion that words have "intention" that is specifically verbal, that they are meant to function as nonwords do not, to symbolize in particular ways. Finding out exactly what an individual word or words "intends" is a matter of hermeneutics, of interpretation, which is precisely one of the things the child has to work through in working with "intention."

An instance of a child's early relationship to writing may be of help here. I recall a Candid Camera television show of a few years ago in which an adult asked a youngster some four years old, "Can you write?" "Yes," she beamed back confidently. "Show me," the man requested. The little girl scrawled a long, twisted, looped-over line on the blackboard provided by the show. "That's fine," her adult interlocutor said pleasantly, "but I can't read it." "I can," the little girl said, and went on, " 'Once upon a time a little girl . . .' " The situation was clear. The child understood that writing had something to do with the production of speech, and, although she had no clear idea of how it worked, she wanted very much to get into the act, and did, in her own way. There are analogies with the learning of oral speech here. Children know that with speech something is going on out there, and they want to get into it but to do so they have gradually to figure out what it is that is going on.

Eventually, McShane shows, with a very limited range of utterances or sound creations which produce desired results, such as a few words constituting personal names and words such as *look*, to direct attention, *more* to request recurrence, *here*, *there*, *no*, and so on, the child begins to master more fully more exact intentional situations in which words can function in quite specific, predictable ways (McShane 140 passim). But this does not lead immediately to structured language, to "grammar," as McShane points out. What leads to grammar, structured language, is the development of naming, which means not simply the utterance of names (such as "mummy" above here) but the development of the concept of what naming is, "a particular conceptual relationship between language and the world" (McShane 147), or, we might say, between the word and the nonverbal. This concept develops gradually. Language learning does not start with naming. In this sense, language learning is not logocentric. In the child, language grows out of the fact that "although the child does not initially possess an intention of using language to name objects . . . nevertheless his or her utterances are treated [by caretakers and others] as if they were attempted naming" (146).

At this point, we become involved in the mysterious intersubjectivity of human beings. It has been noted earlier that in order for me to say anything to you, I have to have in advance some conjectural feedback, have to be able to conjecture what you might say in response to what I am about to say. If I am speaking to a five-year-old, I speak differently from the way I would speak to an adult. I have in my own mind a sense of the child's mind or of the adult's mind, as the case may be. Somehow, I have to be inside another's consciousness in order to have something to say or even to think.

The mysterious intersubjectivity which marks human consciousness and which can only be pointed to but not fully explained here, lies at the basis of all use of names and indeed of all words as words. In learning to speak a language, the child has to learn to interpret intersubjectively. For a sound to function as a word, the speaker has to intend that the sound he or she makes so function—that is, that the sound is not *just* a noise but has some specially intended purpose of its own. And the hearer has to know that the speaker so intends the word to function as a name. Further, the speaker has to know that the hearer knows that he or she so intends. And all this network has to be set up initially without being explained in words, for it lies beneath the use of words as words. It lies in our intersubjectivity, in our being able to be aware of and, in a way, to participate in and interpret the subjective consciousness of other human beings. Hermeneutic or interpretive activity, like intentionality, precedes as well as accompanies naming as such. For the child is interpreting word and context for quite practical purposes before he or she can put together a grammatical utterance.

Our purpose here is not to explicate in detail all that goes on in learning language and the implications of naming, but simply to adduce enough evidence to show that from the start language learning is not essentially an exercise in affixing names and structuring them in relation to one another but is a complex hermeneutic or interpretive process, involving the entire world in which the child is situated, and involving intersubjectivity.

Keller's report (*Story* 34–37) referred to earlier brings out the intersubjectivity inseparable from the objectivity that words involve. All in one moment, the deaf and blind Helen suddenly realized that the "w-a-t-e-r" that her teacher Anne Sullivan was spelling onto her hand as she held her hand under the "water" was a name that meant "the wonderful cooling something that was flowing over my hand." Simultaneously, she knew that there was an existent that a word (in her case apprehended tactilely) could represent, that what she felt flowing over her hand *was* water, that Miss Sullivan knew it was water and knew that Helen knew it was water and knew that Helen knew that she, Miss Sullivan, knew that it was water, and so on. The intersubjective world and the objective, named world bloomed simultaneously, each interpreting the other. The act of naming, not "presenting" but representing, she now grasped.

There are of course incalculably more things to say about how children learn language. The point here, however, is simply to instance how the process is drastically hermeneutical, a process of bringing out something concealed in a given manifestation. At first, language conceals from the child learning it far more than it reveals. Gradually, it reveals more.

11

LANGUAGE, TECHNOLOGY, AND THE HUMAN

Gadamer's point that all language is essentially writable and gains by being written is certainly well taken (*Truth and Method* 354). But by the same token all language is also essentially printable and electronically processible, and gains by being printed and electronically processed. The fact that certain losses are entailed in the gains thus achieved, as has been earlier suggested, does not make the gains less real. If writing is a technology that transforms thought (Ong, *Orality*; *Presence*; "Writing") and if the technology of print further transforms thought (Ong, *Orality*; "Samuel Johnson") and if electronic technology effects comparable transformations in thought, as Heim has shown, it would appear that technology has a much closer interior bond with human consciousness than is commonly allowed for. For instance, modern musical instruments that have made the modern orchestra possible are the result of technology, as never before (Bekker). Yet these technologized instruments express what is truly human in ways impossible without the technology. Technology is not external to, but part of human life, including the operations within intellectual life.

In dealing with language, we are dealing with a phenomenon closely entwined with human technological competence, which takes language from its original oral habitat—nontechnological, for no tools are normally involved in oral speaking—to a technologically managed visual or visual-tactile world and, through this world, into a world of secondary orality, the world of radio and television and VCRs and all the rest, where the use of vocal and other sound is dependent on the technologies of writing, print, and now electronics.

Language is deeply embedded in the nonlinguistic from the start of human history and from the start of individuals' language-learning history. If this connection of language is not attended to and language is treated on purportedly purely linguistic grounds, any language—oral, and/or textual and/or electronic—deconstructs itself from start to finish. The recent work on orality-writing-print-electronic contrasts suggests that the alliance of language and thought with technology must be taken into account in interpretive or hermeneutic procedures, as it has been in the work of Parry, Lord, Havelock, Eisenstein, Heim, and many others. In *The Humiliation of the Word,* Jacques Ellul has underlined some of the problems which have arisen as the word has been moved from the oral to the visual world, but we must remember that the kind of closely reasoned critique which Ellul produces would be quite impossible until the word has been transformed technologically into the visual world by writing and print. *The Humiliation of the Word* is not only thought out in analytic forms of thought unknown before the technology of writing but is also a product of the technological-visual medium of print (now commonly produced through electronic word processing).

What can all this mean in all its aspects for the future of humankind? The intrinsic involvement of language and thought with technology appears to be testimony to the unity of humankind not only with itself but with all the rest of the universe. The old dichotomy of the interior and the exterior remains valid. We know it, each of us, in his or her own life: the interiority of the "I" each of us speaks contrasts with the exteriority of the world with which we are surrounded. As phenomenological studies have made a commonplace, interior and exterior meet in the body, which is included in the interior "I" or "me," as well as in the exterior world. "Quit kicking me," we say, not "Quit kicking my body." Yet parts of this body can be excised while the "I" remains completely intact. All this is well known, if far from entirely explained.

But the involvement of interior and exterior found in the intimate connections between language and thought on the one side and the technologies of writing, print, and electronics on the other is something relatively new to our reflective consciousness. It must enter now into our efforts to interpret, to explain, how language and thought are involved in everything else in and around us. Awareness of these connections must more and more shape our hermeneutic of human existence.

The age in which human existence is now framed, the age in which human life and technology so massively and intimately interact can well be styled not only the information age and the age of interpretation, but. perhaps even more inclusively, the ecological age, in principle an age of total interconnectedness, where everything on the earth, and even in the entire universe, is interconnected with everything else, not only in itself but, ideally, in human understanding and activity. In "The American College in the Ecological Age," Thomas Berry has proposed that education for ecological understanding of the universe and of the human being's place in the universe through the earth on which we live should be the central aim of liberal education in our day. Although Berry does not go into the matter, this would seem to include the human being's place as developed through language and technology. Berry discusses how the ecological period in which we now live culminates and supersedes earlier successive stages, such as, for example, the prepatriarchal matricentric stage, the classical-religious stage, and the scientific stage, that have marked human macrohistory. In our present ecological stage of consciousness into which the world, through human beings, has entered, unification is the wave of the future. Human beings know more about the physical world in which they exist and are more in charge of it as a whole than was possible or even imaginable in earlier days. Divisiveness is outmoded, or should be as far as possible.

In this age, the consuming interest in hermeneutics, as the effort—always desperately incomplete—to achieve fuller and fuller explanation, to relate everything to everything else, is a special manifestation of the unification pattern, the totalizing pattern, which ecology necessarily involves. Paradoxically, the unification toward which we must work, also involves the digitization which marks human knowledge in our time, despite the fact that digitization, as has been seen, proceeds by division into discrete parts. Paradoxically, only through the vast amounts and the massive structures of knowledge which digitization makes it possible to achieve and to manage to a degree can the details needed for massive hermeneutic unification effort be dealt with, although the digitization never fully accomplishes the hermeneutic. It only helps in certain ways to implement it.

For digitization is still digitization. It is fractioning, indeed infrafractioning, apparently destined to be developed more and more as computerization becomes more omnipresent in human life. Digitization can be accomplished more efficiently by machines. But unification must be achieved within the human sensibility, not within a machine. The more important the computer becomes, the more supremely important the human being also becomes. Despite all the work to achieve "artificial intelligence" through the computer, the computer always lacks the living silence in which, as we have seen, human thought and language are embedded, it lacks the unconscious in which human thought and language are also embedded, and it lacks the biological substructures in which human thought and language are embedded (Ong, *Fighting*).

The computer lacks rhetoric, out of which *logos* and logic grew and in which they remain embedded (Ong, *Interfaces* 209, 301). However, the intimate alliance between the interior resources of language and thought and the exteriority of technology made evident by a deeper understanding of the nature and operation of writing, print, and electronics should make it possible to deal with digitization without the hostility to it, and to other technology, that has sometimes impeded deeper humanistic and religious understanding.

12

EPILOGUE

The Mythology of Logos

I

In these reflections, we have been examining hermeneutics largely in terms of *logos* and *mythos*, more or less as these were polarized following the work of Plato, implemented as this work was by thought patterns made possible by the introduction of writing in Greek culture. Which is the more inclusive, *logos* or *mythos*? Either? Neither? And in what sense or senses? These final reflections will attempt to deal with such questions. The reflections will be more suggestive than totally conclusive.

As has been seen, Plato was convinced that the *mythos* of poetry (basically Homer) had lain at the center of Greek education and its concern with *mimesis* or "imitation," and he undertook to move Greek thought away from such *mythos* toward *logos*, the reality of the Platonic "ideas." "For Plato," Havelock summarizes (*Preface* 25) "reality is rational, scientific and logical, or it is nothing." Poetry "disguises and distorts reality and . . . distracts us and plays tricks with us" (Havelock, *Preface* 26). We are today more aware than Plato was that narrative poetry and all poetry is in fact highly structured, while we are also aware that its structure is not that of scientific logic—although structuralist poetics has in our day tried to apply forms of binary analysis (digitization) even to narrative itself.

From this point on, I shall be using "myth" and its cognates, such as "mythology," "mythic," etc., in the quite various, but not unrelated, senses in which they have come to be used today and which the context will in each instance, I trust, usually make adequately specific. The senses are all connected, directly or indirectly with the meaning of the original Greek *mythos*, something uttered, especially a story. (Narrative, a story, a sequence of happenings, is somehow involved in all utterance, for all utterance in one way or another emerges from our experience in the temporal sequence in which we live.)

A story of the sort we commonly call a myth is not at all of necessity historically true (on occasion it may be), but it is a story which commonly means more than it seems to on the surface. A myth about a dragon, for example, may signal all sorts of psychological or physical dangers. Myths commonly refer to matters of deep human concern, although they may do so in a veiled way. As Northrop Frye has liked to point out, myths are faced inward to the life of the human community, not outward in the way in which strict historical narrative or a scientific account is (although these, too, may have their concealed mythological elements). Myths often tend to grow together to present a more or less organic whole, as in the various myths which combine to give us the Greek pantheon.

Achieving total rationality, fully realizing *logos* in a context initially dominated by *mythos* is an arduous and always incomplete process, as Seeskin has abundantly shown Plato's Socrates was well aware. Socrates was modest not in his efforts, but in his claims to full achievement, especially since he thought of *logos* as involving not simply intellectual matters but the formation of the individual's character in relentless intellectual honesty. Thus we here can raise the question as to how far the effort to achieve *logos* was, or could be, in ancient Greece or now, fully and completely successful. The question has a bearing on what we make of hermeneutics.

We have been understanding hermeneutics or interpretation in a general and ordinary sense, as the bringing out of what is concealed in a given manifestation. Although, as we have seen, what is concealed can of course in some instances be brought out, explained, by means other than verbal—by such things as a gesture, for example—nevertheless, as we have also seen, hermeneutics or interpretation moves toward verbalization, favors verbalization. Hermeneutics of course is never complete. It can suffice for a given state of affairs for a given audience at a given real time, and be quite true, but its sufficiency is never absolute. Additional questions can always be put. What we are dealing with in hermeneutics is always thus in some sense a will-o'-the-wisp, something which in its totality is destined to escape us in the sense that verbalized hermeneutics or verbal interpretation of anything in its full relationships with everything else can in principle and in fact go on and on and on. Verbal explicitation of all connections is permanently beyond reach.

Hermeneutics or interpretation, as the bringing out of what is concealed in a given manifestation, is not simply an academic matter. As has been seen, it is concerned with more than texts and with more than academic subjects. When Gadamer insists quite rightly that hermeneutics covers more than the humanities, he makes the point that it includes the natural sciences, too (see Weinsheimer 36). Here, however, we are going still further and considering interpretation not simply as something that grows primarily out of texts or out of scientized discourse but as a part of the fabric of human life. To get through the day in a community of human beings, we are constantly involved, informally as well as formally, in interpreting to one another ourselves and our surroundings, not to mention our verbal utterances. Gadamer (*Truth and Method* 345ff.) discusses at length the more widespread need for hermeneutics in the human lifeworld generally, but he comes to this discussion out of a universe of specific philosophical questions dealt with by Heidegger and many others. Here we crisscross his area of discussion, by moving in from our own center of concern, the effects of the technologies of writing, print, and electronics on hermeneutics or interpretive activity.

Interpretation has become more and more a part of human life as the information we deal with has grown incalculably with the application of the technologies of writing, print, and electronics to the originally nontechnological oral word. These technologies have increased and continue to increase information beyond all measure, and have affected the modes of human knowledge and interpretation. The more information we have on hand, the more interpretation or hermeneutics is possible and called for, and the more technologies change the management of language and thought, the more interpretation itself changes form.

In *No Sense of Place* (311–12), Joshua Meyrowitz, following Michel Foucault, has made the point that television and other modern media have created new social environments, which include new environments of understanding. The new media have changed drastically, for example, who knows what about whom, and from childhood on. The electronic age makes for more and more exposure of knowledge generally. Much of the mystification earlier surrounding such matters as the professions, gender distinctions, the adult world as hidden from children, and so on ad infinitum, is being more and more done away with. For example, with the aid of a sonogram, not only an adult but even a young child today can view his or her younger sister or brother even before birth, in the mother's uterus. Sonograms of this sort have recently been featured publicly on television programs. What was earlier inviolably intimate or totally inaccessible is often now on total public display. The computer is particularly effective in implementing the widespread disclosure of knowledge which characterizes the entire electronic age, since, through computerized simulation and other procedures, it potentially makes all sorts of data equally accessible to an unprecedented degree and even thrusts that data into the private home (Meyrowitz 327). The amount of portrayal of violence, for example, pumped daily by television into millions of homes across the world had no counterpart in earlier ages, even in societies (and there were such) proportionately more violent than many of ours today.

Our increased and boundlessly circulatable data invite—in fact, often demand—increased interpretation or hermeneutics that is virtually nonstop. Print media, radio and television, fax machines, and other devices, abetted by always burgeoning computer programs, constantly supply varying interpretations of the flood of information inundating human consciousness today, from personal, domestic and political events to developments in the physical sciences and all other academic subjects, local to international politics, business, religion, and what have you. The amount of information called forth, for example, by such an event as the Oliver North trial—not counting the masses of shredded material rendered forever unavailable—could not be remotely dreamed of in the forensics of pre-electronic ages. And information always spreads. Despite frantic efforts at containment, there are always leaks.

A sense of a world with an overload of information appears to be built into the fabric of the postmodern consciousness. Samuel Beckett's *Waiting for Godot* (1955), for example, was already paradigmatic. The play is clearly, among other things, a reaction to the information overload in modern culture. In this play of Beckett's, interpretation is to all intents and purposes simply abandoned as too overwhelming a demand to be taken seriously. No one knows who Godot is, why the two main characters in the play are waiting for him, what their other than coincidental relationship to one another is, or virtually how anything or anyone else is clearly to be understood. But the play has been—still is—a rewarding experience for countless audiences. It catches the feel of elements of today's human lifeworld—an overwhelming situation in which there is simply too much information to handle. But interpretation here, as always, is still in desperate demand, and because *Waiting for Godot* calculatingly stymies interpretation, the play has from the beginning certainly generated and frustrated more interpreters than most other dramatic productions.

The increment of information that overwhelms and smothers us today demands proportionate multiplication and intensification of interpretation. The age we live in is commonly described as an information age. But, as earlier noted, it could be described just as appropriately as an interpretation or a hermeneutic age. Today interpretation is so much in demand that interpretations are often programmatically multiple and varied. One of the common features of programming in the media now is the confrontational interview, in which—as in the MacNeil-Lehrer television newscast, for example—an interviewer draws out from various respondents their partly contrasting, partly complementary interpretations of public events or other matters. Today's full-blown application of the technologies of writing, print, and electronics to the originally nontechnological oral word has made interpretation more and more necessary and has implemented it as it could never have been implemented earlier. The details made accessible by computers and other means are beyond measure. Even a straightforward event such as a baseball game floats into the television audience's attention in a maze of interpretive maneuvers—batting averages and other statistics and countless instant playbacks ad nauseam, devices and procedures totally impossible a few decades ago.

Not only in such relatively simple human activities as sports but also in interpreting the whole of human existence, we have enhanced our powers beyond anything realizable in the hermeneutic of earlier ages. Although we can and often do overestimate our own competence in these matters, the use of writing, print, and electronics has enabled us to constitute in our minds an overwhelming mass of details in the structuring of the cosmos over the past 14 billion years or so as well as to reconstruct better than ever before human lifeworlds far distant from our own in time and/ or space, and thereby to give far greater depth to interpretation, both of these other lifeworlds and of our own. For some time anthropologists have been studying comparatively both what used to be styled "primitive" societies and their own high-technology societies, and in previously unattainable depth.

II

But, while these technologies of writing, print, and electronics have abetted hermeneutics or interpretation or explanation and thus have served the purposes of integration of our understanding, they are also in certain basic senses always analytic or fractioning as well and thus are condemned to incompleteness, as anthropologists have often observed (Sass; Tyler, *The Said*). Explanation brings understanding, but explanation alone, by its analytic processes, can distance us from the total, existential situation of a given group's life with which it undertakes to deal. One of the abiding problems of explanation is that it splits issues analytically in order to clarify them, and in the process often impoverishes or denatures the issues, depriving them of some of their full and essential depth. Inadvertently, as we study other peoples, past or present, we dissolve the totality of their existence into items we are able to handle and fail to note the other parts of their lives which remain unassimilable to ours as a whole.

Analytic explanation serves the interests of *logos*, as Plato and his followers used this term to contrast with *mythos*. By contrast with *mythos*, which, as has been seen, at root refers to something uttered, sounded (saying, word, utterance, story, myth), *logos* is at root a term based on a visual or visual-tactile metaphor, referring originally to picking out, gathering, selecting, assorting, separating, and only later, derivatively, to the auditory, oral world, the primary world of speech. In insisting on the difference between *logos* and *mythos* and in touting *logos*, Greek thought after

Plato was advocating by contrast to an oral, sound-processed organization (such as Boman shows so largely governed Hebrew thought and expression), a separation and arrangement technique which, despite other deeply unifying trends in Greek thought, notably in Plato himself, nevertheless eventually led, in the historical sense earlier explained, to the digitization we find in the computer. All this despite Plato's express misgivings about writing as compared to oral speech.

Following the fractioning route of *logos* leads of course paradoxically to some sort of integration—we fraction and analyze with a view to constructing some sort of whole. But, as earlier noted, however sophisticatedly we may use it, fractioning of itself simply has no ultimately holistic terminus. Explicitation cannot achieve full integration of the totality of human life. The ending of the Gospel according to John (21:25) cogently voices the problem: "There are still many other things that Jesus did, yet if they were all written about in detail, I doubt if there would be room enough in the entire world to hold the books to record them." There is no way to break down into individual articulated items the absolute totality of even one person's history, much less of the entirety of human existence or of the entire universe—or even of a baseball game.

III

In significant ways, myth is holistic. The truth conveyed by myth in the quite usual sense of traditional narrative conveying cultural values, structures, and attitudes is of course not truth in the sense in which "objective," scientific treatment is truth. In a given culture, individual myths tend to be grouped together to form a mythology that "transmits a heritage of shared allusion and verbal experience in time" which "helps create a cultural history" (Frye 34). This grouping together of narratives into a mythological whole is the opposite of a fractioning or analytic process. It associates certain narratives with in-articulated, often subconscious beliefs and/or attitudes or lifestyles. It is an amalgamating process: it gives mythology truth of a holistic—and somewhat intangible, fugitive—sort quite different from that of science. The time sense in mythologies often does not refer to ordinary, lived, human time, to the day-by-day. Myths often typically deal with "in-those-days" time.

Myth gives some sort of totalizing expression to the culture's own interior consistency. We recall once more Havelock's insistence that it takes writing, which came long after myth, to separate the knower more definitively from the known and thus to make possible formal logic and science, which programmatically set apart discrete items "objectively" from the knower.

The sense of *mythos* as an unanalyzed bearer of a total culture is one of the senses of *mythos* in ancient Greek culture and a sense against which Plato rebelled, as we have several times observed, in excluding poets from his republic (Havelock). In the poetic use of myth and the audience's appropriation of myth as validating a culture, the hearer (we need to say "hearer," for myth antedates writing by far) is encouraged to identify himself or herself with the content of the myth, not just verbally, explicitly, but also emotionally, psychologically, and in every other nonarticulate way. Ancient oral Greeks fulfilled themselves and kept their culture relatively integral by thus holistically identifying with Achilles or Odysseus or Penelope, not by studying such characters objectively and analytically. Simple absorption into what these characters stood for integrated their hearers into their Greek cultural world. Knowledge was pursued here to identify the knower with the known, not to objectify and evaluate the known object by distancing it from the knowing subject. Evaluation was not the question. Constitution or consolidation of the self was.

But a mythology in the sense just mentioned we ourselves must also have today, even in our literate, typographic, electronic mind-set. We must seek some way of totalizing, however vaguely, our own cultural existence, of embedding logic and science—or, rather the plethora of different sciences—with all their present digitizing apparatuses, into something more inclusively human, and, because of the increasing global awareness of humanity, into something somehow encompassing the mythologies of all cultures. Otherwise, we cannot even speak, as we do speak, about the framework of our informational, interpretive, ecological age, for we cannot round out concepts of this sort—"framework," "ecological age"—in totally scientific fashion.

We feel a need to treat somehow in our discourse the totality of today's global existence and of how we relate to it. But the world's greatest computers can never provide such kind of awareness. It is disconcertingly clear, as we have seen, that digitization or *logos* will come to no totally holistic conclusion, though it will multiply dismayingly the number of matters calling for conclusion. How can we resolve the problem of unification, which grows greater and greater as we in the present age learn more and more about our age and all the billions of years out of which it has evolved?

Somehow, we must remain in contact with *mythos. Logos* cannot be made holistic. The more we explain, the more we generate need for further explanation. *Mythos*, in various forms—proverbs, for example, as well as storytelling, lurking subconscious or unconscious awarenesses, and the deep probings of religious belief—will certainly remain as permanent and desperately needed components of human understanding. As Thomas Kuhn's now classic work, *The Structure of Scientific Revolutions*, has shown, all science is modeled on paradigms which cannot be fully articulated scientifically (see also Blumenthal). Science is a container, but it is also comes in a container which is trans-scientific. Even mathematical definitions and postulates are stated in terms all of which can never be interpreted mathematically with fully articulated explicitness. More succinctly, as has been stated here earlier, all science is only arrested dialogue, its roots in silence, the unsaid, myth, and personal encounter. Science itself is always incomplete articulation. The latest book on quantum physics is simply what one physicist says to other physicists here and now, a group of statements lying fallow for the next scientist who can plow them up more. The articulate remains always embedded in the inarticulate, the said in the unsaid, the verbalized in silence. Willy-nilly, we are permanently committed to *mythos*. In other words there is a myth that encompasses logic, but there is no logic that encompasses myth. This does not mean that myth is illogical, but that it is metalogical. It means than logic cannot fully and explicitly lay hold of all that is expressed by myth. Yet because it is not fully logical, but partly escapes logic, myth is not fully satisfying either.

IV

In accord with what has just been said, we can note that today we often use the term mythology to refer to a body of stories, assumptions, and beliefs developed from human beings' deeper concerns and faced inward toward those concerns, not outward in the way science is faced outward. In its depth of meaning, we hold this mythology for the most part unconsciously. Although it often involves narrative ("myths" in the sense of stories) in various ways, mythology in this sense, as has been seen, is not simply a string or bundle of narratives but includes much more. It is something embedded in and representing a lifestyle. Such mythology enters not only into our art and literature but into many other things as well. Thus we speak of a mythology of science, a mythology of democracy, a mythology of ecology, and a mythology of innumerable other constituents of our lifeworld. Some of these mythologies attach to deep, existential human concerns—religion, patriotism, family life, friendships, lifetime commitments and goals, and so on—others to less deep or less intrinsically valuable matters, as when we speak of a mythology of fly fishing or of golf or of bird watching. Mythology in this sense, while it is not exactly the same as the Greek *mythos*, is related to this Greek term, and not only etymologically. Mythology in this sense would certainly belong to the world of *mythos* which Plato wanted to distinguish from *logos*. It belongs to the world of the poets—in the very large sense, including persons such as newspaper columnists—largely, though not entirely, unanalyzed and ultimately not entirely analyzable, somehow resistant to *logos* or full explicitation. Indeed, as we have seen, Plato himself needed and used such myth to clarify matters for more reasoned processing into *logos*, as in the famous story of the cave in the *Republic*—a mythological interpretation or hermeneutic of *logos*.

Like all major developments in human history, the creation of the technological worlds of writing and print and electronic communication encouraged the development of new concomitant mythologies. In the case of electronic communication, paradoxically, although the computer serves *logos* by its analyzing potential, it surrounds *logos* with an almost boundless mythology, a body of assumptions and beliefs regarding the computer's prowess, often picturing this prowess as being virtually limitless. But it is quite evident that some information processing is beyond human limits, which are always there in one way or another. For example, we hear talk of computer programs to play perfect checkers and/or chess. Yet there are, it appears, humanly insurpassable limits here. In his *Principles of Artificial Intelligence* (115), Nils J. Nilsson notes that for more complex games, such as complete chess and checker games, *and/or* search to termination is wholly out of the question. It has been estimated that the complete game tree for checkers has approximately 1,040 nodes and the chess tree has approximately 10,120 nodes. (It would take about 1,021 centuries to generate the complete checker tree, even assuming that a successor could be generated in one-third of a nanosecond [a nanosecond is one-billionth of a second].)

Regarding chess, Bolter quotes (176) David Levy to the effect that the number of possible games (more than 10,120) "far exceeds the number of atoms in the universe and the time to calculate just one move in the perfect game would be measured in millions of years." As part of what we may call the myth of the computer, we have heard that computers will do away with the use of paper. In some special cases they do, but on the whole they have certainly increased the use of paper immeasurably. In my own case, since I switched from typewriter to the computer, I would calculate that I use around twenty times more paper than before. I used to type first drafts of books on scratch paper, already used on the other side. Now I need lots of print-outs and make far more revisions after the print-outs, as well as before. The elimination of paper has been one of the unrealized parts of the mythology of the computer.

The most significant element in the mythology generated by electronics is perhaps that of artificial intelligence (often referred to as AI), that is, of computer programs that "think" as human beings do (Bolter 12–13 passim). The literature on artificial intelligence is vast and will almost certainly never end (see, e.g., Winograd and Flores). But, as earlier noted, the perspectives we are using here suggest as pivotal reasons, among others, why the computer will never be able to substitute human intelligence: (1) that it lacks the silence in which human verbalization and thought live and which gives both meaning (Valesio), (2) that it lacks the human unconscious which is part of human thought as much as is consciousness, and (3) that it lacks the nonverbal context in which human thought is always embedded, directly or indirectly. Working together with live human intelligence, the computer can certainly aid human understanding massively. Bolter, we have seen, has suggested that the term "synthetic intelligence" could better be used instead of "artificial intelligence" for what the computer can accomplish (238). Since artificial intelligence or AI functions always by aiding ongoing human intelligence, perhaps another term might be "deep-level instrumentation for aiding intelligence."

In connection with mythology and electronic culture, a book such as John Naisbitt's *Megatrends: Ten New Directions Transforming Our Lives* is informative. This thoroughly documented book begins with a chapter on the transformation of our earlier industrial society into our present information society (11–38) and concludes by showing how the computer has converted hierarchical organization into networking organization (189–206, 249–52). *Megatrends* is loaded with statistics and other "hard" information, but the book as a whole unmistakably evokes a mythology rather than a logic. It simply cannot come to any "hard" conclusion but ends framed in a mythology in the sense earlier described here, a body of more or less articulate assumptions and beliefs faced inward toward human beings' greater concerns. It concludes with the summary statement that "We are living in the *time of the parenthesis*" (249). Its final sentence is not a formulation but an exclamation which appears to evoke a mythology again. "My God, what a fantastic time to be alive." The electronic world as a whole eludes formal coverage. It cannot be encompassed in *logos*.

These reflections have proceeded by polarizing digitization and hermeneutics, tracing digitization back to one aspect of Plato's *logos* (in its connection with writing) and thence through print to the computer in our present electronic age. They have suggested that the digitization of our present electronic age has understandably been complemented by the concomitant massive growth in hermeneutics or interpretation which marks our time. Digitization is fractioning, hermeneutics or interpretation is holistic: it attempts to reestablish us—often enough, paradoxically, with the help of digitization—in the seamless web of history where everything relates to everything else, but which, once it is broken, even by interpretation, can never be made whole again.

V

The development of hermeneutics as a kind of discipline over the past few centuries in the West has been rooted largely, although not entirely, in biblical studies and hence a brief word relating to the biblical tradition may be a place to conclude. Of course, from pre-Christian times the Hebrew people had associated the word of God not only with the spoken word—God spoke to Moses and others—but also with the written text. As we have seen, Hebrew thought tended to link text and the spoken word where Greek thought tended to separate them. The ancient Hebrews had devoted a great deal of hermeneutic commentary to interpreting the sacred scriptures, as Jose Faur has detailed. Faur makes the point that, while the Greek gods were illiterate, the God of the Hebrews gave Moses the tablets of the Law in writing on Mount Sinai, and Handelman quotes the rabbinic text, "He [Yahweh] looked into the Torah and created the world" (38). In rabbinic tradition there was a written and an unwritten Torah, and this association of writing with Yahweh gave the text a value and strength far exceeding that allowed it by Plato or the ancient Greeks generally. The Hebrew hermeneutic could in fact often include quite openly *mythos*, could consist less of analysis than of stories, as in the haggadoth and the midrashim, where biblical narrative could be explained not analytically but rather by another narrative. To interpret a story, one often simply told another story, sometimes more mystifying (and thought provoking) than the first, and holistically somehow satisfying.

Nevertheless, the presence of writing among the Hebrews, as elsewhere, did of course make possible a kind of organized, more analytic, interpretation or hermeneutic inaccessible to primarily oral cultures, although the analysis did not take the turn into the Greek *logos* that we find in Plato, for reasons convincingly explained by Boman (68 passim). Print opened the way to further development, to modern, highly self-conscious hermeneutics, for it made possible the authentication of given texts in ways impossible with scribal copies, always of uncertain accuracy, and even of growing inaccuracy—indeed, always condemned through successive copying to greater and greater inaccuracy, despite the desperate efforts at regularization such as those of the well-known Jewish Masoretes. Print made possible interpretation based on comparison of texts more rigorous than had been realizable before print. But it took time for the new print-based hermeneutics to mature; as Gadamer and others note, hermeneutics as a truly special branch of learning came into its own only in the eighteenth century and later, some three hundred years after the invention of printing from movable alphabetic type.

Because, as has been seen, textual hermeneutics must attempt to recreate so far as possible the total lifeworld in which the text—written, printed, electronic—came into existence and to set this world in dialogue with the total lifeworld of the present-day reader, hermeneutics, despite its necessarily analytic procedures, ultimately ambitions serving not as a fractioning but as a totalizing activity. It must try to reconstitute—if always with less than complete success—the total, existential situation in which the text is embedded and try to merge this with the total, existential world in which the text is being interpreted. In his *Oral Poetry: An Introduction,* Paul Zumthor maintains that this is impossible without full human vocalization, which for Zumthor includes song. Song is of prime importance to Zumthor: song is somehow fully matured hermeneutics, full interpretation, fully matured vocalized sound, full *mythos.* One may not agree with this all-out vocalized hermeneutic of hermeneutics, but the observation provides food for thought.

However analytic its procedures—and they are becoming more and more analytic with computer implementation—hermeneutics is thus in ultimate intent permanently involved in *mythos* even more profoundly than in *logos.* But the *mythos* in which hermeneutics is involved is more than merely a matter of fabled time. It includes the time in which we find the real world of historical human action, of dialogue, of real argumentative, rhetorical dispute directly affecting human decisions and existence. Hermeneutics enters into the total reality of existential history. This is what is meant by saying that hermeneutics is fundamentally seeking to be holistic, if more in ambition than realization or accomplishment. In the religious context we are considering, both writing and print in the last analysis thus are utilized by hermeneutics not so much simply to analyze the text as to resituate the text, so far as is approximately possible, directly or indirectly, in the seamless web of real history of which the lives of individual human beings and of human communities and languages themselves are parts. As Tyler and Leith have both demonstrated in detail, the meaning of words ultimately can never be gathered entirely just from other words but relies ultimately on social context and other nonverbal elements. The use of computers does not change this fundamental totalizing drive of hermeneutics but only intensifies it by giving hermeneutics more to work with. Moreover, computers interact intimately with the human, and their own inhuman action makes the human element itself today all the more urgent in the use of computers. Modern culture is mysteriously marked by the complementary drives to digitization (fractioning) and to hermeneutics (human totalizing).

VI

The bibliography of work on the word of God in the Jewish scriptures of the Old Testament is massive, as can be gathered from the citations in Boman and Faur as well as in countless encyclopedia articles. The word of God in Hebrew tradition has been adverted to often through this present work. For our immediate and concluding purposes here, it will be worthwhile noting especially the new kinds of intensity that mark discussion of the word of God in the Christian New Testament. The focus on the *logos* is especially urgent in passages such as John 1:1 and in 1 John 1:1.

> In the beginning was the word; the Word was in God's presence, and the Word was God. . . . The Word became flesh and made his dwelling among us, and we have seen his glory, the glory of an only Son coming from the Father. (John 1:1)

> This is what we proclaim to you: what was from the beginning, what we have heard, what we have seen with our own eyes, what we have looked upon and our hands have touched—we speak of the word (*logos*) of life. (1 John 1:1)

The commentaries on these texts are beyond measure, and here we can venture simply some observations based on what has been seen in the course of the present reflections. Whatever the Platonic influence within and around these (and other) biblical texts, it is clear that we are not dealing here simply with the *logos* that Plato contrasts with *mythos*, that is, with the foundation of logic that is pointed away from the *mythos* of the old purely oral world to rational discourse or science, to Plato's "ideas."

Quite the contrary, the *logos* here is embedded in the unabstracted actuality of history, of fleshly existence ("our hands have touched"). Boman has explicated in detail (58–73 passim) the contrasting semantics and psychodynamics of the Hebrew *dabar* (drive forward> speak> word> deed) and the Greek *logos* (gather> arrange> speak> reckon> think> word> reason) and has discussed the resulting complex richness and contusion of the term *logos* in New Testament Greek. Both *dabar* and *logos* are often translated "word," but they are quite differently skewed.

The *logos* in the biblical sense of the Word of God transcends, although it does not invalidate the rational. While this *logos* is not simply *logos* as set off by Plato against *mythos,* neither does the biblical *logos* here dwell in mythological time but in the same historical time in which human beings dwelt and still dwell. "Our hands have touched . . . the word (*logos*) of life." Jesus, the Gospels circumstantially relate (Luke 2:1–1), is historically dated, as we are: he was born in the days of Caesar Augustus while Quirinius was governor of Syria, and put to death by the historical Pontius Pilate (for example, Matthew 27:11–26).

Moreover, this Word through whom John's Gospel maintains "all things came into being" (John 1:3) is not the impersonal *logos* which Plato contrasts with *mythos* nor is he *mythos* either. He is a personal being, dealing as a person with other human persons, holistic as all persons are. As proposed in the Gospels, Jesus is somehow a kind of hermeneutic of hermeneutics: "I am the way, and the truth, and the life" (John14:5). Persons *present* themselves to other persons, as thoughts or words never "present" their referents to persons but, instead, as has earlier been seen at length, *re*present what they refer to, never bringing it forward to attention in the state in which it actually exists. Persons come across to one another more directly. When you and I talk to one another, we somehow enter into one another's consciousness. In the New Testament view, the one, holistic person who presents himself as "the way, the truth, and the life" is both God and human being. Here hermeneutic, involving both *logos* and *mythos,* is ultimately and fully holistic, not in spoken words at all but in an individual personal existence, involved with the other personal existents to whom he is addressing himself—which means, ultimately, in Christian teaching, with all women and men.

Whatever one makes of all this—and a believer and an unbeliever will presumably make of it ultimately something different—passages such as this make it little wonder that the emergence of hermeneutic as a distinct discipline in the last few centuries has been so intimately connected with biblical scholarship.

And little wonder that biblical scholarship itself in our age, with many other major phenomena of our age, has shown holistic tendencies never so manifest before. Holism in countless ways, many as pervasive as they are subtle, is a mark of our times, not unconnected with the emergence of the information society which provides us with more and more to relate to more and more, and with more and more means of establishing relationships. Ecumenism, improved interracial relations, more constructive international relations, and the ecological outlook are cut of the same contemporary cloth, are each in their own way hermeneutic, relationist, holistic. It appears that in certain ways the climax of holism is the present worldwide force of the ecological movement, which deals with the interrelationship of everything living in the world with everything else in the world. In our day, everything more clearly does relate to everything else than it ever before seemed to, although we cannot of course begin to spell out all the intricacies of the interrelationships and will never be able to compass them all. We are not yet out of the woods. Darkness and suffering are still with us, and doubtless always will be. But, felt differently by different persons, in accordance with their own beliefs as well as their own knowledge. It does seem that hope—Jewish, Christian, other—does lie ahead in this digitizing and dizzying hermeneutic age that appears to be our future.

Illustrations

Figure 1 Schema or outline of logic in Thomas Murner's *Logica memorativa* (Strasbourg, 1509), reproduced from Ong (*Ramus, Method* 87). Note that the schema or outline is iconographic, not yet simply verbalized and/or binary.

P. RAMI DIALECTICA.
TABVLA GENERALIS.

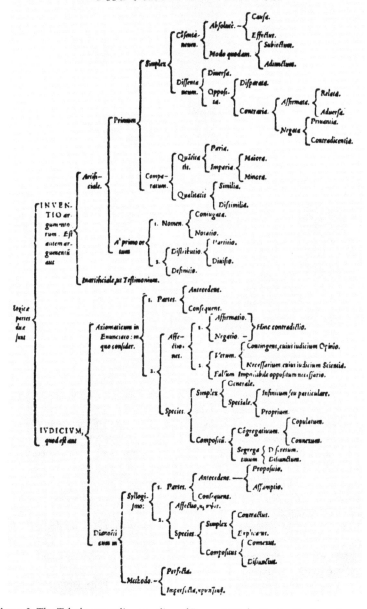

Figure 2 The Tabula generalis or outline of Ramus's Dialectica (or Logica—the terms were commonly in effect synonymous) in a collection of some of Ramus's works, *Professio regia* (Basle, 1576), ed. Johann Thomas Freigius (Freige), reproduced here from Ong (*Ramus, Method* 202). Freige here exhibits Ramus's seven liberal arts in their in-built schematic outline. As against Murner's iconographic outline of logic, here we have simply printed words arranged in abstract space in what is, in effect, a binary computer flowchart—centuries before the computer.

REFERENCES

Bakhtin, M. M. *The Dialogic Imagination.* Ed. Michael Holquist. Trans. Carol Emerson and Michael Holquist. Austin: University of Texas Press, 1981.

Bauman, Richard, and Joel Sherzer, eds. *Explorations in the Ethnography of Speaking.* Cambridge: Cambridge University Press, 1974.

Beckett, Samuel. *Waiting for Godot: A Tragic Comedy in Two Acts.* New York: Grove Press, Inc., 1954.

Bekker, Paul. *The Orchestra.* New York: W.W. Norton, 1936.

Berry, Thomas. "The American College in the Ecological Age." *Religion and Intellectual Life* 6.2 (Winter 1989): 7–28.

Blumenthal, Hans. *Work on Myth.* Trans. Robert M. Wallace. Cambridge: MIT Press, 1985.

Bolter, J. David. *Turing's Man: Western Culture in the Computer Age.* Chapel Hill: University of North Carolina Press, 1984.

Boman, Thorleif. *Hebrew Thought Compared with Greek.* Philadelphia: Westminster Press, 1960.

Buber, Martin. *I and Thou.* 2nd ed. Trans. Ronald Gregor Smith. New York: Charles Scribner's Sons, 1958.

Coulmas, Florian. *The Writing Systems of the World.* Oxford: Basil Blackwell, 1989.

Culler, Jonathan. *Ferdinand de Saussure.* Rev. ed. Ithaca: Cornell University Press, 1986.

——. *On Deconstruction.* Ithaca: Cornell University Press, 1982.

DeFrancis, John. *Visible Speech: The Diverse Oneness of Writing Systems.* Honolulu: University of Hawaii Press, 1989.

Derrida, Jacques. "Critical Response." Trans. Peggy Kamuf. *Critical Inquiry* 13.1 (Autumn 1986): 167–68.

———. *Of Grammatology.* Trans. Gyatri C. Spivak. Baltimore: Johns Hopkins University Press, 1976.

———. *Writing and Difference.* Trans. Alan Bass. Chicago: University of Chicago Press, 1978.

Dillon, George L. *Rhetoric as Social Imagination: Explorations in the Interpersonal Function of Language.* Bloomington: Indiana University Press, 1986.

Diringer, David. *The Alphabet: A Key to the History of Mankind.* 2d ed. New York: Philosophical Library, 1953.

Dreyfus, Hubert. *Mind over Machine: The Power of Human Intuition and Expertise in the Era of the Computer.* New York: Free Press, 1985.

Edmonson, Munro S. *Lore: An Introduction to the Science of Folklore and Literature.* New York: Holt, Rinehart, and Winston, 1971.

Egan, Kieran. *Primary Understanding: Education in Early Childhood.* New York: Routledge, 1988.

Eisenstein, Elizabeth. *The Printing Press as an Agent of Change: Communications and Cultural Transformations in Modern Europe.* New York: Cambridge University Press, 1979.

Ellul, Jacques. *The Humiliation of the Word.* Trans. Joyce Main Hanks. Grand Rapids, MI: Eerdmans, 1985.

Faur, José. "God as a Writer: Omnipresence and the Art of Dissimulation." *Religion and Intellectual Life* 6.3–4 (Spring/Summer 1989): 31–43.

Fisher, Walter R. *Human Communication as Narration: Toward a Philosophy of Reason, Value, and Action.* Columbia: University of South Carolina Press, 1987.

Fletcher, Paul, and Michael Gorman, eds. *Language Acquisition: Studies in First Language Development.* New York: Cambridge University Press, 1981.

Frye, Northrop. *The Great Code: The Bible and Literature.* New York and London: Harcourt Brace Jovanovich, 1982.

Gadamer, Hans-Georg. *Truth and Method.* New York: Crossroads, 1985. (First published as *Wahrheit und Methode,* 1968.)

Gilbert, Neil. *Renaissance Concepts of Method.* New York: Columbia University Press, 1960.

Goody, Jack. *The Logic of Writing and the Organization of Society.* New York: Cambridge University Press, 1986.

Goody, Jack, and Ian Watt. "The Consequences of Literacy." In *Literature in Traditional Societies,* ed. Jack Goody, 27–84. Cambridge: Cambridge University Press, 1968.

Graff, Harvey J., ed. *Literacy and Social Development in the West: A Reader.* New York: Cambridge University Press, 1981.

Handelman, Susan A. *The Slayers of Moses: The Emergence of Rabbinic Interpretation in Modern Literary Theory.* Albany: State University of New York Press, 1982.

Havelock, Eric A. "The Linguistic Task of the Presocratics, Part One: Ionian Science in Search of an Abstract Vocabulary." In *Language and Thought in Early Greek*

Philosophy, ed. K. Robb, 7–82. La Salle, IL: Hegeler Institute, Monist Library of Philosophy, 1983.

———. *The Muse Learns to Write: Reflections on Orality and Literacy from Antiquity to the Present.* New Haven: Yale University Press, 1986.

———. *Preface to Plato.* Cambridge: Harvard University Press, 1963.

Heath, Shirley Brice. *Ways with Words: Language, Life, and Work in Communities and Classrooms.* Cambridge: Cambridge University Press, 1983.

Heim, Michael. *Electric Language: A Philosophical Study of Word Processing.* New Haven and London: Yale University Press, 1987.

Hogrebe, Edmund F. M. "Digital Technology: The Potential for Alternative Communication," *Journal of Communication* 31.1 (1981): 170–76.

Houis, Maurice. *Anthropologie linguistique de l'Afrique noire.* Paris: Presses Universitaires de France, 1971.

Ijsseling, Samuel. *Rhetoric and Philosophy in Conflict: An Historical Survey.* The Hague: Martinus Nijhoff, 1976.

Jackson, Jean. "Language Identity of the Colombian Vaupes Indians." In *Explorations in the Ethnography of Speaking*, ed. Richard Bauman and Joel Sherzer, 30–64. Cambridge: Cambridge University Press, 1974.

Karpen, James L. "The Digitized Word: Orality, Literacy, and the Computerization of Language." Ph.D. diss., Bowling Green State University, 1984.

Keller, Helen. *The Story of My Life: With Her Letters (1887–1901) and a Supplementary Account by John Albert Macy.* Garden City, NY: Doubleday, 1954.

Kermode, Frank. *The Genesis of Secrecy: On the Interpretation of Narrative.* Cambridge: Harvard University Press, 1979.

Kernan, Alvin. *Printing Technology, Letters, and Samuel Johnson.* Princeton, NJ: Princeton University Press, 1987.

Kirk, G. S. *Myth: Its Meaning and Functions in Ancient and Other Cultures.* London: Cambridge University Press, 1971.

Kuhn, Thomas. *The Structure of Scientific Revolutions.* Chicago: University of Chicago Press, 1970.

Leitch, Vincent B. *Deconstructive Criticism: An Advanced Introduction.* New York: Columbia University Press, 1983.

Leith, Philip. *Formalism in AI and Computer Science.* Chichester, England: Ellis Horwood, 1990.

Lloyd, G. E. R. *Polarity and Analogy: Two Types of Argumentation in Early Greek Thought.* Cambridge: Cambridge University Press, 1966.

Lundin, Roger, Anthony C. Thiselton, and Clarence Walhout. *The Responsibility of Hermeneutics.* Grand Rapids, MI: Eerdmans, 1985.

MacLeish, Archibald. *Collected Poems 1917–1982.* Boston: Houghton Mifflin Company, 1985.

McShane, John. *Learning to Talk.* Cambridge: Cambridge University Press, 1980.

Meyrowitz, Joshua. *No Sense of Place: The Impact of Electronic Media on Social Behavior.* New York: Oxford University Press, 1985.

Naisbitt, John. *Megatrends: Ten New Directions Transforming Our Lives.* New York: Warner Books, 1982.

Newbold, R. F. "Nonverbal Communication and Parataxis in Late Antiquity." *L'antiquite classique* (Brussels) 50 (1986): 223–44.

Nilsson, Nils. *Principles of Artificial Intelligence.* Los Altos, CA: Morgan Kaufmann, 1980.

Ohmann, Richard. "Grammar and Meaning." In *The American Heritage Dictionary of the English Language*, xxxi–iv. Boston: Houghton Mifflin, 1969.

Ong, Walter J. "Before Textuality: Orality and Interpretation." *Oral Tradition* 3, no. 3 (1988): 259-69. [With the permission of the editor and publisher, material from this article has been incorporated here and there in this work.—WJO.]

——. *Fighting for Life: Contest, Sexuality, and Consciousness.* Ithaca: Cornell University Press, 1981.

——. *Interfaces of the Word: Studies in the Evolution of Consciousness and Culture.* Ithaca: Cornell University Press, 1977.

——. "Literacy and Orality in Our Times." *ADE Bulletin*, no. 58 (September 1978): 1–7.

——. *Orality and Literacy: The Technologizing of the Word.* London: Methuen, 1982.

——. *The Presence of the Word: Some Prolegomena for Cultural and Religious History.* New Haven and London: Yale University Press, 1967.

——. *Ramus and Talon Inventory.* Cambridge, MA: Harvard University Press, 1958.

——. *Ramus, Method, and the Decay of Dialogue.* Cambridge, MA: Harvard University Press, 1983. First published 1958.

——. "Samuel Johnson and the Printed Word." Review of *Printing Technology, Letters, and Samuel Johnson.* By Alvin Kernan. *Review* 10 (1988): 97–112.

——. "Writing Is a Technology That Transforms Thought." *The Written Word: Literacy in Transition*, ed. Gerd Baumann, 23–50. Oxford: Oxford University Press, 1986.

Oxenham, John. *Literacy: Writing, Reading, and Social Organization.* London: Routledge and Kegan Paul, 1980.

Piaget, Jean. *The Child's Conception of the World.* Trans. Joan and Andrew Tomlinson. London: Routledge and Kegan Paul, 1967.

——. *The Language and Thought of the Child.* Trans. Marjorie Gabain. New York: Meridian, 1955.

Plato. *Gorgias.* Trans. with notes by Terence Irwin. Oxford: Clarendon Press, 1979. [The editor's notes on *logos* (rational account) and *mythos* are invaluable.—WJO.]

Postman, Neil. *Amusing Ourselves to Death: Public Discourse in the Age of Show Business.* New York: Viking, 1985.

Pyles, Thomas, and John Algeo. *The Origins and Development of the English Language.* New York: Harcourt, 1982.

Rader, Margaret. "Context in Written Language: The Case of Imaginative Fiction." In *Spoken and Written Language: Explaining Orality and Literacy*, ed. Deborah Tannen, 185–98. Norwood, NJ: Ablex, 1982.

Reisman, Karl. "Contrapuntal Conversations in an Antiguan Village." In *Explorations in the Ethnography of Speaking*, ed. Richard Bauman and Joel Sherzer, 118–24. Cambridge: Cambridge University Press, 1974.

Ricoeur, Paul. *The Conflict of Interpretation: Essays in Hermeneutics.* Ed. Don Ihde. Evanston, IL: Northwestern University Press, 1974.

———. *Hermeneutics and the Human Sciences.* Ed. and trans. John B. Thompson. Cambridge: Cambridge University Press, 1981.

———. *Interpretation Theory: Discourse and the Surplus of Meaning.* Fort Worth: Texas Christian University Press, 1976.

———. "The Model of the Text: Meaningful Action Considered as a Text." *Social Research: An International Quarterly of the Social Sciences* 38.3 (Autumn 1971): 529–62.

Sampson, Geoffrey. *Writing Systems.* Stanford: Stanford University Press, 1985.

Sanders, Donald H. *Computers Today.* New York: McGraw-Hill, 1983.

Sass, Louis A. "Anthropology's Native Problems." *Harper's Magazine* (May 1986): 49–57.

Saussure, Ferdinand de. *Course in General Linguistics.* Ed. Charles Bally and Albert Sechehaye with the collaboration of Albert Riedlinger. Trans. and annotated by Roy Harris. LaSalle, IL: Open Court, 1986.

Seamon, Roger. "Poetics against Itself: On the Self-Destruction of Modern Scientific Criticism." *PMLA* 104.3 (May 1989): 294–306.

Searle, John. *Minds, Brains, and Science.* Cambridge: Harvard University Press, 1984.

Seeskin, Kenneth. *Dialogue and Discovery: A Study in Socratic Method.* Albany: State University of New York Press, 1987.

Shapiro, Gary, and Alan Sica, eds. *Hermeneutics: Questions and Prospects.* Amherst: University of Massachusetts Press, 1984.

Sherzer, Joel. "*Namakke, Sunmakke, Kormakke*: Three Types of Cuna Speech Event." In *Explorations in the Ethnography of Speaking,* ed. Richard Bauman and Joel Sherzer, 263–82. Cambridge, UK: Cambridge University Press, 1974.

Sontag, Susan. *Against Interpretation and Other Essays.* New York: Dell, 1967.

Stock, Brian. "Language and Cultural History." *New Literary History* 18.3 (Spring 1987): 657–70.

Stubbs, Michael. *Language and Literacy: The Sociolinguistics of Reading and Writing.* London: Routledge and Kegan Paul, 1980.

Tannen, Deborah, ed. *Spoken and Written Language: Exploring Orality and Literacy.* Norwood, NJ: Ablex, 1982.

Tyler, Stephen R. *The Said and the Unsaid; Mind, Meaning, and Culture.* New York: Academic Press, 1978.

———. *The Unspeakable: Discourse, Dialogue, and Rhetoric in the Postmodern World.* Madison: University of Wisconsin Press, 1987. [Note (89) to ch. 3, "Intertextuality, Geography, and the End of Description": "This chapter is part of a longer meditation motivated by the strong, but partly contrapuntal voices of W. Ong and J. Derrida."—WJO.]

Valesio, Paolo. *Ascoltare il silenzio.* Bologna: Il Mulino, 1986.

Versény, Laszlo. *Man's Measure: A Study of the Greek Image of Man from Homer to Sophocles.* Albany: State University of New York Press, 1982.

Weinsheimer, Joel C. *Gadamer's Hermeneutics: A Reading of* Truth and Method. New Haven: Yale University Press, 1985.

Whitelock, P., et al., eds. *Linguistic Theory and Computer Applications.* New York: Harcourt Brace Jovanovich, 1987.

Willey, Basil. *The Seventeenth Century Background: Studies in the Thought of the Age in Relation to Poetry and Religion.* Garden City, NY: Doubleday Anchor Books, 1934.

Wimsatt, William K., and Monroe Beardsley. *The Verbal Icon.* Lexington: University of Kentucky Press, 1954.

Winograd, Terry, and Fernando Flores. *Understanding Computers and Cognition.* New York: Addison-Wesley, 1986.

Yates, Frances. *The Art of Memory.* Chicago: University of Chicago Press, 1966.

Zumthor, Paul. *Oral Poetry: An Introduction.* Trans. Kathy Murphy-Judy. Minneapolis: University of Minnesota Press, 1989. Trans. of *Introduction à la poésie orale.* Paris: Editions du Seuil, 1985.

Editors' note. These authors are listed in the bibliography but are not clearly identified in the current text: Oxenham, Postman, Rader, Sampson, Sanders, Searle, Shapiro and Sica, and Whitelock. These authors were cited in the 1990 version but not in the 1994 version:

Diringer, David. *The Alphabet: A Key to the History of Mankind.* 2d ed. rev. New York: Philosophical Library, 1953.

Egan, Kieran. *Primary Understanding: Education in Early Childhood.* New York: Routledge, 1988.

Karpen, James L. "The Digitized Word: Orality, Literacy, and the Computerization of Language." PhD diss., Bowling Green State University, 1984.

Kermode, Frank. *The Genesis of Secrecy: On the Interpretation of Narrative.* Cambridge: Harvard University Press, 1979.

Kirk, G. S. *Myth: Its Meaning and Functions in Ancient and Other Cultures.* London: Cambridge University Press; Berkeley: University of California Press, 1971.

Lundin, Roger, Anthony C. Thiselton, and Clarence Walhout. *The Responsibility of Hermeneutics.* Grand Rapids, MI: Eerdmans, 1985.

PART II

About *Language as Hermeneutic*

LANGUAGE AS HERMENEUTIC: THE EVOLUTION OF THE IDEA AND THE TEXT

Thomas D. Zlatic

Walter J. Ong did not finalize *Language as Hermeneutic: A Primer on the Word and Digitization*. Although he did produce a complete draft, he continued to revise without coming to closure. Thus this edition is in part a reconstruction, and given the editorial judgments that had to be made, certainly no other editor would produce a completely identical text. The four principal manuscripts used to construct this text are the 1988 *Language as Hermeneutic: Reflections on the Word and Digitization* (*LAH-88*); the 1989 *Language as Hermeneutic: Reflections on the Word and Digitization* (*LAH-89*); the 1990 *Language as Hermeneutic: A Primer on the Word and Digitization* (*LAH-90*); and the unfinished 1994 *Language as Hermeneutic: A Primer on the Word and Digitization* (*LAH-94*). Scholars are invited to review online the original manuscripts and related documents at the Saint Louis University Library Archives, Walter J. Ong Collection at http://cdm.slu.edu/cdm/landingpage/collection/ong.

Identifying four distinct versions of *Language as Hermeneutic* is a bit arbitrary. Each is a still photo of a document moving in time; a movie camera would be needed to capture Ong's ongoing revisions. Or, as Ong himself says in *Language as Hermeneutic*, "I use [sic] to type first drafts of books on scratch paper, already used on the other side. Now I need lots of print-outs and make far more revisions after the print-outs, as well as before" (*LAH* 104).

Our reconstruction is based on this hypothesis. Ong had written in 1990 what he thought was a publishable manuscript but continued to revise particularly because of his growing interest in digitization. By 1994 Ong gave up on the attempt to integrate the 1990 draft with his new insights, and instead published three major articles using material from *Language as Hermeneutic,* thus abandoning on his computer an "unsatisfactory" manuscript.

LAH-88

1980–1988: Toward an Oral Hermeneutic

Though Ong stated that *Language as Hermeneutic* is a synthesis, its direct origins can be traced to the early 1980s. This was a very productive decade for Ong, during which he published four books (*Fighting for Life* [1981]; *A Fuller Course in the Art of Logic Conformed to the Method of Peter Ramus (1672), by John Milton* [coeditor/translator with Charles J. Ermatinger, 1982]; *Orality and Literacy* [1982]; *Hopkins, the Self, and God* [1986]), nineteen articles/chapters, dozens of miscellaneous papers and presentations, and six book reviews. From his output one would not recognize that age and ill health increasingly limited his activities.

Ong's interest in hermeneutics developed in the wake of such movements as structuralism, audience-response criticism, composition studies, and particularly deconstruction, for he saw in its theories a naïveté regarding the primacy of text and a lack of awareness of the history of communications technology. Working from his background in orality and literacy, Ong tried to recontextualize interpretation or hermeneutics within the development of communications technology and, more generally, within the development of human consciousness out of unconsciousness.

In 1982 Ong reviewed Geoffrey Hartman's "fascinating" *Saving the Text: Literature/Derrida/Philosophy,* a counterstatement to Derridian deconstruction that resonated with Ong in its insight that " 'texts are false bottoms' " (276). Here Ong delivered a key aphorism repeated often in his subsequent work on hermeneutics: "all text is pretext," meaning—as aphorisms always do—many things: that texts are never independent of discourse; that context is needed for interpretation; that the code for interpreting texts lies outside the text; that to treat a text as self-contained and self-interpreting is a pretext; and so on.

Ong's courses as a student at Saint Louis University in the 1940s in philosophy, theology, and literature were steeped in a St. Louis Thomism that explored cognition and noetic processes, including how sensory perception and intellection are related.[1] With this influence Ong's scholarly agenda later developed from a central insight he arrived at in the 1950s during the composition of his doctoral dissertation and later his groundbreaking 1957 book *Ramus, Method, and the Decay of Dialogue*. In an interview in 1992 (when he was in the last phases of revising *Language as Hermeneutic*), he described his germinal insight into varieties of knowing.

> The seminal discovery of his long career came nearly 40 years ago. "It happened while I was doing my dissertation research in France," recalls Ong. "I was reading Rudolph Bultmann, the Protestant theologian, who made reference to the idea that knowing, for the Hebrews, had to do with hearing and sound, while the Greeks thought of knowing as related to seeing. I guess it took me about a day, but suddenly I could see how the whole thing fit together." (Nielson 1992, 404; cf. Riemer [1971], 149)

From this flash of intuition Ong developed the sound-based psychodynamics of orality that he contrasted with the visualism of writing and print that dominated Western culture since the Enlightenment. The hyper-visualism is a source of the text-oriented hermeneutics that ignored the aural-oral roots of communication. Oralism, by contrast, was connected to dialogue, self-identity, and personalism, which for Ong were central to communication.

Ong's insights resonated with the "oral hermeneutic" of the social philosopher Eugen Rosenstock-Huessy, who prioritized speech over the reason of traditional investigation.[2] Already in 1960, Ong noted that in Rosenstock-Huessy "one returns here from a world of 'observation' and measurement to an older world of gnomic expression and chthonic wisdom" (140). One such aphorism in Rosenstock-Huessy Ong later prominently featured as an epigraph for *The Presence of the Word*: "experiences of the first order, of the first rank, are not realized through the eye" ("Philosophical Sociology," 1960, 138, 140).

It is this orientation that valorized sound, voice, and dialogue that Ong would later find in Mikhail Bakhtin, Paolo Valesio, and Paul Zumthor, all of whom are cited in *Language as Hermeneutic*.

During this time Ong's focus on oral hermeneutic was filtered through biblical studies, particularly through Werner Kelber's seminal work, *The Oral and Written Gospel* (1983), which had employed Ong's analysis of oral psychodynamics to reinterpret the Gospel of Mark. Ong in his foreword to Kelber's book was enthusiastic about the scholarly possibilities opened up by this oral hermeneutic:

> Because of lack of understanding of oral psychodynamics . . . , neither form criticism nor redaction criticism nor other biblical scholarship has succeeded in producing a truly oral hermeneutic. Indeed, one might say that biblical scholarship generally has not even tried to produce such a hermeneutic, differentiated from a textual hermeneutic, for one has to be acquainted with the mass of extra-biblical scholarship just mentioned to become aware that such a differentiated hermeneutic is even called for or possible. . . . A sophisticated oral hermeneutic opens the way to deeper understanding not merely of orality but of texts themselves. (xiv)

On September 23, 1984, Kelber called Ong's attention to his colleague at Rice University, Stephen Tyler, "whose major work [*The Said and the Unsaid*] is an attack on formalistic, structuralist hermeneutics" (3). A few months later (May 2, 1985), Kelber notified Ong regarding a new anthropological journal at Rice University whose first issue would be devoted to "Oral Hermeneutics" (Doc MSS 64.2.2.1.346).[3] And again in 1988 Kelber alerted Ong to another book by Tyler, *The Unspeakable*. Kelber, enclosed a copy, explaining it "takes major issue with formalist theories of language while developing what amounts to a very oral, rhetorical concept of language" (Doc MSS 64.2.2.1.346). Given that chapter 3 of *The Unspeakable* is "part of a longer meditation motivated by the strong but partly contrapuntal voices of W. Ong and J. Derrida" (*The Said* 89), Ong studied the book closely, taking a special interest in the possibilities for an oral hermeneutic. He underlined this passage, which Tyler acknowledges is inspired by Ong's *Orality and Literacy*:

> Oral discourse has its hermeneutics, but it is a hermeneutics of language-in-the-world, of reflexivity and immanence, of contingent and *ad hoc* transcendence. Holy and mystical speech apart, it has no will to truth except in a secondary and derivative imitation of writing (Ong 1982: 31–77, 139–54). (*The Said* 90–91)[4]

Ong also updated Tyler's index, penciling in after his own name additional pages on which he is mentioned, including the pages that contain the above passage—after which he elaborated: "oral discourse has its own hermeneutics"; he also inserted alphabetically two other entries, "oral hermeneutics, 190" and "hermeneutics, oral, 190." Clearly Ong found here a topic for exploration.[5]

In an outline for the essay "Literacy, Orality, Truth, and Method" (dated January 1, 1986), Ong wondered aloud, "Despite more frequent disclaimers and growing self-consciousness, we still tend to take the text (literature) as the paradigmatic model for hermeneutics or interpretation. What would happen if we were to take oral expression as the primary model?" (Doc MSS 64.2. 1.1.121). In that same year, in a lecture "Biblical Text as Interpretation," Ong expanded on Kelber's contributions to the identification of an oral hermeneutic, and previewed some of the themes of *Language as Hermeneutic*, at times in identical words: interpretation is a manifestation of what is hidden, there is no completely explicit statement, meaning is always negotiated, texts do not have independent status (Doc MSS 64.1.3.1.36). Ong covered much of the same ground in his published 1986 article "Text as Interpretation: Mark and After" as he explored "the central question . . . , the interpretive interaction of text and oral expression, and particularly to the effect of text as interpreting oral discourse antecedent to it" (*Semia* 10), using the work of Kelber, Brian Stock, and Stanley Fish, to make the point that "[o]rality-literacy contrasts and interactions . . . involve not merely 'channels' for units of 'information' but different noetic worlds and different psychodynamics"[6] (21).

In another important published article, "Before Textuality: Orality and Interpretation" (1988), Ong further extended an oral hermeneutic beyond biblical studies and introduced the idea that all language is hermeneutic:

"Because it is a call, a cry, addressed to another person, or the equivalent, an imagined person or persons, the oral word is essentially explanation or interpretation or hermeneutics, a clarification by one person of something that to his or her interlocutor or interlocutors is not evident" (267). In all communication, meaning must be negotiated in a holistic situation.

On another front, also percolating in Ong's consciousness at this time was the binary digitization of the emerging computer era. In *Ramus, Method, and the Decay of Dialogue,* Ong had argued that the pedagogical reformer Peter Ramus, under the influence of print technology, had helped to reorient Western culture toward a visualist apprehension of knowledge and the world. For a new 1983 edition of *Ramus,* Ong wrote a two-page preface in which he identified a resemblance between Ramus' binary dichotomized charts and digital computer programs: "The quantifying drives inherited from medieval logic were producing computer programs in Ramus' active mind some four hundred years before the computer itself came into being"[7] (viii). Oral hermeneutics and digitization were coming together.

This was the milieu for the first extant manuscript of *Language as Hermeneutic (LAH-88),* which seems to have been begun in the middle of the 1980s when Ong began typing notes related to language and hermeneutics on 3x5 "ephemera" cards.

The Text of *LAH-88*

LAH-88, dated April 18, 1988, was saved electronically as LANGHERM (Doc MSS 64.2.1.1.121). It consists of forty-one pages, including a prologue and eight chapters. It has no subtitle, references, or table of contents. The nine chapters are numbered but only Chapter 1 ("Prologue") and Chapter 2 ("Hermeneutic, Textual and Other") are titled. A contemporaneous hard copy contains a few minor edits. On its first page, prior to the prologue (and apparently not meant to be part of a published text) Ong succinctly laid out four points he would cover:

Language interprets the nonlinguistic.
Thought interprets the noncognitive.
Words and concepts begin not simply as labels but as heuristic devices (which make use of labels), and they remain heuristic devices

throughout their history. At no point is the formation of the concept or the history of the meaning of the word complete.

Words and concepts move toward fixity, but they never become fixed: they remain always alive.

"Digitization" is mentioned nowhere in the manuscript.

LAH-89

1988–1989: Interpretation and Being, or Language as Hermeneutic

Ong did not pause in his revision of *LAH-88*. Some of the ephemera note cards that Ong created on language and hermeneutics during the 1980s contain handwritten comments inserted later that refer to *Language as Hermeneutic*: a quote from Margaret Rader has written on it "LANG-HERM.05:3 (as of 5-12-89)"; a Basil Willey quote dated 2-11-85 is marked with "LANGHERM.TXT 10-19-88"; a quote from Plato typed on 11-30-84 is noted to be "in LANGHERM.TXT, 7, 17, 19, 10-19-88" (Doc MSS 64 Ephemera Box 149).

Further insight into the subsequent development and dating of *LAH* can be gained through a review of Ong's graduate courses, symposiums, and lectures during the late 1980s and early 1990s.

Sometime after May 4, 1988, Ong wrote on a deleted section of his review of William A. Graham's *Beyond the Written Word* that this excerpt might be used within a graduate interdisciplinary course at Saint Louis University, A-673: Interpretation and Being, that he planned to teach in the spring of 1989 (Doc MSS 64.2.1.1.121). Sometime after June 1988, he changed the course name from "Interpretation and Being" to "Language as Hermeneutic,"[8] which he taught in the spring of 1989 and had planned to teach again in the fall of 1989, until illness forced him to cancel. The required textbooks were his *Orality and Literacy* and Michael Heim's *Electric Language*; Gadamer's *Truth and Method* was recommended. Ong informed his students that the material he was presenting in the course was related to his next book (Zlatic, personal class notes), and significantly he filed the hard copy of *LAH-88* in his Language as Hermeneutic course folder, not a *LAH* manuscript folder.

Included in the *LAH* course file are nine notes/essays that parallel *LAH-88*,[9] and on January 2, 1988, Ong noted that material checked in the notes had been inserted into a WordPerfect file LANGHERM, presumably *LAH-88*, dated April 18, 1988 (Doc MSS 64.2.1.1.121). In his spring 1989 class plans, in minuscule handwriting, Ong scheduled discussions of various chapters of *Language as Hermeneutics*: LANGHERM #2 LANGHERM #3, LANGHERM.TXT, LANGHERM 12, LANGHERM.13. Though Ong did not teach the course in the fall of 1989 as planned, he had prepared a similar class plan that included *Language as Hermeneutic* chapters but the file names are more structured: LANGH ERM.00, LANGHERM.01, LANGHERM.03, and so on. It is clear the work was evolving (Ephemera Cards, Doc MSS 64 Box 149).[10]

Ong prepared on June 2, 1988, a two-page document of thirty-two subjects for "Interpretation and Being" (again the title was later scratched and replaced in pencil with "Language as Hermeneutic"). Item 27 is an "Introduction":

> There is no way to discuss at any depth in purely analytic and linear fashion the relationship of speech and thought and the social matrix in which these take form. You have to work out of complex cultural patterns more or less familiar to all. Particularly to catch which I have called the "interfaces of the word." This is what I propose to do here. Other cultural patterns could also be used as starting points. These are ones familiar to me and to many of my readers. (Doc MSS 64.2.1.1.121)

And in his "Opening Remarks" Ong informed the students,

> The reflections in this course come not out of the lengthy philosophical tradition (Schleiermacher, Dilthey, Husserl, Heidegger, and others) with which some recent philosophers, most notably Paul Ricoeur, have worked, but instead have been generated more specifically out of work on the evolution of verbal communication through the technologies of writing, print, and electronics. (Doc MSS 64.2.1.1.121)

The Text of *LAH-89*

By March 22, 1989, in the middle of the Language as Hermeneutic course, Ong produced *Language as Hermeneutic: Reflections on the Word and*

Digitization (*LAH-89*). Ong's handwritten note reads: "File name: LANG-HERM.TXT. Word count: 17565 Pg. 72." This draft of thirteen chapters has a new prologue but still no table of contents or references. A subtitle is added: "Reflections on the Word and Digitization." The manuscript exists only as an electronic (WordPerfect) file.

The first nine chapters of *LAH-89* are substantially the same as the first nine chapters of *LAH-88* with amplifications, clarifications, and stylistic revisions. The prologue of *LAH-88* becomes chapter 1 in *LAH-89*, and a new prologue appears in *LAH-89*. The *LAH-88* prologue, now chapter 1, has a new concluding paragraph. Chapters in *LAH-89* now have titles.[11] Chapter nine is expanded with five concluding paragraphs, and four additional chapters are added (10–13). Notably the only text for chapter 10, "*Logos* and Digitization," is the chapter title itself. Other than in the subtitle and the title of chapter 10, "digitization" or "digital" is mentioned only in chapters 12 and 13.

LAH-90

1989–1990: Second Thoughts

At a National Endowment for the Humanities (NEH) Summer Seminar conducted by John Miles Foley, Ong—on July 18–20, 1989—discussed three topics related to *LAH*: "Hermeneutics Textual and Oral," "Logos and Digitization," and "Language as Hermeneutic" (Doc MSS 64.2.1.1.108). In the early1990s he continued to prepare presentations and publications related to hermeneutics and digitization, including in 1990, "Technological Development and Writer-Subject-Reader Immediacies," in which he reiterated the theme, "all text is pretext." Sometime between March 22, 1989 and March 11, 1990, Ong produced his *LAH-90* manuscript (Doc MSS 64.1.4.4.1.1). This is the only extant draft that is complete, though some indications are that even then it was not considered finished. Certainly there was a good deal of ambivalence.

In a memo first dated January 10, 1990, Ong wrote: "After several years of work, off and on, I find this draft (=c. 130 printed pages) of this projected book, *Language as Hermeneutic*, unsatisfactory. I have never sent it to any publisher"[12] (Doc MSS 64.1.4.4.4). Curiously, the day before, John Kavanaugh, S.J., responded to Ong's request for feedback to a portion of the essay, apparently *LAH-90*. On Kavanaugh's response Ong wrote "LANGHERM 10 'Logos and Digitization.'" Although Kavanaugh's comments were highly enthusiastic, perhaps Ong was deflated by his suggestions, but if so, it was a short-lived response. In a subsequent letter the next day, January 11, Kavanaugh offered another suggestion, on which Ong wrote in script, "Langherm 13," suggesting perhaps his interests were revived.

This is conjecture, but in fact, on February 11 and 13 Ong received further oral and written feedback from Le Xuan Hy, S.J. (Doc MSS 64.1.4.4.4.2). Hy politely questioned Ong on some of his statements regarding matters of computer operations and he offered suggestions, such as "Epilogue is a little much. Should it be splitted [sic] into two chapters to deliver more punch in the finale?" "Do you want to elaborate on the new digital-oral more, that of videos and sound rather than writing & printing?" And he cautioned that the comparison between Ramus' dichotomies and computer flow charts may not be accurate. Ong checked Hy's handwritten paragraphs, and after a discussion with him on February 13, 1990, Ong on February 16 "emended and/or corrected" the manuscript (Doc MSS 64.1.4.4.4.2).

On that same day, Michael Macovski sent a request to Ong to submit a section of *Language as Hermeneutic* for a projected collection of essays; Ong on February 22 replied "I am indeed working to finish up my volume on *Language as Hermeneutic*, but I regret to have to say that none of it is in shape for excerpting for your volume *Textual Voices, Vocative Texts*" (Doc MSS 64.1.4.4.4.3). Four days later, February 26, Ong wrote a letter of inquiry to Maud Wilcox at Harvard University Press regarding the publication of *LAH*. The letter was answered by Lindsey Waters on March 9, 1990, two days prior to the dating of *LAH-90* on March 11.

The Text of *LAH-90*

Ong's handwritten note on the *LAH-90* copy tallied "c.163 pp-c. 40,000 w. = 130 printed pages," compared to the 17,565 words on seventy-two pages of the 1989 draft, an increase largely attributable to the inclusion of a "Postscript to Prologue," the text of chapter 10, an expanded epilogue, and a bibliography. With these additions and penciled notes regarding layout at the top of each chapter, it is the most publication-ready of all drafts. There is no electronic copy of *LAH-90* but there is a hard copy with several handwritten revisions (Doc MSS 64.1.4.4.1.1).

In this draft Ong clarified, updated, and expanded. He changed the subtitle from "Reflections on the Word and Digitization" to "A Primer on the Word and Digitization" and inserted a table of contents, Roman numeral subdivisions within chapters, and a list of references. In the prologue he added a thesis in a new concluding paragraph, and the previously mentioned Postscript to Prologue. Most significant, Ong introduced the long chapter 10, "Logos and Digitization," which did not exist in *LAH-88* and had been only a chapter title in *LAH-89*.

Ong had begun his revisions of *LAH-89* almost immediately after its completion. On April 9, 1989, Ong prepared ten "topics for possible addition: *Language as Hermeneutic* (LANGHERM.ADD). The first two ("the death of rhetorical consciousness and culture" and "Exist [sic] from the prison-house of language") were later marked for deletion. Five topics derive from the work of Joshua Meyrowitz on computer effects on consciousness and society, but only brief mention is made of Meyrowitz (in chapter 13).

The third topic, though, was given more consideration: "What digitization does: (1) fractioning, (2) distancing (absence), (3) interiorization (intellectualization of a 'reasonable' sort)." Fractioning had not been discussed in *LAH-88* and though it was mentioned in chapter 12 of *LAH-89*, in *LAH-90* it was promoted to a subsidiary thesis and discussed in more detail in chapters 10 and 13. Chapter 10 was of course the most substantial addition to *LAH-90*. Ong's notes indicate the relationship of computers to human consciousness, and popular conceptualizations of artificial intelligence stimulated Ong's interest in electronic technology.

An important new source in this regard was Philip Leith's *Formalism in AI and Computer Science* (1990). In his 1990 letter of inquiry to Maud Wilcox at Harvard University Press, Ong mentioned that he received an advance copy of this book, which discusses the formalistic constraints of artificial intelligence. Ong cites this work in *LAH-90* and frequently thereafter; it has the latest publication date of any of the references for both *LAH-90* and *LAH-94*. Though Ong continued his research in this area after 1990, it is not reflected in *LAH*.

Two other topics Ong listed for possible inclusion in *LAH-90* were 1) "Present ecological age maximizes hermeneutic aims and efforts" and 2) a conclusion: "unification (hermeneutic) effort religious at root," relating to myth and "a-historical time." Both of these topics were raised in chapter 12 of *LAH-89,* and were expanded on in chapter 13 of *LAH-90.*

Among other changes, Ong renamed the second chapter from "Hermeneutics Textual and Oral" to "Hermeneutics Textual and Other" and expanded a bit on his discussions of Ricoeur and Derrida. It is here that he incorporated for the first time another source to which he would frequently advert, Paul Zumthor's *Oral Poetry: An Introduction.* However, he deleted Thomas D. Blakely's discussion of the Hemba tribe.

The revised third chapter, "The Hermeneutic Imperative of Verbalization," introduced a new reason for why oral and textual words require interpretation, and he included a discussion of how learned Latin differs from "mother" tongues, which had been the subject of his 1959 study, "Latin Language Study as a Renaissance Puberty Rite." In chapter 4, "The Interpersonalism of Hermeneutics, Oral and Other," Ong added the material on President Lyndon B. Johnson's 1966–67 Task Forces on Education to clarify the need for interpretation of all texts. Chapter 5, "Affiliations of Hermeneutics with Texts" included a new paragraph on the tactile and digitization. In chapter 6, "Hermeneutics, Print, and 'Facts,'" Ong clarified his explanation of the nature of a "fact" by quoting Nietzsche's assertion that "There are no facts, only interpretations": Nietzsche's judgment, Ong states, thus is also an interpretation but that does not thus make it unverifiable. Chapter 8, "Meaning, Hermeneutic, and Personal Trust," expands on the reason that Jesus did not leave any writings for his followers: the message must be reinterpreted anew in different contexts, which is more difficult to accomplish in texts.

Chapter 13 is more than four times longer than before (25 pages vs. 6 pages). Most of the new material focuses on *mythos* in relation to science and technology, as he writes, "our own center of concern [is] the effects of the technologies of writing, print, and electronics on hermeneutics or interpretative activity." He introduces discussions of structuralist poetics, which applies "binary analysis (digitization) even to narrative itself"; Meyrowitz's *No Sense of Place*; the effects of media, computers, and sonograms, on social environments; television news; Beckett's *Waiting for Godot*; an age of hermeneutics; artificial intelligence; computer chess games; Naisbitt's *Megatrends*; and information overload. At the end he also expands his discussion of religion as an expression of *mythos.*

On the sheet of paper that Ong listed possible additions to his manuscript, he also recorded the very favorable responses to *LAH-89* by Br. William Rehg, S.J., who was writing a Ph.D. dissertation on Habermas, so apparently Ong had been circulating his draft prior to March 6, 1989.

LAH-94

1990–1994: Hermeneutical Encounter

The extant copy of *LAH-90* is heavily revised in pencil. It is not known when Ong began inserting these handwritten edits into the *LAH-94* version, but it is clear that digitization and hermeneutical encounter complicated the completion of *LAH-94*.

Ong always had an interest in all technology, seeing it as a positive and beneficial manifestation of the human interior, an uttering or outering of the self. Because of its involvement in the processing and exchange of human knowledge, he was particularly interested in communication technology. In each of five decades Ong published books and essays that explored connections between technology and the humanities.[13]

Writing, Ong had declared, is a technology that restructures thought, and similarly, the electronics revolution once again is reshaping what and how we think. Given his moment in time, Ong's focus on the electronic world of secondary orality was particularly on radio, television, and compact disks, and even as late as the early1990s, he still referred to the electronic world as "an age I have hitherto styled the age of 'secondary orality,' but which is better described, as it now appears to me, as an age of secondary orality and secondary visualism—exemplified, for example on television and in videocassettes" (Doc MSS 6.4.2.1.2.12). Increasingly, though, he became more interested in the effects of computers on human consciousness and unconsciousness, particularly through the pervasiveness of binary digitization. Ong associated digitization with division, fractioning, writing, print, formalization, numbers, visuality, spatiality, logic, closure, textuality—all of which he considered essential for human development, but which, if employed unreflectively, could threaten the inviolability of the self. Hermeneutic "encounter" was a corrective to both textualist frameworks and digitization.

Once again, the line of Ong's thinking can be traced through lectures and two series of Graduate Student Symposiums that he conducted in the 1990–91 and 1991–92 academic years.

1990/91 Symposiums

In the summer of 1990, Ong began a brainstorming document listing twenty possible topics for the symposiums, including topics and even chapter titles from *LAH-90*: "Meaning and Interpersonal Trust"; "The Mythology of Logos"; "Rhetoric, Plato, Logos, and Digitization; or Rhetoric, Writing, Print, and Digitization; "Electronics and Language"; "*The Said and the Unsaid*"; "Electronics, Style, Imagination, Thought" (Doc MSS 64.2.1.1.21).

Ong's approach to his material was dynamic: he was working out his ideas as he taught and thus he modified the sessions as he went along, consistent with his principle that knowledge is best developed through conversation and dialogue.[14] The changes to the 1990 Fall and Spring semesters registered a new focus.

Fall 1990 Planned	*Fall 1990 Taught*
History of English as an Academic Subject	History of English as an Academic Subject
Orality, Writing, Print, Electronics	Orality, Writing, Print, Electronics
The Flip Side of Deconstruction	Under Deconstruction

Spring 1991 Planned	*Spring 1991 Taught*
You and Your Students	More Under Deconstruction
Rhetoric, Writing, Digitization	Tools, Body, Brain, and Writing
Hermeneutics and "Facts"	You and Your Students

Most significant is the renaming of "The Flip Side of Deconstruction" to "Under Deconstruction" and its spilling over into two sessions. In Symposium 4 Ong explained his rationale for the name change:

'Under' to be taken here in any and all of the senses which suggest themselves: (1) what lies beneath, *under* deconstruction. (2) Deconstruction as something being built, as being *under* construction. (3) Deconstruction is something being deconstructed, as *under* deconstruction. (3) [sic] Deconstruction is seen as *under*-deconstructed, as not deconstructed enough. (4) What it means to live *under* the reign or the power of deconstruction. (5) Others?

Ong began Symposium 4 with Jasper Neel's *Plato, Derrida, and Writing* (1988); his note card reads:

> The flip side of deconstruction . . . everything Derrida, and deconstructionism generally, assert is subsumable under these propositions: (1) "The Writer's Audience is Always a Fiction [sic]; (2) truth is achieved only in a concrete existential activity consisting of dialogue (with another or with oneself) and the interaction of this dialogue with its nonverbal context.

Ong thus continues his interest in the themes of *LAH* but also pursues new connections. For Symposium 3, "Under Deconstruction," Ong refers to his essay "Language as Encounter in Voice and in Text: Hermeneutics from Sound to Digitization," which states that taking textuality as a paradigm or "analogue for everything," leads to distortion, particularly regarding the nature of the human self:

> Deconstruction: Heidegger's *alethéia*, like Kant's noumenon-phenomenon, < knowledge by analogy with sight only. Coverup: something always behind the surface that you see or behind the surface under that surface, *ad infinitum*.

In "Language as Encounter in Voice and Text" Ong explains that text is the most recent example of reductive models for understanding human activity, which have included classical causation, structuralism, games, drama, ritual, and symbolic action. In these attempts, "the mysterious is reduced handily to the already known" (Doc MSS LANGENCR.TXT).

Eventually Ong clarifies that digitization should also be added to this list.

1991–1992 Symposiums

The 1991–92 graduate student symposiums were a continuation rather than repetition of the 1990–91 series. The original title for the 1991–92

symposiums was another variation of a now familiar formula: "Hermeneutic Encounter in Orality and Text." However, in Symposium 3 (November 19, 1991) Ong announced a new title, "Possible Misprisions in
Today's Literary Theory (misprision in the sense of not saying or revealing
something you ought to say or reveal: e.g., misprision of treason)" (Doc
MSS 64). Examples of such misprisions are the ideas of deconstructionists, textualists, and artificial intelligence enthusiasts that misrepresent the
interiority of the human person.

The symposium topics planned were:

1. Where Does the Study of English Come From?
2. Nouns versus Pronouns
3. Evolution toward Language: Continuity and the Impasse
4. The Alliance of Language and Thought with Sound
5. Three Fields of Hermeneutics*
6. Computer-Assisted Thought and Writing**

   *Changed to Information, Communication, Rhetoric, and Persons
   **Changed to Writing, Print, and Electronics All Restructure
   Thought, March 30, 1992

Symposium 4 shares its title with chapter 5 of *LAH*, but the other symposiums are also linked with that manuscript. In the margins next to each
topic Ong penciled in filenames of sources for those lectures. Most of
these filenames correspond to the electronic folders for the chapters in
LAH-94.

Lecture 2, "Nouns and Pronouns"

LANGHERM.04 (The Interpersonalism of Hermeneutics, Oral and
   Other)
LANGHERM.11 (Hermeneutics in Children's Learning to Speak)
LANGHERM.07 (Hermeneutics and the Unsaid)
HERMENC2.VTD (Hermeneutic Encounter in Voice and in Text; [not
   from *LAH*])[15]

Lecture 5, "Three Fields of Hermeneutics" (Information, Communication, Rhetoric, and Persons)

STYLE.OTD (Style in Oral Speech and Style in Texts; [not from *LAH*])
LANGHEARM.05 (Affiliations of Hermeneutics with Texts)
LANGHERM.09 (Hermeneutic and Communication in Oral Cultures)

Lecture 6. "Writing, Print, and Electronics All Restructure Consciousness"

LANGHERM.12 (Language, Technology, and the Human)[16]

A five-page description of all the symposiums is broken down into eighteen points that are distributed among the six sessions. Each session is also summarized in one or two pages of lecture notes (apart from the first one which is a carryover from the previous year).

The 1991–92 symposiums blended the concept of language as hermeneutic with the new emphasis on language and hermeneutic as *encounter*. Already in the 1990–91 symposiums, Ong had initiated this transition when he titled his work "Language as *Encounter*," rather than "Language as *Hermeneutic*" (emphasis added). Similarly, he supplemented the readings from Language as Hermeneutic in the 1991–92 Symposiums with "Hermeneutic Encounter in Voice and Text" (for Symposium 2) and "Hermeneutic Encounter: Voice, Text, Digitization: Reflections on Verbal Communication" (for Symposium 5).[17]

In his outline for "Language as Encounter in Voice and in Text: Hermeneutics from Sound to Digitization" [LANGHEANCR.OUT], Ong clarified his choice of the word "encounter":

> Explain etymologies of *hermeneutics* and *interpretation*. In-betweenness, encounter. Encounter involves basically an "I" and a "you" ("thou"), so that the names of the interlocutors are basically irrelevant, set off by commas in texts, as the pronouns "I" and "you" are not. . . . The whole naming process is never a matter of speaker-idea-word-thing, but is always embedded in the encounter of two unconsciousnesses." (2)

The word "encounter" had special resonance for Ong, for a number of reasons. The evolution of his focus from "Language as Hermeneutic" to "Language as Encounter" to "Hermeneutic Encounter" harkens back to Ongian themes from the 1960s when he had cast the hermeneutic/digital dialectic in terms of the dialectic of mechanization and the encounter of self with self and with others: "What I mean by man's encounter with himself is in a way a correlative of mechanization" ("Religion, Scholarship" 421). As with the increased interest in hermeneutics due to digitization, "the puzzling fact [is] that, as technology has become more and more dominant, personalist philosophies, philosophies of 'presence,' of encounter, and of dialogue come more and more to the fore" (425). With "encounter" Ong thus invokes a long tradition of personalist trends in philosophy, sociology, psychiatry, and anthropology, mentioning such figures as Martin Buber, Jean-Paul Sartre, Eugen Rosenstock-Huessy, Rollo May, and Ludwig Binswanger. In existential psychiatry and particularly in Germany in the 1950s, "encounter" describes the psychotherapist-patient relationship, a practice with which Ong had been familiar during his nineteen years of co-conducting a series of informal seminars on psychiatry and literature at Saint Louis University.[18] And of course in personalism, "encounter" refers to a negotiation of meaning between interiors, between the "I" and a "Thou," and it reinforces the notion that knowledge and communication are optimized in dialogue or conversation. The importance of "Hermeneutic Encounter in Voice and in Text" is underscored by the fact that on an earlier version (Doc MSS HERMENC1.VTD) Ong had inscribed the subtitle, "Possible Misprisions in Today's Literary Theory," the alternate name Ong gave to the entire 1991–92 symposium series.[19] The misprision is the unreflective use of textuality as a model for language that leaves little place for encounter.

Ong's unfinished essay, "Hermeneutic Encounter in Voice and in Text," is a substantial forty-two page draft that covers many of the same topics as *Language as Hermeneutic*, sometimes using the same passages. One difference is that within this essay, Ong quotes Stephen Tyler and Henry Sussman, both of whom had offered Ong's oralism as an alternative to the textualization of Derrida. Though Ong states that his scholarship was not consciously motivated by such an intention, it is clear at this point that a response to deconstruction was on his mind in his later works.

Under the handwritten heading, "Text as (indirectly) encounter. Words not 'signs,'" Ong in 1990 typed on an ephemera card:

If we take the text as the primary manifestation of language (as is common in a typographic culture), language cannot be rooted in encounter—that is, as sounded discourse between individuals in each other's presence in a certain time and place and nonlinguistic context. Can we read text and interpret it as a kind of encounter? In the world of sound, words are not "signs," a visually based borrowed concept (*signum*), but are exchanges between persons. (Doc MSS 64, Box 155)

Again, Ong asserts that his scholarly pursuits were not intended as a response to Derrida (see "Hermeneutic Encounter"), but he wrote on a notecard for Symposium 4 in the 1990–91 series, "Orality-literacy (incl. print) studies & deconstruction [are] contrapuntal" (Doc MSS 6.4.2.1.2.12). A primary motivation was to demonstrate that an oral hermeneutic clarifies that in writing, print, and electronic communication, *encounter* is still the basis for language use.

For the 1992–93 academic year Ong had planned to teach a graduate reading course: "Hermeneutic Encounter: Voice, Text, Digitization," but it was not offered.

Thus though in 1992 Ong was still engaged with the *LAH* manuscript, he was producing a number of other texts as well, frequently repackaging material from *LAH* and other texts into new combinations, as he experimented with finding a title that integrated his major issues—hermeneutics, encounter, voice, textuality, and digitization; and as he also clarified the relationships between the self, I-thou communication, intentionalism in the development of language, omnipresence of interpretation, the negotiation of meaning through dialogue, the limitations of a textualist paradigm, and the promises and threats of digitization. One senses a waning interest in *Language as Hermeneutic*.

The Digital Turn

During the early 1990s Ong's interest in digitization was being expressed outside of the *LAH* manuscript in a number of essays and presentations. Schmandt-Besserat's *Before Writing* in 1992 may have reflamed Ong's interest in digitization, though already by November 18, 1992, he had been brainstorming on "Digitization Ancient and Modern: Separation and the Rise of Hermeneutics," which evolved by 1995 into a copyrighted text, "Digitization Ancient and Modern: The Prehistory of Writing and the Computer."[20] In this 1992 draft Ong repeated the definition of digitization as calculating by numerically discrete units and the idea that writing begins not with literacy but numeracy.

New in chapter 10 of *LAH-90*, "Logos and Digitization," is a paragraph on digitization and memory, in relationship to Salvador Dalí's most famous painting *The Persistence of Memory* (Doc MSS 64.1.1.1).[21] "Human memory dwells in time and is more than just recall: it is, strictly speaking, non-digitizable, as is the case with time itself" (the essay is printed in an appendix to this volume). Similarly, digitized data are not commensurate with human knowledge. In chapter 10 of *LAH-94* Ong allied "knowledge" with the orality of speech and "data" with the visualism of text.

> Digitization means reduction to separate, numerable forms, to digits. Knowledge thought of as so reduced we commonly designate as "information" or "data" (that is, what is "given"). The term "data" or "what is given" suggests not an oral, auditory world of knowledge allied to spoken words . . . , but suggests rather more directly a tactile-visual world, a world in which items are somehow physically "given" or handed over to us. (100)

In a number of other essays and lectures of this period Ong extended this distinction. In "Orality, Text, Electronics: Hermeneutic Theorems" Ong formulated the equation: "Information : Communication : : Digitization : Hermeneutics" (Doc MSS ORLTXTEL.HTH). Information, fact-gathering, is fragmenting; communication, understanding the facts, is unitive.

In *LAH-94* he paired the information age with the age of interpretation and the age of hermeneutics. A further christening occurs in a passage new to chapter 12:

> The age in which human existence is now framed, the age in which human life and technology so massively and intimately interact, can well be styled not only the information age and the age of interpretation, but, perhaps even more inclusively, the ecological age, in principle an age of total interconnectedness, where everything on the earth, and even in the entire universe, is interconnected with everything else, not only in itself but, ideally, in human understanding and activity. (91)

But for the most part, these new insights were developed outside of *Language as Hermeneutic.*

Probably among the last revisions that Ong made to *Language as Hermeneutic* is the new prologue, "Language, Hermeneutics, and Digitization," which ends abruptly: "By the same token that it is an information age, our age is an interpretation age." Rather than update *Language as Hermeneutic*, it appears Ong chose to develop his ideas elsewhere, including in the 1996 published essay, "Information and/or Communication: Interactions."

The Text of *LAH-94*

It is clear that Ong's ideas were blossoming vigorously and it became difficult to root them in a single pot.

It is not known when Ong began inserting his handwritten edits of *LAH-90,* or when he ceased his revisions. The date assigned here, 1994, is the one at which Ong said he was abandoning the manuscript, but it is possible that Ong ceased working on it prior to that. The latest date of a work cited in *LAH-94* is 1991. *LAH-94* is not prepared as a completed text, as is *LAH-90.* The *LAH-94* version does not exist in hard copy nor in a one complete electronic file. Instead, each chapter is saved independently in the same electronic folder, sometimes in different fonts and layout. Because the files were moved at a later time, only the saved dates, not the dates of composition, can be determined. The earliest saved file date is September 8, 1994, and the last is October 13, 1994. The electronic folder contains fifteen chapter files, including two prologues, two versions of chapter 3, a table of contents, illustrations, references, and supplementary materials.

The folder contents suggest that the draft is unfinished: two prologues and two versions of chapter 3 are not integrated. The table of contents is not updated from *LAH-90.* The list of references has only minor changes from *LAH-90.*

Not included in the references are writers whom Ong prominently cited in his Graduate Symposiums and his scholarship of this period; others are mentioned only in passing.

A glaring omission is Denise Schmandt-Besserat whose 1992 *Before Writing* was the basis for Ong's "Digitization Ancient and Modern: Beginnings of Writing and Today's Computers" (1998), and with which Ong had been familiar before its publication. John DeFrancis whom Ong praised for an "almost superhuman survey of scholarship" in his 1989 *Visible Speech* (1990–91 Graduate Symposium 2, 2) is mentioned once in chapter 2, but though his name is penciled in on the edited copy of the *LAH-90* references, he is not included in the *LAH-94* references. Derek Bickerton (*Language and Species*) to whom Ong frequently adverted in the early 1990s is not mentioned at all, and Joshua Meyrowitz (*No Sense of Place*) is mentioned in the essay but not in the references. Mikhail Bakhtin and Ivan Ilych likewise receive less attention than would be anticipated, given the subject matter.[22] Some citations in the references are incomplete, and particularly telling is that the latest publication cited is 1990 (Leith's *Formalism in AI and Computer Science*, which Ong had read in prepublication typescript).[23]

Two major problems in the 1994 version suggest Ong was beginning to take the essay in a new direction but instead decided to drop the project entirely.

The second prologue in the folder is saved as LANGHERM.00A (the original prologue is labeled LANGHERM.0). This second prologue itself has a title, "Language, Hermeneutics, and Digitization." It could be conjectured that this is a prologue for a different work of that name that was misfiled in the *LAH* computer folder. Or the title might simply apply to the prologue itself, not to a longer work by that name. We are speculating, though, that the new prologue was an attempt to reorient the essay more toward digitization.

The original prologue's thesis is that all language is hermeneutic, with a subsidiary thesis that hermeneutics and digitization are opposite but collaborative forces. In the new prologue, the previously subsidiary thesis is now announced in the first sentence as the thesis, and "language as hermeneutic" is not mentioned. Particularly toward the end of the prologue, the style and tone become "chatty" and even perhaps quirky as he relates a sixty-year-old memory that haunts him. In his 1990 inquiry to Harvard regarding the publication of the work Ong had acknowledged that he intended *Language as Hermeneutic* to be informal, but the awkwardness of this text and the abrupt ending suggest that the prologue was a work in progress.

Further, *LAH-94* has two versions of chapter 3: filename LANGHERM.03 titled "The Hermeneutic Imperative of Verbalization," and filename LANGHERM.03A, titled "Affiliations of Hermeneutics with Text," a slight variant of chapter 5's title, "The Affiliation of Hermeneutics with Texts." In fact, the revised Chapter 3A combines much of the original chapters 3 and 5. However, Ong did not cancel the original chapter 3 or the original chapter 5, nor did he try to assimilate the material from chapters 3 and 5 that were not incorporated into chapter 3A. It appears that Ong may have given up on the project at this point, leaving the fate of chapters 3 and 5 unresolved.

The Current Text of *Language as Hermeneutic: A Primer on the Word and Digitization*

We have approached Ong's *Language as Hermeneutic* with a philosophy consistent with Ong's theorem that texts are not closed systems but are part of on-going never-finished dialogue. There is no fixed text.

For the most part, *LAH-94* is the basis for this text. However, there are some substantial variations.

On the 1990 version Ong had made a number of handwritten additions, deletions, and comments. Some of the additions and deletions are carried over into the 1994 version and others are not. Because Ong never finalized his revision, it is impossible to determine with certitude what changes he would have made had he the time and interest to continue. Editorial judgments were made whether to silently accept or reject proposed changes that were not implemented. The marginal comments presented additional challenges, and once again we strived to give the manuscript the benefit of an editorial review that it would have received had it been sent to a publisher.

The greatest challenges were the materials that Ong began to rework but did not complete: the new prologue, two chapter 3s, and an eviscerated chapter 5. We decided that both prologues should be maintained. The original prologue is consistent with the majority of the material in the manuscript, but the second prologue signals a new line of thought or emphasis. Reading the prologues in sequence does not create a dissonance.

For chapters 3 and 5 we had to exercise the most editorial license as we tried to honor Ong's intentions while providing a coherent text. Ong had combined chapters 3 of *LAH-94* and 5 to form chapter 3A. However, chapter 3A also introduced new material and conversely did not include all of the paragraphs from chapters 3 and 5. Ong left no notes on what his intentions were for chapters 3, 3A, and 5.

We decided that Ong's intentions would be best represented by replacing chapter 3 with chapter 3A, and deleting chapter 5. Thus in this edition there is no chapter titled "Hermeneutic Imperative of Verbalization" as there had been in earlier versions; chapter 5 has become a newly formulated chapter 3; and the total number of chapters has been reduced from thirteen to twelve.

The resulting text of *Language as Hermeneutic* presented here is not polished; it does contain some repetition, false starts, unfulfilled promises, and abrupt endings. In that sense, it is more a record of Ong's thinking than Ong's thoughts. By providing online access to the original manuscripts at the Saint Louis University Doc MSS, we hope to enable scholars to engage in a conversation with Ong and to come to their own conclusions regarding Ong's intentions.

1994–1998: Further Developments

In a sense, *Language as Hermeneutic* was not abandoned but distilled, refined, and supplemented by later lectures, unpublished manuscripts, and three major publications, "Hermeneutic Forever: Voice, Text, Digitization, and the 'I'" (1995), "Information and/or Communication: Interactions" (1996), and "Digitization Ancient and Modern: Beginnings of Writing and Today's Computers" (1998).[24] *Language as Hermeneutic* gives a picture of Ong working toward the ideas presented in these essays and provides a framework to clarify their connections. An attempt to locate *Language as Hermeneutic* within the totality of Ong's publications can be found in the next chapter below. To appropriate Ong's terminology, while the current chapter takes apart or "digitizes" *Language as Hermeneutic*, the next chapter "*Language as Hermeneutic*: An Unresolved Chord" is a hermeneutic or unitive move to discover why Ong envisioned this book to be a synthesis of his life work.

LANGUAGE AS HERMENEUTIC: AN UNRESOLVED CHORD

Thomas D. Zlatic

The person whom this alchemy
Of history, biography,
Or pious hagiography
Would put into a test solution,
Decant and filter, isolate,
Resolve into precipitate,
Dehydrate and desiccate,
Compress, and roll into a pill-
A tour de force consummate skill
Has hatched by patient prosecution
Of strictly scientific study
Defies recovery: to date
Immortal being has eluded
The fingers of the pursuivant,
And all his search is unconcluded.

The cartoon lies unfinished.

The chord is unresolved.

—Walter J. Ong, from "Disposed in Labels: After Reading a Biography" (1942)

Walter J. Ong envisioned *Language as Hermeneutic* as a distillation of his life work. In 1990 he explained to a potential publisher, "Like this book of Havelock's [*The Muse Learns to Write*], mine is a synthesis which I hope will prove useful at multiple scholarly levels, although its tone is at times also somewhat personal" ("Letter to Maud Wilcox").

A 100-page synthesis of 457 publications over a sixty-year period seems a tremendous challenge, particularly because Ong's scholarship spans multiple disciplines and treats such disparate topics as the sensorium, beatniks, Gerard Manly Hopkins, subway graffiti, Joseph Conrad, African talking drums, noobiology, Renaissance education, psychodynamics of orality, puberty rites, noetics, John Milton's logic, and many more. It is little wonder that in 1990 and again in 1994 he put the work aside, finding it "unsatisfactory" ("Note to *Language as Hermeneutic*").

Yet Ong's prodigious scholarly output evinces a remarkable continuity of purpose and themes, as sounded already in one of his earliest publications, the 1942 poem "Disposed in Labels: After Reading a Biography"—which serves as warning to anyone attempting to sum up his life's work. After the most meticulous filtration, dissection, dehydration, and compression of data, and regardless of the medium or sensory modality used to convey the results—attempts to analyze and explicate the human person are always incomplete. Neither the *digitization* of science nor the *interpretative* efforts of the arts can completely capture "immortal being"—the ineffable self, that unresolvable chord. These three points evoked in this early poem—the decontextualized nature of data or "fact," the persistent need for interpretation, and the inexplicability of the human person—resonate still in *Language as Hermeneutic*.

Certainly Ong's ideas over a sixty-year period evolved and extended into wider and deeper spheres of human understandings. Ong was anything but monolithic. He continually engaged with current cultural and intellectual trends as he entered into dialogue with scholars from many fields, propelled by his principle of relationism—that everything is related to everything else—and his conception of scholarship (including science) as conversation or "arrested dialogue." Recognizing that no " 'true' meaning is monistically simple" (*LAH* 49) he was on the front of intellectual currents, whether they be neo-Thomism, New Criticism, rhetoric, phenomenology, psychiatry, orality, media studies, cosmology, sociobiology, anthropology, structuralism, reader-response theory, deconstruction, or hermeneutics.

Is it surprising then that in a short study meant to be a "synthesis" of his life's work, he does not address many of these issues and instead focuses on hermeneutics? No. For much of his remarkable productivity can be seen as an exfoliation of an abiding orientation. As synthesis of Ong's life work, *Language as Hermeneutic* clarifies that Ong's studies in literature, rhetoric, history of ideas, philosophy, theology, anthropology, communications, and so on, frequently had been motivated by his conviction of the absolute nonequivalency of idea and being: that there is more to being that can be put into concepts, that there is more to concepts that can be captured by words, that there is more to words than can be expressed through writing. *Language as Hermeneutic* thus is a call for an "oral hermeneutic," for the necessity of an approach to understanding that incorporates not only *logos* (logic, clarity, digitization, division, treatise) but also *mythos* (myth, rhetoric, ambiguity, integration, aphorism, story).

Ong has been frequently misinterpreted by some who had read only small selections of his works or who had encountered Ong primarily through secondary sources. Recently at a national conference a prestigious and clearly brilliant keynote speaker nonetheless criticized Ong's endorsement of the visualization and quantification of the educational reforms of Peter Ramus, when of course in fact, in his seminal work on *Ramus, Method, and the Decay of Dialogue* and in numerous other studies Ong repeatedly and sometimes brutally excoriated the sixteenth-century pedagogue. Clearly there is a need to revisit Ong's corpus through the lens of his final attempt to explain himself.

This essay demonstrates how *Language as Hermeneutic* offers insights into what over sixty years of publishing Ong thought he was about: that is, greater self-articulation and thus freedom through encounter with, and conscious appropriation of, an increasingly particulate world. *Language as Hermeneutic* not only distills Ong's thinking but also provides a tool for resituating his earlier works.[1]

Ong vigorously resisted attempts to classify himself and his work.[2] He showed some tolerance for the designation that his Saint Louis University literature students applied to his scholarship, "Onglish,"[3] but labels pertain to commodities, and Ong spent a lifetime demonstrating the confusion that arises when people, knowledge, and mental processes are conceived in terms of things.

Ong is perhaps best known for his analyses of four stages of human consciousness paralleling the unfolding of communications technology: from primary orality (in a culture largely independent of writing), to writing, then print, and now electronics,[4] but this was only one facet of a much broader and deeper scholarly project. Late in his career, Ong provided this framework to connect his seemingly disparate interests:

> I guess you'd say I'm a cultural historian. The cultural history that I do involves the study of the evolution of communications media and of forms of communication. . . . But communications are not my ultimate focus. More basically, I am concerned with the evolution of ways of conceptualizing, storing, and retrieving knowledge—human beings' ways of thinking, and why they change. And ultimately I am concerned with the evolution of consciousness, which I think is the central node in history. (Cargas 1990, 97)

Ong's investigations into the "evolution of consciousness" center on the development of the mysterious and inviolable self within thirteen and a half billion years of cosmic evolution, particularly in relationship to the history of communications technology.

Ong noted in 1957 that for him the most important insight of the influential neo-Thomist Jacques Maritain was his opposition "to all monolithic views holding that there is only one way of knowing, one kind of knowledge, whether this be that of scientific experiment, of mathematics or even of mystical vision" ("Eternal Spring," 26). *Language as Hermeneutic* argues for an approach to understanding that is more open and inclusive than models of interpretation predicated on texts, models that promote fixity and closed-system thinking. Whereas logic and print tend to promote closed-system thinking, oral-aural exchange (including rhetoric, dialogue, conversation, and now the secondary orality of electronic culture) are more system-breaking, promoting interactional and transactional open-system thinking, as instanced in literature, television, ecology, ecumenism, phenomenology, relativity, quantum theory, social sciences, education, and other cultural phenomena. Ong's tenet of "relationism" is ecological: all things are potentially inter-related, if not in space and time, through human consciousness, the most closed-off, organized-from-within system that we know of. "Human consciousness is open closure" ("Voice and Opening," 337).

What Ong offers is a postmodern understanding of language and culture that is an alternative to both Derridean labyrinths and posthuman philosophies that envision artificial intelligence as the culmination of cosmic evolutionary processes. Ong, like the deconstructionists, was critical of the naïveté of logocentrism, or as he styled it, "corpuscular epistemology," but his groundbreaking studies on the role of media environments in the structuring of human consciousness enabled him to historicize the deconstructive enterprise itself, identifying the literate biases and assumptions that underlie that thinking. Positioning himself from the perspective of an oral hermeneutic, Ong celebrated the "pretextual." Despite the pretense of writing, language use is always contextualized, and that context itself defies complete explicitation. Attention to the history and phenomenology of orality reveals that language is not intrinsically a set of labels nor a vehicle for the transfer of information; it is a negotiation of meaning between human persons that is open-ended and without terminus. In other words, all language use is hermeneutic. This negotiation of meaning through language is not limited to the verbal, nor is it a completely explicit, conscious, or rational process. Further, all interpretation is interdependent with the communication medium through which the negotiation is conducted. Thus the probes in *Language as Hermeneutic* into the philosophical nature and historical development of language and language use can be considered to be prolegomena to media study.

The Argument

In his original prologue, Ong announced two theses for *Language as Hermeneutic:* primarily, all language use is hermeneutic, and secondarily, that all communications technology is fractioning or digitizing, creating increasing complexity and thus a need for integration at a higher level of complexity and understanding. The primary thesis speaks to the nature of language and its relation to thought. The secondary thesis is concerned with the evolution of language and thought in dynamic interplay with emerging communications technology.

Point the First

The truth of the statement "all language is hermeneutic" is occluded by visualist/textual models of interpretation promoted by a print mentality. Thus Ong explained of his manuscript, "One purpose of the present treatment is to introduce into the study of hermeneutics more reference to the oral" (*LAH* 22).

It is not always recognized, however, that the "oral" is a fuzzy or multi-faceted term in Ong's work, resulting in skewed interpretations of Ong's ideas. The "oral" is not equivalent to what is voiced: the transcription of an illiterate person's testimony may be more oral than the reading aloud of a book composed in writing. That is because "oral" can refer to speech, which like its counterpart writing, is a mode of communication. But the oral can also refer to orality (or oralism), a habit of mind, as is its counterpart, literacy. Thus the set of terms "speech/writing" refers to modes of communication whereas the pair "orality/literacy" refers to the habits of mind that are fostered by such modes (Heckle, qtd. in Welch 1999, 66).

"Primary orality" refers to the mental processes for comprehending, processing, organizing and communicating knowledge by those within a traditional culture that has had no or little exposure to writing—as Ong described in his most widely read and translated book, *Orality and Literacy* (1982), which Ong later said is an effort to explain "oral hermeneutics" in ways not previously attempted.[5] In an oral culture emphasis is not on abstract, formal thought but on concrete, situational thinking that is rooted in the human life world.

In addition to its historical manifestation in primary orality, the "oral" also refers to the spoken word, to sounded human speech. "Spoken word," though, Ong would say is a redundancy, for a "real" word is always sounded, whether physically or imaginatively in the mind of a reader. Ong demonstrates the ramifications of this in his phenomenological investigation of the sensorium, finding that each sense orients us differently to space and time (*The Presence of the Word*). The dominant sense by which knowledge is apprehended influences not only what we know but even our concept of what knowledge is. Again, our access to reality both illuminates and shadows. Sound is "event-ful," a happening, a process, whereas vision orients us more to space (*The Presence*; "I See"). Further, different communications media engage the senses in different proportions with different effects on noetic processes, psychic drives, and personality structures. The visualization and spatialization of writing and print promote the conception of knowledge as an object—manipulatable in space and enduring unchanged through time, even after the death of the author. The text seemingly is decontextualized from human interaction and the give-and-take of dialogue.

As valuable and necessary as is a visual synthesis for the development of Western culture, for Ong, orality remains "a deep well of our humanity" (Letter to Sheila Nayar). As vision drives toward greater and greater explicitation, there is a greater need for a more holistic processing of experience that is uniquely accessible through sound. "Sound is alive but at the same time evanescent and elusive. It is much easier to describe something seen than to describe a symphony. The oral-aural provokes mystery more than any other sense does" ("Hermeneutic Encounter in Voice and in Text").

Finally, for Ong the oral also refers quintessentially to conversation or dialogue, oral-aural communication in existential situations, particularly those involving face-to-face encounters in a shared space or context, in which people together negotiate meaning. The oral in contemporary culture counters the spatialization, exteriorization, commodification, and depersonalization of knowledge that are promoted by writing and print technologies. Oral hermeneutics helps to remind us that all human communication, whether spoken, written, printed, or electronically encoded, is dialogue, conversation. Such communication is not a sharing of information but a sharing of selves. Looking backward from *Language as Hermeneutic*, we can see more clearly in Ong's earlier works that orality is a spring for *mythos*, for an alternate way of knowing that complements *logos*.

Point the Second

Once again Ong's 1942 poem, "Disposed in Labels" is prescient: "to date/Immortal being has eluded/The *fingers* of the pursuivant" (emphasis added). In *Language as Hermeneutic*, the *finger's* futile attempt to "grasp" the totality of a person's being is connected to digitization, which etymologically as well as historically, is associated with counting, to divisioning and fractioning, to tactility and spatiality. Ong contends that the history of communications technology is a record of increasing digitization that manifests itself in analysis, abstraction, logic, and systems. Again, retrospectively, this provides a framework for Ong's fascination with the Western world's transition from a centuries-old age of rhetoric to an age of logic, as the drive toward quantification accelerated with the mathematization of medieval scholastic logic, the invention of print, the enormous popularity of Ramist "method," the realignments of the *artes sermocinales* (communication arts)—especially the shift of dialectic or logic from an *ars disserendi* (art of discourse) to an *ars bene ratiocinandi* (art of reasoning)—and the rise of modern science (see *Ramus*; "Introduction" to *A Fuller Course*; "Renaissance Symbolism"). Such developments resulted in psychological as well as cultural changes: new understandings of the physical universe were paralleled by a corresponding shift in human consciousness. Many of Ong's works speak to this quantification or digitization that encouraged a reconceptualization of mind and mental processes on visual/spatial models, with knowledge being now "envisioned" in terms of structure, system, fields, bodies, and content that could be manipulated by "method" and being displayed by diagrams and charts.

Thus Ong's subsidiary thesis is that digitization (divisive) and hermeneutics (unitive) are countervailing strategies for advancing ourselves and our world. The backdrop or context or "pretext" for *Language as Hermeneutic*, though, is human consciousness, for it is through the dialectical interplay of digitization and hermeneutics that the self achieves greater depths of interiority and thus greater ability to communicate.

We will trace here the development of Ong's oral hermeneutic through five topoi to which he frequently returns: the foundational orientation in personalist thinking; the material and biological base for human thought; the use of aphorisms and conversation to explore and communicate knowledge; the inescapability of the tacit dimensions of all thinking and communication; and the perpetual need for *logos* to be supplemented by *mythos*.

Presence of Personalism

For a Ph.D. candidate writing a dissertation on his works,[6] Ong in 1974 clarified his scholarly interests:

> In one way, my concern with such statements [of a metaphysical nature] and my concern with communication are convertible with one another, as both are convertible also with my concern with personalism. ("Letter to Randolph Lumpp," June 4, 1974, 9)

The "convertibility" of metaphysics, communication, and personalism provides a unique flavor to Ong's organization and style of writings, writings which he construed as a continuing dialogue between one presence or interior to others. Ong's oral hermeneutic is deeply embedded in I-thou relationships.

Walter Ong and Jacques Derrida at times have been, simplistically, pitted against each other, which on the surface is a seemingly plausible dichotomization in that Ong is the author of a book titled *The Presence of the Word*, and Derrida is famous for his critique of logocentrism and the metaphysics of presence. However, both men are postmodern thinkers acutely aware of the provisional nature of all knowledge. For instance, like Derrida, Ong was critical of logocentric thinking, finding it to be the antithesis of hermeneutics: Logocentrism, or as Ong styled it, "corpuscular epistemology"

> is the naïve belief that direct connections exist between words and things, that things are presented rather than *re*-presented in language. Logocentrism places small value on hermeneutics, reserving it for the foreign, ancient, and arcane. Ong's "presence of the word" has nothing to do with logocentrism. (Ong, private correspondence, November 1, 1993)

Rather, for Ong, presence bespeaks personalism; the "paradigmatic sense of presence is the presence of one conscious human being to another" (*LAH* 24).

In oral exchange it is more obvious than in writing that negotiation of meaning is never a completely verbal nor only a cognitive process. Like Bernard Lonergan, Ong recognized the distortions that result from attempts to separate concept from being or explanation from understanding. Meaning is not an object free-floating in space, to be snatched and wrapped in language for delivery to another person. Meaning is negotiated in a context that is itself interpretative but beyond complete formulation and understanding. And the process of negotiation is a cognitive, psychological, somatic, and pragmatic undertaking, conducted by human beings whose interpretation is influenced by a living, organic memory that wells up out of both consciousness and unconsciousness. Human communication is not primarily an exchange of messages, but a sharing of interiors, an effort to establish relationships that result in an intensification of one's sense of self.

Communication between humans, as Ong defines it, is anchored in mystery. Among the most recondite mysteries for Ong is the human self, the inexplicable "I," as described by Gerard Manly Hopkins, with whom he had strong affinities (see Ong, "Hopkins's Articulate Self"): "my self-being . . . that taste of myself, of I and me above and in all things, which is more distinctive than the taste of ale or alum, more distinctive than the smell of walnutleaf or camphor, and is incommunicable by any means to another man" (*Poems and Prose* 145). "This absolutely central, unique, and assertive feature of human consciousness" ("Hopkins's Articulated Self" 127) is not a definition of self (*Hopkins, the Self* 27); nor the decentered, divided, and deconstructed self that has been identified, for instance, by Jacques Lacan and others, nor a self-image or a construction (*Hopkins, the Self* 6) but the "self that obtrudes when one awakens from sleep, the self that does not need to be discovered at all" (*Hopkins, the Self* 4). This taste of self becomes more acute as consciousness evolves out of unconsciousness, partly through interaction with others. This self-contained "I" is outer-directed, seeking through outerings or utterings to engage another interior, a Thou. In other words, for Ong it is clear that communication is inherently rooted in personalism:[7]

> All human communication is an interiorizing operation. . . . "communication" is more than the mere movement of information," imagined as a commodity shuttled through a "medium" from one point to another in a field.

Human communication proceeds from the interior consciousness of one human being to the interior consciousness of other human beings. ("Reading, Technology," 139)

Interiority and intentionality distinguish communication from a mere exchange of information: "by communications we understand here not simply new gimmicks enabling man to 'contact' his fellows but, more completely, the person's means of entering into the life and consciousness of others and thereby into his own life" (*Presence* 15). This is why, during the writing of *Language as Hermeneutic,* he so frequently created working titles that included the word "encounter" to describe communication. Ong offers that an oral hermeneutics can help us to re-recognize that language is primarily a call or cry of one inviolable human interior to another, an encounter between an I and a Thou.

Thus Ong rejects the notion that humans achieve language through a naming process, for instead, intentionalism underlies language. Referencing Heidegger, Ong writes, language itself is at its deepest level not primarily even a system of sounds. There is a primordial attunement of one human existent to another out of which all language comes. Man is rooted in "speaking silence" (*Presence* 2–3). Prior to speech there must be an attunement of one consciousness to another. The speaker must fictionalize in his or her own consciousness the hearer, must take on the role of the hearer; anticipating feedback, he or she must be speaker and hearer at the same time, or as Ong frequently quoted Lavelle, "the speaker listens while the hearer speaks" ("Voice as Summons").

An oral hermeneutic attempts to recapture a sense of the inherently and deeply interpersonal nature of human communication that is blurred by textual models of interpretation. Ong makes this point clear in chapter 8 of *Language as Hermeneutic,* "Meaning, Hermeneutic, and Interpersonal Trust," when he asserts that "ultimately, meaning and hermeneutic are based on personal intersubjective trust" (*LAH* 58). In a cynical age that values a hermeneutics of suspicion, such a statement may appear naïve, but Ong's earlier works clarify that the trust or belief that underlies human communication is not so much propositional, "belief that" some *thing* is true, but interactional, trust in the sincerity of the other, "belief in" some *one.* Again early in his career, in "The Jinnee in the Well Wrought Urn" (1954), Ong recognized that writing and print mask but do not ever completely eliminate the transactional nature of human communication. While respectful of the New Critics' tenets regarding the autonomy of the literary work, he contended nonetheless that the personalist nature of all art always obstinately asserts itself. We encounter not only a work of art but also the artist or jinnee communicating from within it, for "each work of art is not only an object but a kind of surrogate for a person" (24). In his richly textured essay on "Voice as Summons for Belief" in the same collection, Ong further explained it is reductive to imagine that any piece of literature is merely an object to be handled: "A literary work can never get itself entirely dissociated from this I-Thou situation and the personal involvement which it implies" (53):

> Belief is thus not something superadded to communication and thought, but something endemic to all human thinking. . . . All human intellectual activity implies faith in the possibility of communication and faith in someone with whom we can communicate. ("Voice as Summons," 55)

Thus Ong shifts the focus from belief in statement to belief in speaker, a move in some ways paralleled by both Ricoeur and Tyler as they distinguish truth from veracity or honesty. Ricoeur employs this distinction between "belief in" and "belief that" in his analysis of "attestation" which he finds fundamental in his ontological investigation of "oneself as another" (20). Attestation, related to testimony, is concerned with veracity, not truth; it is without epistemic certainty or pretense to foundational knowledge, and it always entails a "threat of suspicion"; "Tests of sincerity . . . are not verifications but trials that finally end up in an act of trust, in a final testimony, regardless of the intermediary episodes of suspicion."[8]

Stephen Tyler relates the distinction between honesty and truth to modes of communication, suggesting that truth is more of a concern for literate cultures whereas oral cultures value honesty. In an oral culture, "truth is conceived not as an independent entity but as an honesty based on the harmony of words and actions of the one who speaks truly: "There is no agentive force outside of the context of telling; one may be a liar but not a 'truther' " (*The Unspeakable* 190). We can become "hoodwinked by writing" (40) into thinking that hermeneutic is external to the conversational process rather than immanent.

Truth is anchored not in abstractions and statements but in human beings—and thus in matter and time.

A Matter of Time and the Time of Matter

In a 1996 interview Ong provided yet another entrée into his work, this time through the entirety of cosmic evolution:

> In the areas we have touched on (my publications do treat of other matters), academically I should like to be remembered for this, among other things: furthering understanding of the relationships between verbal as well as other types of human expression and the total evolution of the cosmos that we human beings are part of and are still learning more and more about daily. (Kleine and Gale 83)

Language as Hermeneutic is written on the fundamental premise that hermeneutics and digitization, like all human knowing, are matters of time.

In *Language as Hermeneutic* (98) Ong quotes a remark that William Kurtz Wimsatt, Jr. made to him: "I am a space man, you are a time man,"[9] for its pithiness captured his radically temporal orientation to reality. Ong boldly speculated that evolutionary thinking may in fact be the "central corporate discovery of all mankind" ("Evolution and Cyclicism," 125). In Ong's understanding of the then 12.5 billion years of cosmic evolution,[10] there has been an increasing complexification and interiorization of matter to the point that in human beings matter becomes not only conscious but also reflective of its own consciousness.

Ong tries to escape visualist or spatial understandings of time by invoking interiorization. The past is not before or after us, or even outside of us; it is in the present and in us, as we ourselves are in time. "We can control the dimensions of length, breadth, thickness, but we cannot control time at all. We have to fit into it," he wrote (Ong, "Church and Cosmos," 16). "Space is mostly beyond us . . . but time is in us: the material in our own bodies is five to ten billion years old" (Ong, "Knowledge in Time," 14).

It is clear that his investigations into matter-in-time and time-in-matter are natural extensions of his commitment to personalism; the billions of years of cosmic evolution culminate in the human being's ability to utter "I." The interiorization of the self occurs in and through time by engagement of the self with the nonself, including other selves.

Ong firmly rejected idealistic efforts to circumvent time and matter in order to directly capture knowledge in some ideal, timeless realm. As a student in the 1940s, Ong framed his speculations on time and matter within a metaphysics and epistemology situated within the context of a flourishing "Saint Louis Thomism," a style of Thomistic philosophy marked by a particular interest in the role of sensation in noetic processes. Invigorated by the New Criticism that his teacher Marshall McLuhan brought to Saint Louis from Cambridge, Ong, in "The Meaning of the New Criticism" (1946) conducted a metaphysical inquiry into the structure and function of poetry, asserting that the New Critics served as a corrective to Cartesianism's dichotomization of mind and matter that perpetuated for centuries the error that "the idea, and not being itself, had taken the measure of knowledge" ("Meaning," 346).

In this Cartesian redefinition, forgotten was the importance of matter in concept formation: "abstractions always come to us in ways which reflect their origins out of material existents. They are not things hung together on pieces of string, but things found in judgments, the predicate of which always comes as form (more abstract) to its subject as matter (more concrete) ("Meaning," 348). Lost was the Aristotelian/Thomistic realization that *"nihil in intellectu quod non prius aliquomodo in sensibus"* means that concepts are "derived via the senses from material things and maintain always some commerce with the material" ("Meaning," 357). Meaning is derived not from logic, proposition, or definition but from induction, ultimately by pointing, and in this process context, intentionality, and sense knowledge are all crucial—a central point expanded on in *Language as Hermeneutic.*

A judgment, then, composed of a subject and predicate, is a temporal affair that does not allow for the instantaneous apprehension sought by idealists. In his later essay, "Metaphor and The Twinned Vision" (1955), Ong again takes Cartesians to task for being oblivious to the fact that the judgment reveals the binarism "endemic to human intellection" (196). "In a world of 'pure intelligence,' where intellect was not embedded in material existence, there would, indeed, be no necessity for the composite thing called enunciation or judgment: understanding would be effected immediately by a simple concept, an intellectual monad, not a dyad" (197). Words further implicate us in matter and time. The materiality and temporality of the spoken word prevent a purely logical understanding of reality:

> a further special relation with matter is set up artificially by the use of the spoken word. A large number of our abstractions are made and much of our knowledge is achieved under the guidance of speech. But concepts are not carried *on* words. They are submerged in the matter of words and must be re-abstracted from them, reclaimed from this new matter. The study of the use of words, of communication or symbolism or semantics, involves *the study of an abstractive process.* . . . The Cartesian-Kantian dualism had obscured the fact that concepts and judgments cannot be prepared in one mind and handed over like tokens to another. In their movement from intellect to intellect, they must pass through matter *en route*: the vehicle which bears from intellect to intellect the judgment compounded of logical matter and form is itself a material thing. ("Meaning," 350–51)

Although Ong was critical of New Critics on other matters,[11] he did applaud their efforts to dethrone the architectonic logic that governed poetry and to rediscover the indispensable murkiness or ambiguity that comes from sense knowledge and the infra-intellectual. Engagement with the "total meaning" of a poem requires "the submergence in matter, which alone makes ambiguity possible" ("Meaning," 362). Being must be reinserted over idea. Ong's claim—that language study must be *"the study of an abstractive process"* because concepts are "submerged in the matter of words [and] must be re-abstracted from them, reclaimed from this new matter"—is an insight that later is reformulated with deeper implications as, "all language is hermeneutic."

The rootedness of knowledge in time and matter is most extensively pursued in *Fighting for Life: Contest, Sexuality, and Consciousness* (1981), Ong's foray into noobiology, or the biological underpinnings of noetic processes. Through the lenses of biology, anthropology, psychology, social sciences, and academic history, he investigated the material base for noetic processes, focusing on adversativeness and contest. While acknowledging parallels with the then popular E. O. Wilson's *Sociobiology: The New Synthesis*, Ong clarifies that, contra some claims from sociobiology, the material base for intellectual activity is not an argument for materialism or determinism. Thought and human freedom are dependent on matter but not reducible to matter, for "human self-consciousness is biologically unprocessable because it is genetically free-floating," the "I" is not traceable to genetic materials (*Fighting* 10). Human beings are truly microcosms, consisting of

> the genetic heritage, which reaches back into the inorganic world, and the biologically unprocessable, genetically free-floating self-consciousness which is the only situs of human intelligence and of its dialectical complement human freedom. (*Fighting* 11)

The temporality and materiality of human understanding also warranted Ong's conviction that knowledge is an unending, ongoing process: there are no completely explicit statements and there is always more to be said. Such a premise underlay Ong's study of the history of communications technology. Knowledge is contoured by the communications technology used to think about and share that knowledge. Since any encoding system changes what is encoded, further reinterpretation, reexplanation, and rediscovery are always required as new media gain ascendancy

Regardless of the communication medium, knowledge is always wrapped up with time, matter, the senses, biology, technology, the unconscious, culture, and silence—some of which is beyond encoding in language. In fact, Ong contends, immersion in time and matter is intrinsic even to profound philosophical speculation that would seem to be more timeless and ethereal: "serious philosophical statement deeply involves not only consciousness but also the unconscious (more "bodily," less freed than consciousness) (*Fighting* 33).[12] Truth runs deep. And for the exploration of these depths, aphorism and dialogue may be the best approach.

"Knowledge Broken": Aphorisms, Dialogue, and Conversation as Hermeneutic

Before settling on "Language as Hermeneutic" as the title for the course he taught while composing his corresponding manuscript, Ong had named it "Interpretation and Being," which hints at the metaphysical interests of the course and later of his book. In his 1974 letter that identified communication, personalism, and metaphysical statement as being "convertible" in his thinking. Ong also speculated that metaphysics ultimately might be the anchor for his scholarly investigations:

> On the other hand, I am not quite sure that the evolution of the media is at the center of my thinking. As a matter of fact, I don't believe it is. What is at the center? Metaphysics, I suppose, and I am sure that metaphysics somehow ultimately rests on aphoristic statements. (Letter to Randolph Lumpp, June 4, 1974)[13]

The use of aphorisms in philosophical thinking, wisdom literature, and even medicine has a long history, extending from Hippocrates through figures such as Jesus and Francis Bacon, to Nietzsche and Wittgenstein. Though Ong's colleague Marshall McLuhan was more renowned for such pithy, oracular statements, both men as scholars in Renaissance literature and rhetoric were intrigued by the aphorism, a verbal art form straddling the borders between literature and philosophy that substitutes for argument and demonstration such literary/rhetorical devices as metaphor, metonymy, hyperbole, oxymoron, paradox, juxtaposition, and wit.[14] The aphorism blended *logos* and *mythos*, digitization and hermeneutics.

McLuhan's 1944 Cambridge dissertation on Thomas Nashe within the context of the trivium explored the importance of aphorisms for both metaphysics and science, in the tradition of Francis Bacon whose aphoristic style was a way "of keeping knowledge in a state of emergent evolution" (McLuhan 57n45). McLuhan noted Bacon's contrast of the aphorism with the "method" of his day: "Aphorisms, representing a knowledge broken, do invite men to inquire farther; whereas Methods, carrying the show of a total, do secure men, as if they were at farthest" (qtd. in McLuhan 200–201). Further, the aphorism "was to portray, not a thought, but a mind thinking, or, in Pascal's words "*la peinture de la pensée*" (qtd. in McLuhan 201n31). The aphorism as "knowledge broken"—stripped from argument and proof—creates cognitive dissonance that stimulates knowledge as a process rather than a content. Not surprisingly, then, in his reminiscences of McLuhan as a former teacher, Ong singled out as McLuhan's most effective pedagogic trait: the use of aphoristic statements to upset one's paradigms, to get people thinking ("McLuhan as Teacher").

The aphorism as broken knowledge is a vehicle for an oral hermeneutic that privileges dialogue over digitization and is open to the unspoken and unspeakable that resonate in and under both thinking and conversation. Ong's predilection for metaphysical statement wrapped in aphorism helps us not only to grasp the import of *Language as Hermeneutic*, but also to understand better the connection between two of Ong's earlier works whose topics might otherwise seem unrelated, rhetoric and logic in *Ramus, Method, and the Decay of Dialogue* and noobiology in *Fighting for Life: Contest, Sexuality, and Consciousness.*

Fighting for Life's investigation of the biological underpinnings of human mental activity focuses on adversativeness, particularly on agonistic structures in human consciousness, unconsciousness, and behavior. Human thinking is rooted in adversativeness—in struggle or opposition, partly because human truth itself, at its depths, is dialectically structured: "the truly profound and meaningful principles and conclusions concerning matters of deep philosophical or cultural import are . . . invariably aphoristic or gnomic, and paradoxical. Their meaning is both clear and mysterious, and dialectically structured" (31). But, Ong continues, "by dialectically structured I do not mean containing a contradiction. . . . I mean that the ultimately profound statements are always duplex: they say, at least by implication, two things that are related to one another by asymmetric opposition" (31). For instance, one might profess that experience is the best teacher, and still maintain experience is the worst teacher:

> The opposition between the two statements is not symmetrical (is-is not) but asymmetrical (is-but). When you look carefully at the one statement, the somewhat askew qualification buried within it shows, revealing that the statement is really duplex. And when stated in duplex form, at least one of the two resulting contrasted statements will have new duplicities within it. (32)

Similarly, "The medium is the message" may be true, but is not complete or final. "The medium is *not* the message" is also true, in some ways, ways that must be negotiated in dialogue—of which there is no end.

Language as Hermeneutic reaffirms the "is-but" structure of asymmetric opposition in aphorisms as an alternative to the flat contradiction, "is-is not," of binary thinking, which Ong identified with the sixteenth-century logician and educational reformer, Peter Ramus. In his massive Harvard doctoral dissertation, *Ramus, Method and the Decay of Dialogue* (1954), Ong documented how the printing press influenced a reconceptualization of knowledge in terms of vision and space, as exemplified by Ramus's method. To illustrate, Ong contrasted aphoristic thought and communication with the *method* of Ramus, who stripped the personalist cast from rhetoric and dialectic and oriented humans in a world of silent space (227, 318). A major motivation for Ong's antipathy to Ramus' method was Ramus' rejection of aphoristic thinking—his denial of the "duplex" nature of understanding and rejection of mystery and dialogue: "To [Ramus'] mind the sense that utterances can somehow touch mysterious depths which analysis can never quite fathom (without itself opening still greater depths) is of course lost" (*Rhetoric, Romance* 163). Ong noted in particular the contrast between aphorism and analysis:

> One of the *most significant points of difference* [emphasis added] between Ramus' program and other programs generally is Ramus' failure to provide any such collection [of sententiae] for the student to work with. . . . Whatever is caught in any expression is, for Ramus, not usable *unless it has first been analyzed*. The passion for analysis militates against Ramus' resort to aphorisms and other "pointed" sayings. (*Rhetoric, Romance* 155–56)

Ong is unrelenting in his critique of Ramus' method that trivialized aphorism:

> If an apothegm or a proverb or an aphorism should by any chance come to mind, before one uses it one had best write it down and analyze it grammatically, rhetorically, logically, mathematically, or "physically." What it "contains" is what comes out of the analysis, not what it actually says before it is analyzed. . . . To this mind the sense that utterances can somehow touch mysterious depths which analysis can never quite fathom (without itself opening still greater depths) is of course lost. All statement is flat, plain, and if it is not this, it is deficient as statement. (*Rhetoric, Romance* 163)

Before settling on the title *Ramus, Method, and the Decay of Dialogue*, Ong in a 1952 letter to his parents, asked, "What do you think of this as a title, possibly: *The Clunch Fist of Method: Ramus and the Modern Mind*? (Clunch means clenched—old form, from a quotation. I'll have to explain the title, but that's what a book is for, to explain)" ("Letter to his parents"). The clunch fist of Ramus's logic and method contributes to the "decay of dialogue," in that it continues and accelerates the fractioning process begun at least by the time of ancient Greek philosophers who broke knowledge into pieces for easier manipulation. Aphorisms thus are part of an oral hermeneutic, a strategy to supplement the apprehensions of visualist/tactile understandings of the world with the resonances of approaches modeled on sound rather than texts. Ong's own aphorism "all text is pretext" calls attention to the necessity of dialogue to fill in the inevitable gaps and incompleteness of any statement, written, oral, or electronic.

When in the 1980s Ong began research into *Language as Hermeneutic*, he created a series of notecards on aphorisms. It is significant that his definition of "aphorisms" was written under the heading "hermeneutics": "a truth which contains its own reflection on itself—and hence incorporates within itself a dialectic which renders it bottomless as well as intellectually appealing" (Notecards 9-30-84). In this same set of cards, Ong recorded from Crossan's influential book, *In Fragments: The Aphorisms of Jesus,* statements such as, in the aphorism the hearer/reader is "challenged to hermeneutics" (14); the aphorism "is always a heuristic matrix and a hermeneutical challenge" (22); "it defies all the systems" (10); it is "a form of epistemological conflict" (11); whereas method is more suited for proof and belief, aphorisms as knowledge broken "point toward action" (14–16).

The aphorism is thus a hermeneutical tool, the language of metaphysics. In fact, Richard Gray maintains the aphorism's importance in the development of hermeneutical thought in the German Romantic and post-Romantic periods, and he argues that the aphorism can instance Heidegger's hermeneutical circle: "as the part that calls for contextualization in a whole, the aphorism challenges the reader to project a contextual whole under which the part can sensibly be subsumed" (54–55). Ong adds that the aphorism also helps to undermine an uncritical reliance on interpretative models based on vision or text that were generated in the age of print, for which he recommends as a corrective a supplementary "oral hermeneutic."

Ong's insights resonated with the "oral hermeneutic" of the social philosopher Eugen Rosenstock-Huessy, who prioritized speech over the discursive reasoning of traditional investigation. In a 1960 review, Ong noted that in Rosenstock-Huessy

One returns here from a world of "observation" and measurement to an older world of gnomic expression and chthonic wisdom. Rosentock-Huessy's "conclusions" tend to be of the nature of apothegms—not apothegms uttered in a vacuum but brought to bear on particular developments in culture and thought . . . if this is proverbial wisdom, it is a highly informed and sophisticated one, much more so than other such wisdoms in the past because it is generated out of, and brought to bear on, a mass of particular details inaccessible to earlier ages. ("Philosophical Sociology," 140–41)

Note: "observation" and "measurement"—digitization—are implied by the "mass of particular details," but the interpretation is framed within oral discourse" ("Philosophical Sociology" 138, 140). This rang true for Ong for whom sound provided a more intimate connection with time and interiority, with depths of meaning that visualist analysis cannot reach. The aphorism blends chthonic oral wisdom and postprint awareness—that is, *mythos* and *logos*.

But while advancing an oral hermeneutic Ong made clear he was not retrospective in his thinking, as some critics have charged. Though sometimes used interchangeably, the terms "aphorism" and "proverb" are linked to different media environments. The proverb is an expression of conventional wisdom of a traditional (oral) culture that brings discussion to a close, while the aphorism is an insight from a clearly individual (literate) perspective that stimulates thinking: "Proverbs give no reason for none is needed; aphorism does not because none is possible" (Crossan 25). Ong characterizes Rosenstock-Huessy as a thinker who is able to communicate through aphorisms from a postprint perspective. Thus Ong's oral hermeneutic is not a call for the resurrection of an unreflective oral mentality, as some have charged, but an attempt to expose the limitations of visual models for understanding that promote fixity and closed-system thinking. Hermeneutically challenging, anti-systematic, dialectical, epistemologically conflicting, open-ended, time-bound, action-oriented, and sensitivity to silence and mystery—these traits warrant the inclusion of aphorisms into an oral hermeneutic.

Aphorism as "knowledge broken" not only prefigures the first thesis of *Language as Hermeneutic* ("use of language from the very beginning is interpretation or hermeneutic") but also applies to the book's subsidiary thesis (that communications technology is fragmenting in that it decontextualizes knowledge from human dialogue and thereby atomizes knowledge into data). However, knowledge broken through technologies of the word still can be evocative. The overwhelming proliferation of digitized and mathematized binary data make more urgent a unitive effort toward integration.

Already in 1957 Ong claimed that "radically, all human knowledge is held in a dialogue setting . . . it is by taking part in the dialogue that we learn" ("Scholarly," 74–75; Zlatic, "Talking Literature"). Dialogue is time-bound, asymmetrical, open-ended, unsettling, nonsystematic, negotiable, and sensitive to silence and mystery. It inhabits the middle ground of soft oppositions in which Ong locates rhetoric between unreflective *mythos* and formalist *logos*:

> The ultimate paradigm or model for dialectical relationships is not a flat contradiction of formal logic but something from the personal, human life-world, conversation itself, dialogue about a particular matter, in which each statement by one interlocutor needs qualification from the other interlocutor's statement in order to move toward fuller truth. (*Fighting* 32)

Ong found that Bakhtin's work harmonized with an oral hermeneutic:

> This person-to-person dialogue M. M. Bakhtin rightly maintains lies at the ultimate base of all utterance, written as well as oral, scientific as well as casually conversational or formally literary. . . . Dialogue is thus itself a form of hermeneutic, indeed the ultimate model of hermeneutic. Dialogue . . . is hermeneutic in hermeneutic's natural habitat. . . . (*LAH* 41)

Further, knowledge as dialogue or conversation has implications for I-thou relationships. Dialogue, at its optimum, is "encounter," the richly laden term from personalist philosophies and existential psychiatry that Ong became increasingly focused on during the composition of *Language as Hermeneutic*. The "I" and the "thou" in dialogue are beyond complete verbalization. Their ineffability necessitates mystery and silence.

Language as Hermeneutic: The Rest Is Silence

The silence speaks. Listen to the silence. A presence is never mute. These aphoristic paradoxes spoke to Ong, for they too implied the primacy of being over idea, and truth over propositional statement. Since there is more to reality than can be completely known or expressed, a proposition is an abstraction from the plentitude of being; propositional statement expands and clarifies meaning but also delimits and confines being by ignoring silence, the silence that is tied to what it means to be human. *Language as Hermeneutic* is a call to attend to the silence that gives meaning to the utterance.

Ong cannot be more emphatic in stating "The truth of the most clear-cut proposition is *never* within the words alone, but in the words-plus-existential-context" ("Hermeneutic Forever," 19). One thinker who stimulated Ong's conception of hermeneutics was Stephen Tyler, who clarifies that "speaking silence" means a sign cannot be a sign without a sender intending it to be a sign and the receiver knowing it was so intended, and this understanding precedes words, which are later given meaning by their nonverbal context. The context for saying is itself, in its totality, beyond saying. Ong agreed with Tyler that "the initial error in linguistic analysis arises from abstracting the system of linguistic signs from their context and treating them as independent formal entities" (*The Said* 461), and Ong double-lined this passage from Tyler: "yet it is just the illusion of this reduction that the written forms of speech produce. Writing tempts us to locate intersubjectivity in the structure of the written code itself or in some relation between the code and its object" (464).[15]

Context in face-to-face dialogue—paralinguistics, kinesics, intentions, goals, environment, location, history, psychology, health, power relationships, world views, mood, and much more—is unspeakable in its entirety and beyond capture though digitization. Thus the need of an oral hermeneutic to supplement hermeneutics based on visual/spatial modeling that obscures the fact that all language use is hermeneutic.

Truth reverberates through but also beyond articulated language. Perhaps useful here is David Groarke's claim that the aphorism is an alternative approach to philosophy that posits the primacy of intuition or insight over deductive argumentation, which has been variously identified in Western philosophy as nous, intellectus, intellegentia, intuition, understanding, the natural light of reason, and phronetic insight. In referencing Plato's distinction between intuition (noesis) and discursive knowledge (dialectic), Goarke argues "Dialectic does not displace insight; it is a prelude to insight. It works as a kind of propaedeutic that stimulates the mind; it primes students so that they can experience the telltale flash of intuitive insight" (416).

Ong echoes this point when lauding his teachers, two of the most widely known literature professors of the twentieth century. Upon the death of Perry Miller, his Ph.D. director at Harvard, Ong sent to Miller's wife, Betty, this tribute, explaining how Miller's students

> used to strain at his lectures to make sure they were getting, or almost get-ting, that little bit more that he wasn't quite saying because it was the unfor-mulated something in his awareness, his vision, which was leading him on and, with him, those who listened to him . . . but there was more still to be expressed beyond. (Letter to Betty Miller)

And regarding Marshall McLuhan, a vibrant new young instructor at Saint Louis University where Ong was completing masters' degrees, Ong sounded the same theme: "As I suppose is the case with most in-fluential teachers, McLuhan had an inarticulable message that lay much deeper than the factual material he dealt with in his courses" ("McLu-han as Teacher" 130; Zlatic "Ong as Teacher"). No doubt Ong had these two great friends in mind when he came to write this in *Language as Hermeneutic*:

> Plato says that truth, such as the philosopher desires, is "not something that can be put into words like other branches of learning: only after long part-nership in a common life devoted to this very thing does truth flash upon the soul like a flame kindled by a leaping spark, and once it is born there it nourishes itself thereafter." Plato put this in his own way, but many persons in academia and many others today generally have enough existential conti-nuity with Plato's own world to be able to understand him here without any particular further explanation. (34)

Medium as Context/Environment

Ong resisted using the term "media," believing that the word clouded the human interactions that are endemic in human communications (*In-terfaces* 46), but with Marshall McLuhan and Neil Postman he is gener-ally regarded as a founding figure in media ecology, the study of media as environment, though it appears that Ong's primary interest in media developments is a subset of his fascination with the inscrutable self who communicates. Again, his interest in communication media is convertible with metaphysics and personalism.

Media are part of the "unspeakable" context or environment. Thus various ways of mixing meaning and meaninglessness in various writing systems will encourage various kinds of hermeneutics. For instance, writing is a technology that restructures thought and consciousness itself, a human technology that enhances the sense of self ("Writing Is a Technology"), and under the influence of print, Ramus, Descartes, Kant, Lockean psychologists, and Newtonian physicists created visual models of reality that image a world of contents and containers in which knowledge has tight borders, sharp, distinct edges, and above all, complete clarity as a criterion of truth.

It is a truism that writing silences language, exchanging an eye for an ear and space for time. It might be more accurate to say that writing renders silence to irrelevance. In spoken dialogue silence is a structural component of the oral, whether in the hesitation, pause, or pregnant cessation of speech—silences that can be more meaningful than the spoken words. Beyond enunciation, silence includes tacit dimensions, those factors taken for granted, that need not be said or cannot be said because of temporal restrictions or because the speakers are not even aware of them. When in writing all is silent, silence is mute. Or, at least, harder to hear.

For as Ong points out, texts still "speak." His dictum that "words alone cannot deliver the most clear-cut proposition" is even more true of writing. Writing decontextualizes, but in order to be interpreted by the reader, it must be recontextualized into the fabric of living. Further, there are not even any words on the page or screen but only visible marks that must be decoded as they are voiced in the mouth or mind of a reader, and the code is not contained in the writing but in the reader who resurrects and resituates the conversation ("Before Textuality," 264). Communication is encounter.

In a frequently republished essay, "The Writer's Audience Is Always a Fiction" (1975), Ong explores this idea of writing as interrupted discourse, demonstrating the changing masks or roles that readers and writers must assume when they do not share a circumambient actuality. Not only the fiction writer/reader must wear masks: "the historian, the scholar or scientist, and the simple letter writer all fictionalize their audiences, casting them in a made-up role and calling on them to play the role assigned" ("Writer's Audience," 17). In all cases, regardless of the medium, communication involves conversation and context, though oral communication requires fewer machinations:

> No matter what pitch of frankness, directness, or authenticity he may strive for, the writer's mask and the reader's are less removable than those of the oral communicator and his hearer. For writing is itself an indirection. Direct communication by script is impossible. ("Writer's Audience," 20)

An inability to appreciate the oral and contextual leads in part to the byzantine interpretations of deconstructionism. Postmodern in outlook and critical of logocentrism, Ong went further, historicizing deconstruction itself, setting it within the context of the history of communications technology, which deconstruction largely ignores. If one assumes that texts are self-contained, they will inevitably self-destruct endlessly: "texts have meaning only in so far as they emerge from and are converted into the extra-textual. All text is pretext" ("Text as Interpretation" 9).

Electric and electronic culture presents new contextual challenges. With a myriad of variations of simultaneity and distance, of admixtures of oral and visual and tactile sensory data strung out multi-dimensionally over space and time, context becomes even more unwieldy. Explanatory categories such as secondary and now tertiary orality, along with secondary and tertiary visualism evidence that electronic coding, as all encoding, changes what is encoded and requires different interpretative methods or hermeneutical operations. But Ong's oral hermeneutics provides a better understanding of what is at stake in all these maneuvers. In all the noise of contemporary culture, it is even more important to attend to the silence.

Mythos and *Logos* in an Electronic Age

A twenty-year-old unfinished manuscript that the author himself found "unsatisfactory" would not seem to offer many rewarding insights on electronic technology, even if it was written by one of the twentieth century's foremost American scholars in language and the humanities. Given the frenetic pace of technological developments, obviously Ong was unable to envision, and thus significantly underestimated the scope and power of electronic technology today.[16] But in media studies Ong was less interested in the ephemera of technological machinery than in the more enduring relationship of technology to human consciousness. Once again, he offers prolegomena for media ecology.

Technology as Humanizing

Ong not only accepted technology but celebrated it.[17] Technology is humanizing. Technology is not foreign to the human organism, but is both "outside us and inside us" ("Technology Outside"). Communications technology is taken "into" consciousness influencing how we structure and process knowledge, reshaping our psychic drives and personality structures, and expanding tremendously the amount of information available for reflection. Technology itself, when thus interiorized, is made part of consciousness in such a way that, rather than humans being transformed into machines, machines are humanized: "Life envelops and enlivens the non-living" ("Reading, Technology," 144).

As early as 1962 in a Modern Language Association report on trends in education,[18] Ong argued against a defensive posture regarding the use of technology in humanistic disciplines. He was already developing the insight of *Language as Hermeneutic* that communication encompasses more than can be captured in quantified or mathematical encoding: "Communication is not the same as the conveying of information, since it is constituted by necessarily personal and historical relations which are unique and thus cannot be encoded or decoded" ("New Definitions," 86). At this time, Ong framed the dialectic not in terms of digitization and hermeneutic but exteriorization and interiorization. Developments in communications technology result in both a growing depersonalization as well as a growing interiorization of consciousness, as marked in part by personalist philosophies:

> We must have more and more machines in our communications processes, but we must at the same time master them more and more by growth in our interior resources. The way to this mastery of necessity involves fuller understanding of the history and structure of communications in relation to the human psyche. ("Breakthrough in Communication," 16)

Logos as Word and as Organization

Language as Hermeneutic notes that while *mythos* and *logos* originally were interchangeable, *mythos* derived from "word of mouth" (an auditory image) whereas *logos* derived from "arrangement of discreet units" (visual-spatial). Eventually, *logos* was reserved for rational discourse, whereas *mythos* was relegated to "story." Ong finds all technologies of the word to involve manipulation and ordering of discreet units that is registered in the Greek sense of *logos*. However, Ong's ideas on the complementary nature of *logos* and *mythos* precede the advent of our computerized world. Ong's "The Myth of Myth: Dialogue with the Unspoken," written forty years earlier, had identified myth with the unsaid, myth being "the non-explicit complement accompanying any body of expression"; it is "that which fills in the voids between man's abstractions" (133). "It means," he insisted, "that any body of connected human statement will, first, be limited, and, secondly, will have certain things implicit in it, no matter how far it is refined. Total human statement is impossible" (134). And again in his Preface to *The Barbarian Within*:

> What is said tells off against what is not said, reminding us that total explicitness is impossible to human beings: one always means (implicitly) more than one says (explicitly) or, in another sense, says (implicitly) more than one means (explicitly). In being to some degree necessarily occult, myth is the by-product of this limitation of human voice. It exists by virtue of what it says not explicitly but symbolically. *Mythos* complements *logos*. (9)

What Ong does in *Language as Hermeneutic* is to examine this dichotomy of *mythos* and *logos* within the context of an electronic world where *logos* (as organization or arrangement), is maximized in the computer which the French insightfully designate as an *ordinateur*, an "arranger." In a last major publication, "Digitization Ancient and Modern," Ong defined digitization as the numerical processing or manipulation of distinct units (data), and quoted Florian Coulmas, "Basically, microchips are merely a technical improvement on clay tokens" ("Digitization," 4). And in the 1990 letter proposing the publication of his manuscript, he wrote to Maud Wilcox: "The computer has thus been in the making for over 2,000 years, ever since technology first impinged on the spoken word."

But in this electronic world *mythos* survives. For instance, *mythos* is wrapped up with information theory itself:

> Mechanical models for communication-processes such as are used in information theory are helpful, but are all grossly deficient and of themselves misleading because they have no way of representing the interiority essential to all human communication, the individual personal consciousness itself, utterly different in each one of us. ("Reading, Technology," 139)

Information specialists such as Claude Shannon, James Gleick, and David Carr acknowledge that information theory cannot create purpose or "meaning." Ong agrees: technology not only can store but also even breed knowledge, but meaning itself is related to intentionality. "In other words, information theory carries within it the concept of 'intention,' an elusive psychological and philosophical concept which information theory itself simply cannot grasp. Information theory is wrapped up not in information but in an enigma" (Review, *The Noise* 217). Regardless of how sophisticated electronic technology becomes, what it lacks, irremediably, is *mythos*, which requires an "unconscious that underlies the consciousness" (*Interfaces* 45). Although many myths surround electronic technology and its uses, within the computer itself there is no myth, and it is myth that deals with the nonexplicit component that lurks in all human knowledge.

Ong cited Philip Leith to argue that the foundation of communication science is sociological, rooted in human goals and activity:

> But if communication can generate information systems, it can never generate information systems which do not retain some connection with communication. Philip Leith (1990) has shown, for example, that the foundation or the ground of a computerized information system is not fully formalized, not mathematical or "scientific" (as all "information" is inside a computer system), but is necessarily sociological, which means generated by communication beyond the realm of simple information. ("Information," 6; see also "Hermeneutic Forever," 23)

Similarly, Doris Schoenhoff in *The Barefoot Expert: Interface of Computerized Knowledge Systems and Indigenous Knowledge Systems*, investigates the psychic and noetic challenges in introducing computers into a largely primary oral culture. In the book's preface Ong again points out how an oral hermeneutic can provide a fuller understanding of the relationship of computers to the human:

> Computers have developed at the end of a long noetic tradition tracing back largely to the ancient Greek formalization of knowledge by a logic which encouraged the view that truth is maximized in propositional statements. (An alternative persuasion might be that truth is maximized in human living and/or in deep personal relations.) . . . This kind of conscious personal encounter is not enframed in computer language. Computer language is enframed in personal encounter. (Ong, "Preface," ix–xi)

Language as Hermeneutic is an attempt within the digitization of contemporary media environments to maintain a place for the "oral"—for personhood and intersubjectivity, for the unsaid and silence—for *mythos*. In Ong's oral hermeneutics, *mythos* and *logos* are in dialectical relationship with meaning generated by both the explicit and implicit, cleavage and integration, propositional analysis and human interaction.

Computers and the Nonencoded Self

Ong was not a determinist, technological or otherwise; he did not believe electronic technology would ineluctably usher in human progress or doom. The promise and threat of technology lie not in technology itself but in the human conceptualization and use of technology. Decision making for Ong is at the peak of personhood, and knowledge is one requirement for good decisions: as Ong frequently stated, "The truth shall set you free." Without a grounding in the nature of human communication and without an awareness of its distinction from information transfer, we may promote not the hominization of technology but the technoligization of the human—that is, we may mistakenly interpret human consciousness in terms of machinery, however exquisite and ethereal circuitry may become:

> To make machines even moderately convincing as models of consciousness, you have to leave out a lot, most notably the centre of consciousness itself,

the sense of "I" . . . which each human consciousness has in its unique way, the source and boundary of all in me that counts most, which reduces to no model, to nothing else at all, but is simply itself, inaccessible except from within. ("Reading, Technology," 144)

We should not underestimate the tremendous calculating and memory potential of computers that even now can best television game show champions. And machine-voiced interactive phone systems or pocket devices that can mimic human conversation likely will become sophisticated enough so that it will be impossible to distinguish the simulated conversations of Siri's offspring (Alexis) from those of human interlocutors.

To clarify Ong's point, we can look at Siri in terms of his evolving definition of "secondary orality," the term he originally used to refer to the orality of radio and television, orality that is mediated through writing and print to produce consciously controlled "programmed spontaneity," but that he later extended backward to include orality after the invention of writing and print, and forward to include the orality of computers.[19] It is tempting to see in Siri technology a manifestation of secondary orality, especially since Ong acknowledged computer-generated words might be "assimilated" to that category. Given the totality of Ong's thought, though, it may be more accurate to think of such voice technology in terms of "audibility" rather than orality. Sounded words in and of themselves are not equivalent to orality as Ong defined it. For instance, though he preferred the term "secondary visualism," he understood the application of "secondary orality" to soundless computer-mediated communication that had the immediacy of face-to-face communication (such as instant messaging) because of the simultaneity of interactivity between two human consciousnesses.[20] However, he cautioned that while such interactions seem to approach the intimacy that results from "the immediate interchange of living voice," "the utterly devastating problem" is the inability to be certain of the identity of the interlocutor.[21] *A fortiori*, Siri's message is sounded, but it is not expression, an outering or uttering, from one interior to another:

> The conscious self-reference of an interior consciousness, its ability to refer reflexively to its own interiority (which registers, for example, when a person says "I," and which is totally and completely other when another person

says "I") escapes digitization. . . . A digitizing program is never thus fully re-flexive, as human language is. (Ong, "Time," 213).

Siri and her progeny "live" in a world of information, not communication. In other words, those who predict that artificial intelligence (AI) will replace and surpass humans sometimes begin with a circumscribed understanding of human knowledge and consciousness. For the individual and the human race, language develops out of the nonlinguistic setting in which words are used to explain the situation even as the situation gives meaning to the words. Computers lack that nonverbal context as well as the rhetoric, out of which *logos* grew (*Interfaces* 301).

> Despite all the work to achieve "artificial intelligence" through the computer, the computer always lacks the living silence in which, as we have seen, human thought and language is embedded, it lacks the unconscious in which human thought and language are also embedded, and it lacks the biological substructures in which human thought and language are embedded. (*LAH* 93)

Computers have no interiority; their "memory" is mechanical encoding, not the organic, "living memory" of humans that wells up partly out of the human unconscious (111).[22] The processing and transfer of information is a mechanical operation that can be facilitated through waves, wires, and genes; it is not the same as sharing interiors in human communication.

In *You Are Not a Gadget*, Jaron Lanier, a father of virtual reality technology, provides some confirmation of Ong's insight when he describes "lock-in"—the establishment of structuring programming that is difficult to modify because of its impact on subsequent hardware:

> Lock-in removes ideas that do not fit into the winning digital representation scheme, but it also reduces or narrows the ideas it immortalizes, by cutting away the unfathomable penumbra of meaning that distinguishes a word in natural language from a command in a computer program. (10)

This penumbra of meaning falls within the scope of what Ong labels *mythos*, what is needed to preserve the richness of human experience that can be occluded by the nonetheless necessary spatializing and fractioning methods of digitization. In his 1990 letter of inquiry regarding the book's publication, Ong wrote:

> The book's conclusion is that it is no accident that our own era is both (1) the greatest age ever of digitization (taking things apart numerically) and (2) compensatingly, the greatest age ever of hermeneutics (relating everything back to everything else again—to the unbroken web of history). And hermeneutics dominates. Myth (which preceded logic by tens of thousand [sic] of years and which is holistic) still envelops logic. (Letter to Maud Wilcox)

Language as Hermeneutic, a logical, informed, analytic presentation, nonetheless concludes

> *Mythos*, in various forms—proverbs, for example, as well as storytelling, lurking subconscious or unconscious awareness, and the deep probings of religious belief—will certainly remain as permanent and desperately needed components of human understanding. (139)

There is no complete statement. There is no last word. These tenets help to clarify why Ong eventually found his attempt at synthesis in *Language as Hermeneutic* to be "unsatisfactory." The chord remains unresolved.

An After Word

In addition to being an internationally respected scholar of the first order, Walter J. Ong was a Roman Catholic priest of the Society of Jesus, a Jesuit.[23] Thus while in his academic writings he insisted on respect for the integrity and independence of a discipline's methods and practices, even within his secular works he frequently and effortlessly interwove religious references, reflections, and applications, as he did in *Language as Hermeneutic*. His principle of relationism—that all things are connected with everything else—warranted his belief that all knowledge, religious and secular, intersected while remaining distinct.[24]

His Christocentric orientation of hopeful optimism distinguishes him from other intellectuals with whom he otherwise shared deep-seated beliefs. Like Jean-Paul Sartre's, Ong's thinking was saturated with existential freedom, and like the Czech communications theorist Vilém Flusser he understood intentionality to be central to human communication, but unlike them Ong did not believe death is the ultimate reality or that communication is simply a method to distract ourselves from the reality of our deaths. Not fear or decay but love governs the universe. Within an "apostolate" of scholarship, media study for Ong was a quest not only for knowledge but also for justice—and even love. In 1984 Ong confided,

> The cross-cultural understanding which orality-literacy studies make possible enriches the human spirit and opens the possibility for greater understanding and love between diverse peoples and for greater understanding of the intimacy with which technologies relate to human life. But it is not a cure-all for human misunderstanding and greed and ambition. I am under no illusions that orality-literacy studies will be any more redemptive or any freer of human failings than other purely human efforts. Still, the more human human beings are, the more there is in them to be redeemed. Orality-literacy studies can enlarge our humanity and open it more to redemptive powers beyond mere human reach. ("Orality-Literacy Studies," 380)

Ong recognized the intersection of his oral hermeneutics with the dialogism of Mikhail Bakhtin and the speech philosophy of Eugen Rosenstock-Huessy. These three scholars appear to agree: ultimately, our future depends on more than either *mythos* or *logos*, separately or combined. An oral hermeneutic is a supplement or corrective to digitization and visualist interpretations, but it too has its limits.

> Our evident inability to create a hermeneutic adequate to interpret the information flooded into human consciousness shows the plight we are permanently in. Human life must be ultimately managed humanly by more than information-plus-hermeneutics, which is to say by what it always been managed by when it has been humanly managed, that is, by interpersonal and intergroup personal interaction and the love of human beings for one another that has held human society together, when it has been humanly held together, from the start of humankind. Information and also hermeneutic are, so far as accessible, helpful and necessary, but in the last analysis they are inadequate to the world lying ahead. (Ong, "Information," 15)

PART III

Appendices

TIME, DIGITIZATION, AND DALÍ'S MEMORY

Walter J. Ong

The Time "Dimension"

In this post-Einsteinian age, we are aware, as Plato and his heirs for over two millennia had not been, that time is a constituent and not merely an adjunct of material being. Over succeeding periods of time, matter enters into different and apparently irreversible states. When we think of the universe today, time has always to be figured in, as peremptorily as the dimensions of length, breadth, and thickness. This attention to time appears imperative today for any serious cosmology.

It is common knowledge that, according to the currently most likely findings in cosmology, the matter in the universe is some 15 billion years old, our planet Earth having taken shape out of this matter some 4.6 billion years ago (Orgel). These figures are documented in astronomical and other physical research, even though the figures are not absolutely precise; they are not mythological projections. The matter in our bodies is approximately 15-billion-year-old-matter, dating, it appears, as other matter in the universe, from the so-called big bang, the primordial explosion marking the beginning of the universe that we know. But the matter in our bodies has since much matured and is now in a different state from what it first was at the time of the "big bang."

The matter around us and in us is something which started out in a state of unimaginable high temperature and density, and which within a few seconds after the "big bang" was well into the process of expansion and cooling that continues today. After our planet Earth took shape some 4.6 billion years ago, out of matter then some 10.4 billion years old, the earth had to cool down still more for almost another billion years before, around some 3.6 billion years ago, DNA, a prerequisite to all material life that we know, could form, perhaps after an initial formation of RNA, the so-called messenger DNA (Orgel). Living material beings are all built up out of DNA, including our bodies, which are part of ourselves (if someone kicks my body, I do not say, "Stop kicking my body," but "Stop kicking me"). The matter in our own bodies incorporates history into its very being, for it has to be organic matter, and it appears that matter can be organic matter only when it has achieved a certain age. We find no evidence of matter in an organic state in early cosmic history.

Thus our bodies are time-filled. They bear in themselves some 15 billion years of cosmic history, and, at this end of the 15 billion years, some 3.6 billion years of organic development. All matter is time-filled, each sort in its own way. Time is not simply a surrounding medium or a flowing river through which material being floats, but is a constituent of material being. We have no evidence that matter of any other kind than our time-filled matter could exist. Talk of matter that does not include a time component is pure, nonevidential speculation. An evolving universe such as ours is the only kind of universe for which we have any evidence, the only kind we are sure can exist.

Since material beings, therefore, are constituted by time just as much as by length, breadth, and thickness, there is some reason to style time a "fourth dimension." Yet human experience of time differs from human experience of the "dimensions" of length, breadth, and thickness in significant ways, one of which is in the relationship of the human experience of time to digitization, that is, to reduction in terms of discrete numerical units. We cannot humanly sense time as a "dimension" in the way length, breadth, and thickness are dimensions. For having length, breadth, and thickness means that objects can be cut physically into discrete, separate pieces of which all are present after they are cut. Time, as we experience it, cannot be cut into separate pieces that coexist. Time will not stop to be so cut.

For this reason we can, for example, never fix mathematically the exact moment at which yesterday became today. Mathematically we can only reduce the distance between 11:59 p.m. and midnight to a smaller and smaller and smaller fractional digit, to 11:59.9999999+ seconds, without ever finally arriving at an exact point at which yesterday suddenly becomes today. Put in another way, this is to say that to have today present you have to abolish yesterday as present. To separate the two parts of the plank, you simply divide them and move them apart from each other in space, where they both remain present. There is no way to move today apart from yesterday in space, so that both yesterday and today remain present. Moving toward a hoped-for exact point where you can thus separate one day from another is moving asymptotically toward a goal that can never be reached. The closer you get to the goal, the surer you are that you will never reach it. Existentially, we can readily know that this is today and that there was a yesterday which is gone. But in our real lives we cannot move from yesterday to today digitally.

Time, as dealt with here, is being considered phenomenologically, that is, not simply as something abstracted for scientific purposes but as lived, as experienced by human beings—often enough in complex ways which defy total explication but which we can and do deal with in relating to other human beings in daily life. Such time can be styled "human time" or even "real time" as contrasted with time subjected to the operation we call digitization. We are dealing with such "human" or experiential or phenomenological time when we say, for example, "Time hangs heavy on my hands." Of course, scientific description and understanding of time are also valid in their own ways and superbly useful for scientific purposes, although they may not figure in the ordinary nonscientific human experience of time.

Time will not wait to be dissected. Because of its ceaseless and uninterruptible motion, experienced or phenomenological human time simply does not take to digitization as length, breadth, and thickness do, no matter what efforts we make. "Time marches on," as the old newsreels used to proclaim portentously. All this is not to deny that it has proved exceedingly useful to pretend that time can be stopped, broken into units disengaged from one another—in other words, that time is digitizable, although in reality it cannot be.

By way of contrast, at this point attention to sound and hearing is helpful and even imperative. All sensation, including sight and touch, takes place in time. But sound is bound to time as no other sense is. I can stop a gesture of my arm and have remaining a pose which was formed by the gesture. The pose can be apprehended by sight and by touch as well. If I stop sound in order to examine it more carefully, there is nothing to hear or otherwise sense, nothing to be examined. All I have is nonsound, silence. Each of the human senses relates differently to time. One great difference in their relationships shows in the contrast between sight and touch on the one hand and hearing on the other.

The senses of sight and touch, which acquaint us with length, breadth, and thickness, are the senses relied on to give meaning to the concept of "digitization." To digitize is to treat in terms of discrete numerical units. The term *digit* comes from the Latin *digitus*, which means a finger or a toe—still one of the meanings of *digit* in English.

By way of a not entirely irrelevant aside, it is worth noting that the fingers, and the toes, are not entirely separated from one another. In many (not all) cultures, children learn to count by applying discrete numbers (by digitizing) their fingers and toes. Use of these members is not purely accidental or a matter of physical convenience. Children do not take immediately to separation: they like their lifeworld intact, as innumerable psychological studies have shown. Blankets and teddy bears or other "intermediate objects" bridge the gap threatening to break up the totalized world centered on the original union, infant and mother. For children fearing separation, learning to digitize in early childhood with fingers and toes can be reassuring: although these are totally distinct at their tips, they grow together at their bases so that they are not totally separated, after all, but are part of the child's body, so that the child can with some reassurance deal with them as individual units.

Eventually, the child must count resolutely so as to enforce digitization by keeping items really separate from each other. Here is where sight and touch are indispensable. With sight and touch we can register objects spatially distinct from one another, for example, as separate blocks or pieces. Sight fixes items in space, and, although it can register motion, it is somehow maximized inimmobility. Thus we photograph a running horse and then stop separate frames of the film the better to *see* what the running "really" is—even though running does not mean standing still at any instant at all. Sight moves resolutely away from the total human continuity registered in time.

Dalí's Persistence of Memory

Digitization is here to stay, bringing with it, as writing and print earlier did, a new culture and a new way of experiencing the world. The new experience registers in the subconscious and unconscious even more deeply than in consciousness.

A fascinating example of the way digitization is embedded in the subconscious and the unconscious can be seen in a well-known painting by Salvador Dalí, many of whose paintings, as well as explanations of his paintings, engage the subconscious and unconscious so conspicuously. Mention of a conspicuous unconscious may appear oxymoronic, but his aficionados know Dalí himself as a conspicuously programmed oxymoronic figure.

Let us recall that we do constantly, and productively, impose on human time a digitized frame that is divided into numerically distinct, numerable, separate parts. In a high-technology world, digitized time is so ubiquitously incorporated into the fuller human lifeworld that it is often taken to be actuality (or, nowadays, "virtual reality"), even though the fit between digitized time and human time is far from perfect. When digitization is so well done that the digital units are infinitesimal, the fit, though less than total, becomes negligible in many or most instances. This is the point of high-technology digitization: to employ units which are more and more infinitesimal until virtually nonobservable, so that perceptually the division between units becomes virtually nonexistent, and instead of division one seems to have full continuity.

In today's human lifeworld, perhaps the most conspicuous and widespread and insistent experience of the digitization of what is ultimately undigitizable is the visual "timepiece," such as a watch or clock. A watch or other timepiece neatly divides time into pieces, with seeming bits of nontime in between its seconds or minutes or hours. For most people today and more across the world, digitized time is the only kind of time adverted to and thus virtually supplants "human time," the lived time independent of timepieces.

But the watch has a difficult time of it in Salvador Dalí's painting titled *The Persistence of Memory*, completed in 1931 (Lake 1969, 21). This familiar painting features the limp faces of three watches, one of which is draped over the edge of a table-like rectangular block, another over the dead branch of a tree as though the watch face were a kind of rag, and another over the curved back of the dead body of an animal-like or partially human figure on the ground, while ants are scavenging the back of a fourth watch lying, undistorted and partially opened, on the rectangular block. This group of large objects, which obtrusively dominate the painting, are set on a dark, flat surface stretching out as a background of featureless landscape which bleeds off in the far distance into a narrow strip of sea punctuated at the distant right by a small row of cliffs. The effect of this painting is haunting and curiously unnerving. The limp watches—Dalí himself called them "melting watches" (Lake 22)—create the impression that digitized time has been rendered impotent. There is no way for the hands of a watch with a curled, contorted face to function at all. The swarm of ants inside the one noncontorted watch signal that, in fact, digitized time is dead: the ants are working on a stopped watch, that is, on the corpse of digitized time. The all but featureless landscape and sky and sea, and the undistinguished cliffs induce a dream-like state of mind to envelop the four limp, disabled watches, which, with insistent visual clarity, occupy the greater part of the painting and dominate the whole.

To judge from my own experience, in press accounts of Dalí and his work after he died January 23, 1989, this painting was one of the most frequently reproduced: it was known to have caught public attention perhaps more strongly than any of his other works. Why? The painting was completed, as has been noted, in 1931. This was a time when digitization was not at all so much an object of general attention as it has since become. Certainly, Dalí's work, which often on the surface seems so unorganized, depends on the subconscious and unconscious more conspicuously than much other art. In a mysterious way Dalí was onto the subconscious/unconscious line of development making for greater and greater digitization. Later, he knew of the work of F. H. C. Crick and J. D. Watson in their discovery of DNA, which led to the incredibly complex work with countless digital computers still under way today in the human genome project. Somehow, Dalí was deeply attuned to coming developments in digitization. Regarding *The Persistence of Memory* in connection with the Crick and Watson discoveries, Dalí commented to Lake (22): "I foresaw the whole idea and now they are getting around to proving it scientifically."

For many persons, as earlier noted, to think of time is to think of clocks and/or watches, "timepieces." Clock time is not the same as the deep unconscious or subconscious or even conscious awareness of time as an infrangible continuum which in reality has no detectable "parts" or "instants" (*stare* in Latin, from the root of which our *instant* comes, means to stand still, to be immobile). Both in the jerking sweep second hands of mechanical timepieces and in the discontinuous numbers on the blinking faces of digital watches, time is divided by nontime, is treated as though it were coming in little jerks separated by a timeless something. But, however handy and informative and otherwise convenient it may be to think of time as a composite of little dissected pieces, human experience in depth knows better. The omnipresence of clocks and watches, and their overwhelming usefulness forces us normally to repress our deeper awareness of time as incapable of arrest or division into parts, and thus as fundamentally and obstinately nonsubmissive to any digitization whatsoever.

For persons in an alphabetic writing and print culture the clock or timepiece concept of time is relatively easy. Such persons are familiar with texts, and texts represent in visible, immobile form words that oral cultures know only as sounds, bound to time. Oral cultures have no experience of reducing always moving sound, whether in words or elsewhere, to immobile characters on a visible surface. Hence the extreme difficulty, a commonplace in cultural anthropology, which oral cultures experience in organizing their life, even a single day of it, in "clock time." Persons from writing cultures interpret this indifference to clock time as laziness. Literate persons complain that persons from an oral, nonwriting culture (which literates commonly designate as "primitive") commonly do not show up at an hour that has been clearly specified in literates' terms. This is hardly strange. For persons in an oral culture, their entire experience of time is free of any digitization experience. They live in free-flowing, human time, not artificial clock time. It's late when it begins to get dark.

In Dalí's painting, the rigid digitization that timepieces render convincing and in effect operatively real has totally collapsed. A limp watch may be recognizable as a watch, particularly because of the design of its face, however distorted, but the magic of its digitization is lost: these watches clearly won't work. The hands cannot turn, for, to do so, they would have to negotiate unmanageable angles and curves. Sectioned time, watch time, clock time, is seen for what we have been unconsciously aware it really is, more than fragile—unreal. Its hard-nosed digitizing performance, commonly taken for granted as in effect constituting time, is here revealed as the unreality it is, is undermined, destroyed. The unconscious sense of real time asserts itself as different from the dissections that watches represent. The revelation is unnerving. We have been living under false pretenses. No matter that in daily life the pretenses worked—somehow. Or did they? Could this mean that something is really wrong with our lives?

Dalí had the genius to title his painting *The Persistence of Memory*. This title gets to the heart of the digitization issue through the collapsed digitized time that the painting presents.

Beneath all digitization, living human memory remains always within nonartificial human time, using digitization productively but not reducible to digitization. Human memory is involved with time more totally and unequivocally than is digitization. True human memory has persisted all along, Dalí's title for his painting intimates, unnoticed beneath the digitized constructs, and, with the demise of these constructs, simply "persists," takes over alone once more.

Digitized computer "memory" is not human memory, but is simply recall: it brings back the past as though the past had been constituted of digital computer units, which of course was not at all the real human past that "happened" to you or me. My personal memory of yesterday is not of itself digitized, neither experienced nor reconstructable as simply a series of discrete numerical units retrieved one-by-one from the past. Digitized "memory," which is of course exceedingly useful and beautiful, brings back a past which is an artificial past, however deftly related to the real human past. The digitized past is presumed to be invested with discontinuity whereby it was shaped in discrete units to be digitally stored. Human memory does not work by building recall out of discrete units, units which Dalí's painting discredits. For human beings are alive in continuous time, and my memory of yesterday, is, and has to be, colored and shaped by things that happened before and since yesterday and that are normally involved in my recollection of yesterday. Everything I experienced yesterday forms a kind of continuum with what was in my awareness before and is colored by this awareness and by what has come into my awareness since. My memory of a personal interaction yesterday cannot dissociate itself entirely from interactions with the same person before and after yesterday. This kind of human performance in which successive events interpenetrate one another indefinitely is not a corruption of memory. This is what human memory is.

We borrow the concept of memory from real human experience to tailor the concept of digital "memory," which is basically simply linear production. As they actually exist, human memories of one's past often enfold or blend each other. No human being could possibly recall as distinct units all the details of his or her experience of a lived yesterday in the way a computer recalls what is stored in its RAM—which, for that matter, can never by any means digitize anywhere near *all* the components of yesterday or even all of those tumbled into my memory.

In *The Book of Memory: A Study of Memory in Medieval Culture* and in "Inventional Mnemonics and the Ornaments of Style: The Case of Etymology," Mary Carruthers has shown that in treating of memory the Middle Ages included the equivalent of what, since the Romantic Movement, has been called the creative imagination. Any artist or writer knows that the source of creativity—which means of freshness—is memory. This sounds, and is, paradoxical. The freshness of new creativity comes somehow out of the past. But where else could the source be? I work out of what has become known to me, what I can remember—if only from a moment ago. For human memory is not a dead chest of drawers loaded with dead objects. Memory is where things both remain themselves and magically change. Computer "memory" is not this sort of thing. Computer "memory" never feels or murmurs, "Where are the snows of yesteryear?" Computer "memory" is unaware of the longings of the heart that cohabit with human memory, as so many stories told by human beings show. Human memory produces many seemingly wild associations. It establishes existential continuity between past and present and even the imagined future: it does not always separate these aspects of time. For they cannot be separated. In the human imagination, every "instant" runs into the next because existentially there is no such thing as an "instant," something atemporal between two supposedly broken off, discrete units of time that itself takes no time. We are saturated with unfractioned time for good. And human beings always have been.

Words and Time

Human words are doubly bound to time. First, like everything human, they are embedded deep in cosmological and historical time, coming into being close to our end of the 15 billion years from the beginnings of the universe. *Homo sapiens*, the producer of words, appeared on this globe most probably some 150,000 years ago (Stringer). Fully human words were perhaps uttered first at this time, around 150,000 years ago at the advent of *Homo sapiens*, or perhaps somewhat later. Human words, whenever they were first uttered, have a prehistory in language-like vocalization among other animals before *Homo sapiens*, as Bickerton has detailed. While the crucial elements of human language, grammatical structure (115–117, 120, 126, 163), and subject-predicate relationship (12, 39, 97) are conspicuously lacking in subhuman "protolanguages," some such prehuman protolanguages have definite referentiality—the vervet monkey has three separate calls to signal separately the present of pythons, martial eagles, and leopards (Bickerton, 12–15). Human language thus appears not without some antecedents in infrahuman species, antecedents which are clearly related to, but have not arrived at full language.

Second, spoken human words are also individually and operationally and inseparably bound to time because they are sounds. In a magisterial work, *Visible Speech: The Diverse Oneness of Writing Systems,* canvassing virtually all the crucial evidence on the nature of writing systems across the world, John DeFrancis, professor emeritus of Chinese at the University of Hawaii, has reviewed meticulously and clarified certain basic matters concerning writing. He notes that "Full spoken language is the defining characteristic of the human species" (7) and then goes on to discuss in exquisite detail writing itself. He characterizes "full/unlimited/real writing" as "only that writing which permits expressing any and all thought" (47). Writing conveys meanings in two ways: (a) by the use of visual symbols "which represent sounds and function as surrogates of speech" (49), and (b) by the use of certain nonphonetic information (such as, for example, punctuation). "Pictographs used as pictographs" cannot lead to full writing, but "pictographs used as phonetic symbols lead to full writing" (50). If inscribed marks do not represent *sound as sound,* they cannot be construed as full writing.

A pictograph used as a phonetic symbol is styled a rebus. That is to say, if I draw the sole of a foot and use the drawing of the sole for its sound value, making it represent also *sole* in the sense of *alone, sole* in the sense of a species of fish, and *soul* as against body, I am using use the pictograph of the sole of the foot as a rebus, for its sound value, so that it can represent other objects sounded the same verbally. Full writing is writing that encodes sound as such in visual symbols, and the use of the rebus is the first step toward such encoding. But, DeFrancis points out, historically, across the globe, most uses of rebuses have been dead ends (50, 274–75), never developing enough to become full writing.

Full writing itself, then, is embedded not simply in text but initially in sound. This emergence from an embedding, from an interior, is crucial to the function of words. Sound is "uttered" (i.e., "outered"—for *utter* is simply a by-form of *outer*). Sound signals the condition of the interior of the being or object from which it emerges. Its embedding suggests the interiority and reflexiveness of language and of persons who utter language as this interiority connects with sound. One of the characteristics of language is its reflexivity, its ability to talk about itself and about the person from whom it is emanating. A digitizing program is never fully reflexive, as human language is (see Schoenhoff and Leith).

In its soundedness, its resonance, its coming from within, sound advertises the reflexivity of human beings, each of whom, unless physically or otherwise impaired, can reflect on himself or herself. They each can say "I," every one of them referring with this word to someone different from that someone which every other user refers to by the same word.

As an always ongoing event in time, existing only when it is going out of existence, sound advertises the existence of another world beyond digitization. This is the world which Dalí's painting, *The Persistence of Memory,* reopens to us.

References

Bickerton, Derek. *Language and Species*. Chicago and London: University of Chicago Press, 1990.

Carruthers, Mary. *The Book of Memory: A Study of Memory in Medieval Culture.* Cambridge: Cambridge University Press, 1990.

———. "Inventional Mnemonics and the Ornaments of Style." *Connotations: A Journal for Critical Debate* 2:2 (1992): 103–14.

DeFrancis, John. *Visible Speech: The Diverse Oneness of Writing Systems*. Honolulu: University of Hawaii Press, 1989.

Heim, Michael. *The Metaphysics of Virtual Reality*. New York: Oxford University Press, 1993. [In citing this excellent book I shall have to disavow its attribution to me of a view of the future "based on the Christian narrative of Garden→Fall→Paradise Regained" (70). Although I look to the future with Christian hope, in many of my published works I have made clear that I do not look forward to a return to anything. Christianity is radically future-oriented, to the resurrection, which is to establish material being in a transformed state such as never existed before the resurrection of Jesus. With due respect to Milton's epic title, it is to be noted that Christianity has never preached a return to the Garden of Eden or to any past. What lies ahead is the future, and newness.—WJO]

Lake, Carlton. *In Quest of Dalí*. New York: Putnam, 1969.

Leith, Philip. *Formalism and Computer Science*. London: Ellis Horwood, 1990.

Ong, Walter J. *Interfaces of the Word*. Ithaca: Cornell University Press, 1977.

———. *Orality and Literacy: The Technologizing of the Word*. London: Methuen, 1982.

Orgel, Leslie E. "The Origins of Life on Earth," *Scientific American* 271.4 (October 1994): 766–83. [To some degree, figures for the age of the universe and the age of life differ among different cosmologists. This study uses Orgel's figures as adequately normative for its purposes.—WJO]

Schoenhoff, Doris M. *The Barefoot Expert: The Interface of Computerized Knowledge Systems and Indigenous Knowledge Systems*. Contributions to the Study of Computer Science, 3.Westport, CT: Greenwood Press, 1993.

Stringer, Christopher B. "The Emergence of Modern Humans." *Scientific American* 263.6 (December 1990): 98–104.

PICTURING ONG'S ORAL HERMENEUTIC

Thomas D. Zlatic

Walter Ong was drawn toward Salvador Dalí's masterpiece, *The Persistence of Memory*, which eerily depicts limpid, melting timepieces over a surreal barren landscape.[1] In chapter 10 of the 1990 version of *Language as Hermeneutic*, "Logos and Digitization," Ong differentiated human memory from computer recall by referencing Dalí's painting. And, after abandoning his plans to publish *Language as Hermeneutic*, Ong in 1994 offered to the journal *Connotations* his essay "Time, Digitization, and Dalí's Memory," an expanded reflection on *The Persistence of Memory*. The editors rejected it, judging it to be more philosophical than philological: an "essay on human time"[2] (Leimberg). They were correct. This hitherto unpublished essay is a meditation on how time and memory can be an index of our humanity. As does *Language as Hermeneutic*, "Time, Digitization, and Dalí's Memory" explores how an oral hermeneutic can help not only to preserve but also to enhance our humanity in the digital age of artificial intelligence.

Memory had long been of interest to Ong, in part because of his education at Saint Louis University within a milieu of a "Saint Louis Thomism" that focused on the relation of the senses to noetic processes.[3] The fascination with memory stayed with him, for as he later wrote, "Memory, in its initial role and in its transformations, is in one way or another a clue to nearly everything that went on as discourse moved out of the pristine oral world to literacy and beyond" ("Oral Remembering," 14). In his media studies, Ong appreciated scholars such as Frances Yates, Mary Carruthers, and Werner Kelber who explored shifting understandings and valorizations of memory through the centuries, partly in relation to the communications technology within cultures situated within primary orality, residual orality, writing, and print. Within an oral culture, memory was enshrined as a storehouse of knowledge and even up through the early age of print, memory retained its centrality in human thought and communication. Even though medieval *memoria* took a step toward digitization by associating memory with scanning a visual field, it remained connected through rhetoric to the human life world, and was linked not only to invention (or creativity) but to character development as well—or as Ong said, to the "heart" rather than the "head" (Review, *The Book of Memory,* 123–24). On the other hand, Ong's antipathy to Ramus's "method" owed more than a little to its reduction of memory to an afterthought. Later with the celebration of imagination in the age of Romanticism, memory—"mere memorization"—was scorned.

As noted by the editors of *Connotations,* Ong also took a more metaphysical approach to memory, exploring its relationship to time and the unconscious. Historically, oral mnemonics and the various arts of memory or "artificial memory" extending from Simonides to the present, could be employed to retrieve specific information, but the memory, trained or untrained, is not limited to recall. The distinctive feature of the natural (that is organic) human memory is that its relationship to time is unitive rather than fractioning.

In the opening sentence of the Dalí essay Ong repeated a major theme of his metaphysics: time is not merely adjunct to but a "constituent of material being."[4] Organic matter is possible only after billions of years of evolutionary processes; time is built into our bodies as matter moved toward greater and greater complexification and interiorization, culminating in the deeply interiorized human self. It is not just that we are in time but that time is in us. This embodiment and interiorization of time is consistent with the thinking of Teilhard, about whom Ong wrote:

> The Jesuit paleontologist and cultural historian, Pierre Teilhard de Chardin, has gone further in interpreting personal, interior consciousness as the focus of the entire evolutionary process, cosmic, organic, and historical. . . . [attending to] the way the physical universe evolves toward "inwardness" and consciousness and to the way consciousness itself evolves as man fills and organizes the earth. (*Knowledge and the Future of Man* 21–22)

Although time may legitimately be considered a fourth "dimension," unlike the other three it is a continuing process that is not composed of discrete pieces and is thus not susceptive to calculation by division, that is, to digitization. Human memory and consciousness, embedded in time, similarly resist analysis (i.e., breaking into pieces) and thus digitization. This intuition, welling up out of his unconsciousness as well as being formulated in consciousness, is what Dalí pictured in *The Persistence of Memory*.

Thus Ong's Dalí essay is an elaboration of the two theses he offered in *Language as Hermeneutic*: 1) two dialectical forces operating on the contemporary human mind are digitization and hermeneutics, and 2) all language is hermeneutic. In his later years, Ong, with seemingly a bit of modest pride, reminisced:

> I recall many talks with Hannah Arendt and remember her observation to me on one occasion, "Walter, you have a dialectical mind." I thought this was true and still believe it is true still, but it was good to have this unsolicited diagnosis from one of the chief world authorities on the subject of dialectic.[5]

As we have discussed, much of his thinking engages paired terms, and his oral and written hermeneutic are differentiated by the relationships that sound and vision have with time and space: time-sound-knowledge-memory-negotiation-community are dialectically paired with space-vision-information-recording-digitization-alienation. Or to align them differently: time/space, sound/vision, knowledge/information, memory/recording, hermeneutics/digitization, community/alienation. These are instances of the larger dialectic that directs much of Ong's thinking: cleavage and integration, the one and the many.

Natural memory, like language, is rooted in time, and its relationship to knowledge is not fixed but fluid—it is a process rather than a product, whereas retrieving recordings is a spatially conceived activity in which information is isolated and dissected. Ong was not hostile to digitization. He aspired to be a "bridge builder" (between secular and religious knowledge and between the humanities and technology) (Letter to Kenneth Woodward; Nielson), and he saw the value and necessity of digitization in the development of consciousness. However, it is the dialectical interplay of time and space, vision and sound, digitization and hermeneutics that deepens the interiority of human consciousness, stimulating integration at deeper levels of complexity. This is the message Ong hears in *The Persistence of Memory*:

> As an always ongoing event in time, existing only when it is going out of existence, because of its resistance to digitization, sound advertises the existence of another world beyond digitization, a world of resonances with meaning. This is the world which Dalí's painting, *The Persistence of Memory*, reopens to us. (193)

In his submission letter to *Connotations*, Ong described "Time, Digitization, and Dalí's Memory" this way: "It contrasts the digitization of time represented in Dalí's nonfunctional 'melting watches' with actual human memory . . . , of itself non-digitizable. (Computers do not have human memory but only recall, which is a different and lesser thing)" (Letter to Leimberg). Human memory, unlike computer recall, is active, imaginative. As Ong stated in *Language as Hermeneutic*, all language use is hermeneutic partly because the constantly changing contexts for statements change the meaning of the statements. Memories, and memories of memories, similarly are relived in changing contexts and are filtered through both conscious and unconscious motivations, and they are organized in nonlinear fashion according to the dictates of present concerns, as registered in Mark Twain's quip: "When I was younger I could remember anything, whether it happened or not; but I am getting old, and soon I shall remember only the latter" (*Autobiography*, 1269). Rather than a simple retrieval of data or facts, human memory is a living, evolving expression of identity, an interiority that in its functioning is not only retrospective but creative, not isolating but integrating present associations with previous ones. Human memory is inventive, creative. Mechanical digitized memory is wonderfully astounding in its capacity and speed but it is also limiting; it produces an "artificial past," for it cannot encode the shadows or echoes of meanings that attend to all thinking and discourse. As we have seen, computer structuring programs "lock-in" or reduce the number of digital representational schemes available for the development of subsequent programs, but lock-in also narrows the ideas it immortalizes, by cutting away the unfathomable penumbra of meaning that distinguishes a word in natural language from a command in a computer program (Lanier 10). Natural human memory, on the other hand, recalls not just words but the shadows and resonances of past and present associations that the words evoke, not just the content of a message but the context for a human interaction, including the unsaid and sometimes unsayable.

> Dalí had the genius to entitle his painting *The Persistence of Memory*. This title gets to the heart of the digitization issue through the collapsed digitized time that the painting presents. Beneath all digitization, living human memory remains always within non-artificial human time, using digitization productively but not reducible to digitization. Human memory is involved with time more totally and unequivocally than is digitization. True human memory has persisted all along.[6] (Ong, "Time, Digitization," 190)

Ong's "metaphysical" reflections on time and memory in the Dalí essay are reverberations from his oral hermeneutic that locates meaning not on surfaces or in circuitry but in the negotiation between unique interiors. Communication is rooted in personalism, and personalism is rooted in the nature of language itself. Language begins with intentionality, in the attunement of one human consciousness to another, and it develops out of silence, the nonlinguistic setting in which words are used to explain the situation even as the situation gives meaning to the words. Computers lack that nonverbal context. And, "the computer lacks rhetoric, out of which *logos* and logic grew and in which they remain embedded" (*LAH*, 93). Digitized encoding can be copied exactly and, given sufficient terabytes or petabytes, can be shared endlessly and completely, but human memory, like the human self, is distinctive, unique, irreproducible in its totality, and impervious to complete revelation.

Once again, within his studies on personalism and human memory, Ong's faith, like a yeast, extends his secular scholarship without changing or distorting its substance. Ong understood Christianity to be a religion of memory, recalling Jesus's words at the Last Supper, "Do this in remembrance of me." But this memory is not of specific words or facts (which are abstractions from being) but of a person. Ong previously had referenced Gabriel Marcel's distinction between two types of belief: "faith that" something is true versus "faith in" someone, that is, faith based on propositional knowledge versus faith based upon interpersonal communion ("Voice as Summons for Belief"). For Ong, focus solely on the recall of verbatim words or recorded "facts" is a reduction of memory. Of course scholars must contextualize the words of the Bible within its own time, for instance by awareness of the psychodynamics of orality (as for instance Kelber has attempted), but for the believer the words must also be recontextualized within the present, within the framework of contemporary knowledge and communications technology. Because there are no completely explicit statements and because the meaning of words always is negotiated in part by the present context, the memory that Jesus commands is subject to ongoing interpretation. The purpose of living memory is not definition but encounter ("Hermeneutical Encounter"). It is not only retrospective but future-oriented. Ong takes Jesus's words, "I am the way and the truth and the life" (John 14:6) to mean that "full truth, self-contained truth is not a statement at all, but *is* nothing less than a *person*"—and this is paradigmatic for all human speakers, regardless of religious belief ("Hermeneutic Forever" 19–20). The "I" who speaks cannot be digitized or reduced to statement or creed.

So, with digitization, Ong's concern was not that machines would become hominized but that humans could become technologized. In *Language as Hermeneutic*, Ong explained therefore that just as the data or information produced by digitization requires hermeneutics to integrate and communicate knowledge, so to come to deep understanding, *logos*, that is fractioning reason, will always need to be accompanied by unitive *mythos*—by myth, literature, religion, paradox, aphorisms, and so on, which work by indirection to utter the silence that gives meaning to words[7] (*Language as Hermeneutic*, ch. 12). And to alert us to the unique, interiorized human person that escapes digitization.

Research continues on the plasticity of the human brain in response to omnipresent electronic technologies that we employ, and debate certainly will continue on whether Google is "making us stupid." But perhaps the question we should be asking is, "are Google, Twitter, Facebook and other digitally mediated experiences making us forget?" Or rather, by decontextualizing our experiences of the world and one another and by mediating those experiences through digitization, are electronic media inhibiting us from forming memories that extend deep into our conscious and unconscious minds, living memories that echo and resonate understandings and relationships that escape digitization?

Neither a technophobe nor an alarmist, Ong welcomed digitization, though he was more aware than most of us of the need to temper its vision and to supplement it with an oral hermeneutic more adept at speaking the unspeakable. The visual maps of digitization are not the territory of human reality—it is nice to have them around to get where we are going, but it cannot choose for us our destination. Optimistic as always, Ong suggested that the first answer to the problem is awareness, awareness of what is happening, why it is happening, and how it might be changed. The truth shall set you free, free to cultivate *mythos* in its various forms to preserve the richness of human experience that can be occluded by spatializing and fractioning methods of interpretation. Dalí's painting pictures for us Ong's oral hermeneutics: despite exhaustive digitization, memory persists. We need to remember that.

NOTES

Language as Hermeneutic: The Evolution of the Idea and the Text

1. Ong describes the formative influence of Saint Louis University in "McLuhan as Teacher."

2. See Stahmer, "Speech Is the Body"; see also Stahmer's "Vocal Communication," a review of Ong's *The Barbarian Within*.

3. The May 1986 issue of *Cultural Anthropology*, devoted to "The Dialectic of Oral and Literary Hermeneutics," included essays by Tyler ("On Being Out of Words") and C. Jan Swearingen ("Oral Hermeneutics During the Transition to Literacy").

4. Ong's marked copy of *The Said and Unsaid* is in the Saint Louis University Archives.

5. Ong's oral hermeneutic is discussed in Zlatic, "Faith in Pretext."

6. The same essay was also published for a different audience in *Oral Tradition*.

7. In his 26 February 1990 letter to Maud Wilcox at Harvard University Press, Ong commented that the connection he proposed in his 1983 preface between the binary digitization of computers and Ramus' dichotomies was spurring others' scholarship, including Leith's.

8. On his working notes for this course, book order forms, reserve lists, and course proposal, he cancelled the title "Interpretation and Being," substituting "Language as Hermeneutic" (Archives 64.2.1.1.121).

9. Course-related files in the Language as Hermeneutic folder at Saint Louis University include "Discourse and Silence"; "Holism in Our Approach to and/or Understanding of Language and Thought"; "Words Are Ultimately Defined by the Nonverbal"; "Intertextuality as Retrieval of Orality"; "Literacy, Orality, Truth, and Method"; "Technology of Writing

and Its Sequels"; "Theorems on Language, Technology, and Community: The Embedding of Thought in the Material World"; "Words Are Ultimately Defined by the Nonverbal"; "Writing and Reading Texts are Speech Events." The files are available online at http://cdm.slu.edu/cdm/landingpage/collection/ong.

10. In the Saint Louis University spring 1988 course catalog Ong is listed as teaching ENG A612, "Orality, Text, Electronics"; however, no other information about the course can be found in the otherwise scrupulously maintained Ong files, now in the Ong archives. Among the Language as Hermeneutic course papers, though, is a half-page document, "Orality, Text, Electronics: Hermeneutic Theorems." In his 1990 letter of inquiry to Harvard University Press, Ong mentions that his manuscript developed out of two successive seminars that he had taught. Language as Hermeneutic in the spring of 1989 is certainly one of the two, but it is unclear what the other might be.

11. Chapter 6 is neither named nor numbered, but it is between chapters 5 and 7, so this omission appears to be an oversight.

12. The 130 pages listed is the length of *LAH-90*. The second date given is 1994.

13. For instance, "The Challenge of Technology" (1958); "Wired for Sound: Teaching, Communications, and Technological Culture" (1960); "New Definitions in the Humanities: The Humanities in a Technological Culture" (1962); *Rhetoric, Romance, and Technology* (1971); "Technology Outside Us and Inside Us" (1978); "Reading, Technology, and the Nature of Man: An Interpretation" (1980); *Orality and Literacy: The Technologizing of the Word* (1982); "Writing Is a Humanizing Technology" (1983); "Writing Is a Technology that Restructures Thought" (1986); "Technological Development and Writer-Subject-Reader Immediacies" (1990).

14. See Zlatic, "Ong as Teacher."

15. At the top of the manuscript is the date "10-12-92" and the note, "supersedes 10-12-91."

16. Ong later changed the readings for Symposium 6.

17. This is an early version of "Information and/or Communication."

18. Ong conducted the seminars with Dr. Charles K. Hofling, professor of neurology and psychiatry at Saint Louis University (to whom Ong dedicated his book on Hopkins). For Ong's interest in psychiatry, see also James L. Foy, "Teilhard de Chardin, Phenomenology and the Study of Man," and Ong's response, "Comments on Dr. James L. Foy's Paper." Ong's interest in encounter is also evidenced in the subtitle for his book *American Catholic Crossroads: Religious-Secular Encounters in the Modern World* (1959).

19. "Hermeneutic Encounter in Voice and in Text" is a mostly complete forty-two page draft, with references, the latest having been published in 1990. The essay is heavily edited in pencil, and attached is a slip of paper that supplies section headings; the latest penciled-in reference is 1991.

20. The essay was eventually published in 1998 as "Digitization Ancient and Modern: Beginnings of Writing and Today's Computers." On an advertising flyer for *Before Writing* Ong wrote, "being ordered as of 8-2-91" (MSS Doc 64.1.2.3.826).

21. Ong expanded on this idea, and on November 29, 1994, offered "Time, Digitization, and Dalí's Memory" to the journal *Connotations*, but it was not published. On May 15, 1990, Ong was taking notes on Carlton Lake's book *In Quest of Dali* (Ephemera, Doc MSS 64 Box 155). The book is cited in "Time, Digitization, and Dalí's Memory" but not in *LAH-90*, suggesting that *LAH-90* was completed prior to May 15 and that Ong was already expanding his discussion of Dalí. The fact that the book is not cited in *LAH-94* seems to indicate a waning interest in that latter work.

22. Ong was particularly appreciative of Bakhtin's insights: in his notes for the 1991–92 Graduate Symposiums he acknowledged a similarity—and difference—between Bakhtin and

him: "dialogic grounding of all discourse, use of language (Bakhtin, but more existential slant)" (Doc MSS 64.2.1.2.13).

23. The references for *LAH-90* and *LAH-94* are identical, except in the latter Ong deleted the citation for a manuscript by David R. Olson. In his working copy of the *LAH-90* references he had marked for insertion: Buber, *I and Thou*; DeFrancis; and *The Presence of the Word*. But none of these was included in the *LAH-94* references.

24. Other relevant works published during this time are Review of *The Book of Memory: A Study of Memory in Medieval Culture*, by Mary J. Carruthers; Foreword to *Faith and Contexts*, vol. 1; Foreword to *The Barefoot Expert: The Interface of Computerized Knowledge Systems and Indigenous Knowledge Systems*; "Do We Live in a Post-Christian Age?"; "Church and Cosmos: Reflections on Frames of Reference"; "The Elusive Presence of the Word: An Interview with Walter Ong" by Michael Kleine and Frederic Gale; Foreword to *Electric Rhetoric: Classical Rhetoric, Oralism, and a New Literacy*, by Kathleen E. Welch; and "Hopkins's Articulate Self."

Language as Hermeneutic: An Unresolved Chord

1. See Zlatic, "The Articulate Self." Ong confirmed in a 1997 letter to Rev. Barry J. McGannon, S.J., that this dialectic was an opening for understanding, as he put it, of "what I am about."

2. For the most complete factual account of Ong's life, see Farrell, *Walter Ong's Contributions;* see also Farrell, Foreword, in *Faith;* and Introduction, in *Walter J. Ong's Work.* See also Harp, *Constant Motion;* Soukup, *Orality and Literature,* "The Contexts," and "Walter J. Ong"; Kelber, "Walter Ong's Three Incarnations of the Word"; Tyler, *The Unspeakable;* Sussman, *High Resolution;* Johns, Foreword; Golumbia, "Toward a History of 'Language'"; Cargas, "The Christian as Scholar"; Kleine, "Ong's Theory" and "Elusive Presence"; Swearingen, "Oral Hermeneutics"; Riemer, "Walter Ong"; Gronbeck et al., *Media, Consciousness, and Culture;* Weeks and Hoogestraat, *Time, Memory, and the Verbal Arts.* This analysis also borrows freely from my essays, "The Articulate Self"; "Faith in Pretext"; "Talking Literature and Religion"; and "Ong as Teacher."

3. See a 2002 letter to Roman Kowal, in which Ong explained the term "Onglish."

4. Ong's groundbreaking work on communication history and technology has influenced a number of scholars, but his proposed stages of consciousness according to media development were not meant to be absolute, discrete or closed-off categories. He did not argue for (but against) a "great divide" between people in oral, scribal, print, or electronic cultures. What Ong found most interesting were the "interfaces of the word," that is, how the oral, written, print, and electronic interact differently at different times and places, depending on local circumstances. See "Complications and Overlappings," in *The Presence of the Word; Interfaces of the Word;* and "A Comment on 'Arguing about Literacy.'" See also Harp, *Constant Motion,* and Farrell, *Walter Ong's Contributions.*

5. When asked about the desirability of a new edition of *Orality and Literacy,* Ong deferred, explaining that the book was still very popular because "Other writers do not treat oral hermeneutics as I have done" (Letter to Liz Thompson). Chapter 4 of *Language as Hermeneutic* is titled "The Interpersonalism of Hermeneutics, Oral and Other"; chapter 2, "Hermeneutics, Textual and Other," was initially titled "Hermeneutics, Textual and Oral." Ong's oral hermeneutic is discussed in Zlatic, "Faith in Pretext." For further exploration of oral hermeneutic, see Kelber, Swearingen, Rosenstock-Huessy, Stahmer.

6. Randolph Lumpp, "Culture, Religion, and the Presence of the Word: A Study of the Thought of Walter Jackson Ong" (Ph.D. diss., University of Ottawa, 1976).

7. This personalist orientation is obvious in three chapter titles in *Language as Hermeneutic:* chapter 1, "Orality, Writing and Presence"; chapter 4, "The Interpersonalism of

Hermeneutics, Oral and Other"; and chapter 8, "Meaning, Hermeneutic, and Interpersonal Trust."

8. Ricoeur (72). Ricoeur pointedly restricts his investigation of self and attestation to *philosophical* analysis; he comes even closer to Ong's position when, moving beyond philosophy that envisions response as an answer to a question, he posits a response that is an answer to a call (24–25).

9. The remark is quoted on the dedication page of Ong's *Interfaces of the Word*, and is recalled in *Language as Hermeneutic*.

10. Over Ong's long publishing career, scientific estimates of the age of the universe varied. In *Language as Hermeneutic* Ong settled on 15 billion years. Current estimates range from 11–18 billion years, with 13.8 being most commonly given.

11. E.g., "One of the most widespread and fundamental errors of . . . New Critics . . . has been the assumption . . . that to put an utterance in writing is to remove it from this state of oral discourse and thus to 'fix' it, to specify and totalize its meaning (*LAH* 44). Similarly, MacLeish's assertion that "A Poem should not mean / But be," mistakenly implies that meaning is "all act and no residual potential" (*LAH* 43).

12. See Harp for a discussion of embodied knowledge in Ong, Sartre, Merleau-Ponty, and Lonergan.

13. In his June 10, 1974 letter to Lumpp, Ong emends this passage, omitting reference to aphorisms (Doc MSS 64.2.2.1).

14. For instance, in 1968 in a never-delivered conference paper, "Aphorisms Regarding the Media and the Senses," Ong toyed with a series of aphoristic paragraphs on the sensory base for concepts.

15. Ong's copy is in the Saint Louis University Special Collections at Pius XII Memorial Library.

16. For instance, Ong's citation in *Language as Hermeneutic* of computer experts' conclusion that the computer's calculation of the perfect chess or check game is "wholly out of the question" (qtd. in *LAH* 104) might be qualified today based on more recent developments such as parallel processing and quantum computing.

17. Because of Ong's study of the *"presence* of the word" and his investigations of the pyschodynamics of the "oral mind," some assume he was longing for the Rousseauistic world of the "noble savage" untainted by writing. For Ong's dismissal of criticisms that he promoted a "Great Leap" theory through his identification of stages of consciousness development, see his Letter to Victor J. Vitanza.

18. Ong wrote the last section of this report, "New Definitions in the Humanities: The Humanities in a Technological Culture."

19. The coinage is one of Ong's most fecund. A number of subcategories for orality and literacy have been used by Ong and then others, including primary orality, residual orality, secondary orality, secondary literacy, secondary textuality, secondary visualism, tertiary orality. However, these constructs were never meant to be closed fields, as Ong explained in an interview: "When I first used the term 'secondary orality,' I was thinking of the kind of orality you get on radio and television, where oral performance produces effects somewhat like those of 'primary orality,' the orality using the unprocessed human voice, particularly in addressing groups, but where the creation of orality is of a new sort. . . . This is what I originally referred to by the term 'secondary orality' " (Kleine and Gale 80). On a note card titled "Notanda for Informal Response," Ong in 1995 wrote somewhat cryptically: "Secondary orality (orality interacting with writing, print, and electronics): not only in the electronic age (to which I first applied the term, directly to radio and television) but also in the manuscript and print ages and postmodern deconstruction. Paul, close of 2 Thess." In a similar blurring of boundaries, Ong extended the concept of secondary visualism: visualism of manuscript age,

and much more of print age (exactly repeatable visual statement) and of electronic communication (graphics)" (Notanda, Doc MSS 64.1.3.6.6).

20. Ong continued in his 1995 interview:

> I have also heard the term 'secondary orality' lately applied by some to other sorts of electronic verbalization which are really not oral at all—to the Internet and similar computerized creations for text. . . . Computerized communication can thus suggest the immediate experience of direct sound. I believe that is why computerized verbalization has been assimilated to secondary "orality" even when it comes not in oral-aural format but through the eye, and thus is not directly oral at all. . . . To handle such technologizing of the textualized word, I have tried occasionally to introduce the term "secondary literacy." (Kleine and Gale 80–81)

Elsewhere, including correspondence with Doris Schoenhoff, author of *The Barefoot Expert* (for which he wrote the foreword) Ong further experimented with terms such as secondary visualism and secondary textuality but acknowledged that he thus far was unable to come up with a "provocative" term for the contemporary electronic age (July 21, 2000).

21. "A reason for compulsive preoccupation with intimacy: rapidity of electronic interchange of thought between two persons creates an environment like—but not the same as—that voice, vocal exchange, sound, in face-to-face interaction. But virtual reality is by definition not face-to-face. Cf. Bukatman, "Terminal Identity (subconscious suppressed)" (Notanda, Doc MSS 64.1.3.6.6.

22. Memory played a significant role in Ong's personalism, communication studies, history of consciousness, philosophy, and religion. See below in the appendix for Ong's hitherto-unpublished essay, "Time, Digitization, and Dalí's Memory," which was developed from an idea first raised in *Language as Hermeneutic*.

23. See Ong's "Post-Christian," 152–53; "Yeast," 347; "Father Hecker," 63–64; "Apostolate," 149. For discussions on the harmony of Ong's faith and scholarship, see Soukup, "The Contexts of Faith" and "Walter J. Ong, S.J.: A Retrospective"; Farrell, *Walter Ong's Contributions*; Zlatic, "Articulate Self" and "Talking Literature and Religion."

24. For instance, Ong's interest in evolution was related to his incarnational theology and Christo-centric universe that reminds some commentators of Teilhard de Chardin—another Jesuit who impregnated hard and meticulous science with theological reflection. Also, the premium that Ong placed on a conversational model for seeking knowledge is given more resonance in light of the fact that the founder of the Jesuit order, Ignatius Loyola, proposed that conversation be taken as a model for spirituality, with Ignatius' term "converser," meaning not simply talk but communing, a sharing of interiors (Conwell 1997, 216). Of course personalism, for Ong as for Martin Buber, was rooted in religious sensibility.

Picturing Ong's Oral Hermeneutic

1. An earlier version of this essay appeared in *Communication Research Trends*; it is reprinted here with permission.

2. The history of Ong's submission of the article is complex. In January 1992, Ong had published in *Speculum* a favorable review of Mary Carruthers' *The Book of Memory* in which he suggested relationships between *memoria*, computers, hermeneutics, *mythos*, and *logos*. Later that year *Connotations* published Carruthers' "Inventional Mnemonics and the Ornaments of Style: The Case of Etymology," and the editors invited Ong to respond. Ong said his commitments would not allow this, though in his files is a seven page document (Carruthe.RSM) in which he writes, "Here I propose merely to add some comment in the hope of suggesting some further depths underlying the cultural and psychological issues which

she discusses." A year later Ong instead offered the Dalí piece as an indirect response to Carruthers.

Ong linked other essays to the Dalí essay. About his unpublished essay, "Digitization and Hermeneutics: Reflections on Epistemic Coincidence," Ong noted to himself that the major points were already covered in "Time, Digitization, and Dalí's Memory." On his unpublished essay "Digitization, Sound, and Time: From Tallying to Computer," he wrote as an epigraph, "A Memorial for Salvador Dalí"—although later he scratched it out. Dalí is also invoked in "God's Known Universe and Christian Faith: Pastoral, Homiletic and Devotional Reflections" (1991).

3. Ong described the formative influence of Saint Louis University in "McLuhan as Teacher," and in his letter to Lumpp. See also Farrell, *Walter Ong's Contributions*, 38–44.

4. For instance, see Ong, "God's Known Universe" and "Knowledge in Time"; see also Zlatic, "The Articulate Self."

5. Letter to Farrell (2001). Decades earlier, Ong had recounted Arendt's comment in letters to James M. Curtis (September 19, 1970) and to Randolph Lumpp (April 4, 1971). In a 1993 letter in which he provided Kenneth Woodward some "foci" for an article Woodward was writing about Ong's thought, Ong offered this appraisal: "In sum, Ong's work deals with antithesis and conflict, as focused in verbal communication, but his work is synthesizing and unifying in bent."

6. At a conference a skeptical copanelist challenged Ong regarding his valorization of sound over sight by pointing to a projected image in the room and remarking: "See, a picture is worth a thousand words." Ong quickly retorted, "But you had to use words to make that point." In *Orality and Literacy* Ong added, "a picture is worth a thousand words only under special conditions—which commonly include a context of words in which the picture is set" (7). Here too it is worthwhile to note how the title—that is, the *words*, "*The Persistence of Memory*"—open up interpretations by widening and deepening the context for the image.

7. Ong had advanced a version of this theme forty-four years earlier in "The Myth of Myth: Dialogue with the Unspoken," originally published in 1950.

SELECT BIBLIOGRAPHY

Note: Documents identified as Doc MSS 64 are located at the Saint Louis University Library Special Collections. Walter J. Ong Manuscript Collection (http://cdm.slu.edu/cdm/landingpage/collection/ong).

Beckett, Samuel. *Waiting for Godot: A Tragic Comedy in Two Acts.* New York: Grove Press, Inc., 1954.

Besnier, Niko. "Language and Affect." *Annual Review of Anthropology* 19 (1990): 419–51.

Bickerton, Derek. *Language & Species.* Chicago: The University of Chicago Press, 1990.

Cargas, Harry James. "The Christian as Scholar—the Humanist as Christian: An Interview with Walter Ong." Interview by Harry James Cargas. *Cross Currents: Religion and Intellectual Life* 40.1 (Spring 1990): 96–108.

Carruthers, Mary. *The Book of Memory: A Study of Memory in Medieval Culture.* Cambridge: Cambridge University Press, 1990.

——. "Inventional Mnemonics and the Ornaments of Style: The Case of Etymology." *Connotations: A Journal for Critical Debate* 2.2 (1992): 103–14.

Chambers, Tod. "The Bioethicist's Audience Is Always a Fiction." *Language, Culture, and Identity: The Legacy of Walter J. Ong, S.J.*, ed. Sara van den Berg and Thomas M. Walsh, 99–114. New York: Hampton Press, 2011.

Conwell, Joseph F., S.J. *The Impelling Spirit: Revisiting a Founding Experience, 1539, Ignatius of Loyola and His Companions.* Chicago: Loyola Press, 1997.

Coulmas, Florian. *The Writing Systems of the World.* Oxford: Basil Blackwell, 1989.

Crossan, John Dominic. *In Fragments: The Aphorisms of Jesus.* San Francisco: Harper, 1983.

EME: Explorations in Media Ecology, Ong Centennial Issue, 11.3–4 (2013): 189–291. [Essays by Paul Soukup, Abigail Lambke, Sheila Nayar, Jerry Harp, Calvin Troupe, Thomas J. Farrell, Thomas D. Zlatic, and Eberly Mareci.]

Farrell, Thomas J. "An Introduction to Walter Ong's Work." In *Faith and Contexts: Selected Essays and Studies by Walter J. Ong, S.J.,* ed. Thomas J. Farrell and Paul A. Soukup, vol. 1, xix–lv. Atlanta: Scholars Press, 1992.

——. *Walter Ong's Contributions to Cultural Studies: The Phenomenology of the Word and I-Thou Communication.* Cresskill, NJ: Hampton Press, 2000.

Farrell, Thomas J., and Paul Soukup, eds. *Of Ong and Media Ecology: Essays in Communication, Composition, and Literacy Studies.* Cresskill, NJ: Hampton Press, 2012.

Foy, James L. "Teilhard de Chardin, Phenomenology and the Study of Man." *Bulletin of the Guild of Catholic Psychiatrists* 10.3 (July 1963): 155–70.

Golumbia, David. "Toward a History of 'Language': Ong and Derrida." *Oxford Literary Review* 21 (1999): 73–90.

Gronbeck, Bruce E., Thomas J. Farrell, and Paul A. Soukup, eds. *Media, Consciousness, and Culture: Explorations of Walter Ong's Thought.* Newbury Park, CA: Sage, 1991.

Harp, Jerry. *Constant Motion: Ongian Hermeneutics and the Shifting Ground of Early Modern Understanding.* Cresskill, NJ: Hampton Press, 2010.

Havelock, Eric A. *The Muse Learns to Write: Reflections on Orality and Literacy from Antiquity to the Present.* New Haven: Yale University Press, 1986.

——. *Preface to Plato.* Cambridge: Belknap Press of Harvard University Press, 1963.

Hayles, N. Katherine and Jessica Pressman, eds. *Comparative Textual Media: Transforming the Humanities in the Postprint Era.* Minneapolis: University of Minnesota Press, 2013.

Heckel, David. "Ong and Derrida: Orality, Literacy, and the Rhetoric of Deconstruction." Paper presented at the Conference on College Composition and Communication, St. Louis, March 1988.

Hopkins, Gerard Manley. *The Poems and Prose of Gerard Manley Hopkins.* Ed. W. H. Gardner. Baltimore: Penguin, 1967.

Johns, Adrian. Foreword. In *Ramus, Method, and the Decay of Dialogue: From the Art of Discourse to the Art of Reason,* by Walter J. Ong, S.J., v–xiii. Chicago: University of Chicago Press, 2004.

Jousse, Marcel. *Le Style oral rythmique et mnemotechnique chez les verb-moteurs.* Paris: Fondation Marcel Jousse, 1925. Reprint 1981. Published as *The Oral Style,* trans. Edgard Sienaert and Richard Whitaker. New York: Garland, 1990.

Kelber, Werner. *The Oral and the Written Gospel: The Hermeneutics of Speaking and Writing in the Synoptic Tradition, Mark, Paul, and Q.* Bloomington: Indiana University Press, [1983] 1997.

——. "Walter Ong's Three Incarnations of the Word: Orality—Literacy—Technology." *Philosophy Today* (1979): 70–74.

Kleine, Michael, and Fredric G. Gale. "The Elusive Presence of the Word: An Interview with Walter Ong." *Composition FORUM* 7.2 (1996): 65–86.

———. "Ong's Theory of Orality and Literacy: A Perspective from Which to Re-View Theories of Discourse." In *The Philosophy of Discourse: The Rhetorical Turn in Twentieth-Century Thought,* ed. Chip Sills and George H. Jensen, vol. 1, 230–45. Portsmouth, NH: Boynton/Cook Publishers, 1992.

Lake, Carlton. *In Quest of Dali.* New York: G.P. Putnam's Sons, 1969.

Lanier, Jaron. *You Are Not a Gadget: A Manifesto.* New York: Alfred A. Knopf, 2010.

Lavelle, Louis. *La parole et l'écriture.* Paris: L'Artisan du livre, 1942.

Leimberg, Inge. Letter to Walter J. Ong, S.J. 2 January 1995. Saint Louis University Library Special Collections. Walter J. Ong Manuscript Collection (Doc MSS 64).

Leith, Philip. *Formalism in AI and Computer Science.* Chichester, England: Ellis Horwood, 1990.

Leys, Ruth. "The Turn to Affect: A Critique." *Critical Inquiry* 37.3 (2011): 434–72.

Lord, Albert. *The Singer of Tales.* Cambridge: Harvard University Press, 1960.

McLuhan, Marshall. *The Classical Trivium: The Place of Thomas Nashe in the Learning of His Time.* Ed. W. Terrence Gordon. Corte Madera, CA: Gingko Press, 2005.

Meyrowitz, Joshua. *No Sense of Place: The Impact of Electronic Media on Social Behavior.* New York; Oxford: Oxford University Press, 1985.

Naisbitt, John. *Megatrends: Ten New Directions Transforming Our Lives.* Warner Books, 1982.

Nielson, Mark. "A Bridge Builder: Walter J. Ong at 80." *America* 167.16 (November 21, 1992): 404–6.

Ohmann, Richard. "Grammar and Meaning." In *The American Heritage Dictionary of the English Language,* ed. William Morris, xxi–iv. Boston: American Heritage, 1969.

Ong, Walter J. *American Catholic Crossroads: Religious-Secular Encounters in the Modern World.* New York: Macmillan, 1959.

———. "Aphorisms Regarding the Media and the Senses." Undelivered paper prepared for the Modern Language Association, 1968. Saint Louis University Library Special Collections. Walter J. Ong Manuscript Collection (Doc MSS 64).

———. "The Apostolate of Secular Arts and Sciences." In *American Catholic Crossroads: Religious-Secular Encounters in the Modern World,* 118–56. New York: Macmillan, 1959.

———. *The Barbarian Within: And Other Fugitive Essays and Studies.* New York: Macmillan, 1962.

———. "Before Textuality: Orality and Interpretation." *Oral Tradition* 3.3 (1988): 259–69.

———. "Breakthrough in Communications." In *In the Human Grain: Further Explorations of Human Culture,* 1–16. New York: Macmillan, 1967.

———. "Carruth.RSM." [notes on a response to Mary Carruthers] Saint Louis University Library Special Collections. Walter J. Ong Manuscript Collection (Doc MSS 64).

———. "Church and Cosmos: Reflections on Frames of Reference." *Review of Ignatian Spirituality* (Rome) 27.3 (1996): 9–17.

———. "Comments on Dr. James L. Foy's Paper." *Bulletin of the Guild of Catholic Psychiatrists* 10.3 (July 1963): 171–75.

———. "A Dialectic of Aural and Objective Correlatives." In *The Barbarian Within: And Other Fugitive Essays and Studies,* 26–40. New York: Macmillan, 1962.

——. "Digitization Ancient and Modern: Beginnings of Writing and Today's Computers." *Communication Research Trends* 18 (1998): 4–21.

——. "Disposed in Labels: After Reading a Biography" [poem]. *Sewanee Review* 50.3
(July–September 1942): 302–4.

——. "Do We Live in a Post-Christian Age?" *America* 174.3 (February 3, 1996): 16–18,
29–34.

——. "The Eternal Spring of Thought." *Saturday Review* 42 (August 22, 1959): 26.

——. "Evolution and Cyclicism in Our Time." *Thought* 34.135 (Winter 1959–60):
547–68.

——. *Faith and Contexts: Selected Essays and Studies.* 4 vols. Ed. Thomas J. Farrell and
Paul A. Soukup. Atlanta: Scholars Press, 1992–99.

——. "Father Hecker and the American Situation." In *American Catholic Crossroads:
Religious-Secular Encounters in the Modern World,* 46–66. Westport, CT: Greenwood Press, 1959.

——. *Fighting for Life: Contest, Sexuality, and Consciousness.* Ithaca: Cornell University Press, 1981.

——. Foreword. *Electric Rhetoric: Classical Rhetoric, Oralism, and a New Literacy,* by
Kathleen E. Welch, 13–24. Cambridge: MIT Press, 1999.

——. Foreword. *Faith and Contexts.* Vol. 1: *Selected Essays and Studies, 1952–1991.*
Ed. Thomas J. Farrell and Paul A. Soukup, ix–xi. Atlanta: Scholars Press, 1992.

——. "God's Known Universe and Christian Faith: Pastoral, Homiletic and Devotional
Reflections." *Thought* 66.262 (September 1991): 241–58.

——. "Hermeneutic Encounter in Voice and in Text." Saint Louis University Library
Special Collections. Walter J. Ong Manuscript Collection (Doc MSS 64.1.4.4.2.3).

——. "Hermeneutic Forever: Voice, Text, Digitization, and the 'I.'" *Oral Tradition* 10.1
(March 1995): 3–36.

——. *Hopkins, The Self, and God.* Toronto: University of Toronto Press, 1986.

——. "Hopkins's Articulate Self." In *Hopkins Variations—Standing Round a Waterfall.*
Ed. Joaquin Kuhn and Joseph J. Feeney, 125–29. Philadelphia: Saint Joseph's University Press, 2002.

——. "'I See What You Say': Sense Analogues for Intellect." In *Interfaces of the Word:
Studies in the Evolution of Consciousness and Culture,* 121–44. Ithaca: Cornell University Press, 1977.

——. "Information and/or Communication: Interactions." *Communication Research
Trends* 16.3 (1996): 3–17.

——. *Interfaces of the Word: Studies in the Evolution of Consciousness and Culture.*
Ithaca: Cornell University Press, 1977.

——. Introduction. *A Fuller Course in the Art of Logic Conformed to the Method of
Peter Ramus (1672),* by John Milton. Ed. and trans. Walter J. Ong, S.J., and Charles
J. Ermatinger. In *Complete Prose Works of John Milton,* Vol. 8: *1666–1682,* ed.
Maurice Kelley, 139–407. New Haven: Yale University Press, 1982.

——. "The Jinnee in the Well Wrought Urn." *Essays in Criticism* (1954): 309–20. Reprinted in Ong, *The Barbarian Within: And Other Fugitive Essays and Studies.* New
York: Macmillan, 1962.

——. "Knowledge in Time." Introduction to *Knowledge and the Future of Man: An International Symposium,* ed. Walter J. Ong, S.J., 3–38. New York: Holt, 1968.

———. "Latin Language Study as a Renaissance Puberty Rite." *Studies in Philology* 56.2 (1959): 103–24.

———. Letter to Betty Miller. December 11, 1963. Saint Louis University Library Special Collections. Walter J. Ong Manuscript Collection (Doc MSS 64).

———. Letter to Inge Leimberg. November 29, 1994. Saint Louis University Library Special Collections. Walter J. Ong Manuscript Collection (Doc MSS 64).

———. Letter to James M. Curtis. September 19, 1970. Saint Louis University Library Special Collections. Walter J. Ong Manuscript Collection (Doc MSS 64).

———. Letter to Kenneth Woodward. May 29, 1993. Saint Louis University Library Special Collections. Walter J. Ong Manuscript Collection (Doc MSS 64).

———. Letter to Liz Thompson. October 5, 2001. Saint Louis University Library Special Collections. Walter J. Ong Manuscript Collection (Doc MSS 64).

———. Letter to Maud Wilcox. February 26, 1990. Saint Louis University Library Special Collections. Walter J. Ong Manuscript Collection (Doc MSS 64.1.4.4.1.1).

———. Letter to Parents. 14 Janvier 1952. Saint Louis University Library Special Collections. Walter J. Ong Manuscript Collection (Doc MSS 64).

———. Letter to Randolph F. Lumpp, May 23, 1974. Saint Louis University Library Special Collections. Walter J. Ong Manuscript Collection (Doc MSS 64.1.1.3.6).

———. Letter to Randolph F. Lumpp, June 4, 1974. Saint Louis University Library Special Collections. Walter J. Ong Manuscript Collection (Doc MSS 64.1.1.3.6)

———. Letter to Randolph F. Lumpp, June 10, 1974. Saint Louis University Library Special Collections. Walter J. Ong Manuscript Collection (Doc MSS 64.2.2.1.430)

———. Letter to Rev. Barry J. McGannon, SJ, October 10, 1997. Saint Louis University Library Special Collections. Walter J. Ong Manuscript Collection (Doc MSS 64).

———. Letter to Roman Kowal. February 22, 2002. Saint Louis University Library Special Collections. Walter J. Ong Manuscript Collection (Doc MSS 64).

———. Letter to Sheila J. Nayar. November 13, 2000. Saint Louis University Library Special Collections. Walter J. Ong Manuscript Collection (Doc MSS 64).

———. Letter to Thomas Farrell. March 23, 2001. Saint Louis University Library Special Collections. Walter J. Ong Manuscript Collection (Doc MSS 64).

———. "Letter to Victor J. Vitanza." *PRE/TEXT* 8.1–2 (Spring–Summer 1987): 155.

———. "McLuhan as Teacher: The Future is a Thing of the Past." *Journal of Communication* 31.3 (Summer 1981): 129–35.

———. "The Meaning of the 'New Criticism.'" *Modern Schoolman* 20.4 (May 1943): 192–209.

———. "Metaphor and the Twinned Vision (*The Phoenix and the Turtle*)." *Sewanee Review* 63.2 (Spring 1955): 193–201.

———. "The Myth of Myth: Dialogue with the Unspoken." In *The Barbarian Within: And Other Fugitive Essays and Studies*, 131–45. New York: Macmillan, 1962.

———. "New Definitions in the Humanities: The Humanities in a Technological Culture." Report by the Commission on Trends in Education. *PMLA* 77.2 (May 1962): 76–87.

———. Note to *Language as Hermeneutic*. Saint Louis University Library Special Collections. Walter J. Ong Manuscript Collection (Doc MSS 64).

———. "Notecards." September 30, 1984. Saint Louis University Library Special Collections. Walter J. Ong Manuscript Collection (Doc MSS 64).

——. *An Ong Reader: Challenges for Further Inquiry*. Ed. Thomas J. Farrell and Paul A. Soukup. Cresskill, NJ: Hampton Press, 2002.

——. "Oral Remembering and Narrative Structures." In *Analyzing Discourse: Text and Talk*, ed. Deborah Tannen, 12–24. Washington, DC: Georgetown University Press, 1982.

——. *Orality and Literacy: The Technologizing of the Word*. New Accents Series. London: Methuen, 1982.

——. "Orality-Literacy Studies and the Unity of the Human Race." *Oral Tradition* 2.1 (1987): 371–82.

——. "Philosophical Sociology." *Modern Schoolman* 37.2 (January 1960): 138–41.

——. "Post-Christian or Not?" In *In the Human Grain: Technological Culture and its Effect on Man, Literature, and Religion*, 152–53. New York: Macmillan, 1967.

——. "Preface" to *The Barefoot Expert: Interface of Computerized Knowledge Systems and Indigenous Knowledge Systems*, by Doris Schoenhoff, ix–xi. Westport, CT: Greenwood Press, 1993.

——. *The Presence of the Word: Some Prolegomena for Cultural and Religious History*. The Terry Lectures, Yale University. New Haven: Yale University Press, 1967.

——. *Ramus, Method and the Decay of Dialogue*. Cambridge: Harvard University Press, 1958. Reprint New York: Farrar Straus and Giroux, 1974.

——. *Ramus and Talon Inventory: Short-Title Inventory of the Published Works of Peter Ramus (1515–1572) and of Omer Talon (ca. 1510–1562)*. Cambridge: Harvard University Press, 1958.

——. "Reading, Technology, and the Nature of Man: An Interpretation." *Literature and its Audience*. Special issue of *The Yearbook of English Studies* 10.1 (1980): 132–49. Alabama: University Alabama Press, 1982.

——. "Religion, Scholarship, and the Resituation of Man." *Daedalus* 91.2 (1962): 418–36.

——. "Renaissance Ideas and the American Catholic Mind." *Thought* 29.114 (Autumn 1954): 327–56.

——. Review, *The Book of Memory: A Study of Memory in Medieval Culture*, by Mary J. Carruthers. *Speculum: A Journal of Medieval Studies* 67.1 (January 1992): 123–24.

——. Review, *Information*, by William R. Paulson. *Modern Philology* 87.3 (November 1989): 215–18.

——. Review, *The Noise of Culture: Literary Texts in a World of Information*, by William R. Paulson. *Modern Philology* 87.3 (November 1989): 215–18.

——. *Rhetoric, Romance, and Technology: Studies in the Interaction of Expression and Culture*. Ithaca: Cornell University Press, 1971.

——. "Scholarly Research and Publication in the Jesuit College and University." *Jesuit Education Quarterly* 20.1–2 (October 1957): 69–84.

——. "Secondary Orality and Secondary Visualism." Unpublished lecture presented at the Aquinas Institute of Theology, Saint Louis University, October 6, 1995. Saint Louis University Library Special Collections, Walter J. Ong Manuscript Collection, DOC MSS 64.1.3.6.2.

——. "System, Space, and Intellect in Renaissance Symbolism." In *The Barbarian Within: And Other Fugitive Essays and Studies*, 68–87. New York: Macmillan, 1962.

——. "Technology Outside Us and Inside Us." *Communio: International Catholic Review* 5.2 (Summer 1978): 100–121.

——. "Text as Interpretation: Mark and After." *Semeia: An Experimental Journal for Biblical Criticism* 39 (1987): 7–26.

——. "Time, Digitization, and Dali's Memory." 1994. Saint Louis University Library Special Collections. Walter J. Ong Manuscript Collection (Doc MSS 64).

——. "Voice and the Opening of Closed Systems." In *Interfaces of the Word: Studies in the Evolution of Consciousness and Culture*, 305–41. Ithaca: Cornell University Press, 1977.

——. "Voice as Summons for Belief." In *The Barbarian Within: And Other Fugitive Essays and Studies*, 49–67. New York: Macmillan, 1962.

——. "The Writer's Audience is Always a Fiction." In *Interfaces of the Word: Studies in the Evolution of Consciousness and Culture*, 53–81. Ithaca: Cornell University Press, 1977.

——. "World as View and World as Event." *American Anthropologist* 61 (1969): 634–47.

——. "Yeast: A Parable for Catholic Higher Education." *America* 162 (1990): 347–49, 362–63.

Paine, Albert Bigelow. *Mark Twain, A Biography: The Personal and Literary Life of Samuel Langhorne Clemens*. Vol. 3. New York: Harper & Brothers, 1912.

Paulson, William R. *The Noise of Culture: Literary Theory in the World of Information*. Ithaca: Cornell University Press, 1988.

Picard, Rosalind. *Affective Computing*. Cambridge: MIT Press, 1997.

Ricoeur, Paul. *Oneself as Another*. Trans. Kathleen Blamey. Chicago: University of Chicago Press, 1992.

Riemer, George. "Walter Ong." An edited interview conducted by George Riemer. In *The New Jesuits*, ed. George Riemer, 147–86. Boston: Little, Brown, 1971.

Schmandt-Besserat, Denise. *Before Writing*. 2 vols. Austin: University of Texas Press, 1992.

Schoenhoff, Doris. *The Barefoot Expert: Interface of Computerized Knowledge Systems and Indigenous Knowledge Systems*. Westport, CT: Greenwood Press, 1993.

Soukup, Paul, S.J. "The Contexts of Faith: The Religious Foundations of Walter Ong's Literacy and Orality." *Journal of Media and Religion* 5.3 (2006): 175–88.

——. "*Orality and Literacy* 25 Years Later." *Communication Research Trends* 26.4 (2007): 3–18.

——. "Walter J. Ong, S.J.: A Retrospective." *Communication Research Trends* 23.1 (2004): 3–23.

——. "Why 'Hermeneutic Forever'? Walter Ong and Understanding Interpretation." *Communication Research Trends* 33 (2014): 16–21.

Stahmer, Harold M., Jr. "Speech Is the Body of the Spirit: The Oral Hermeneutic in the Writings of Eugen Rosenstock-Huessy (1888–1973)." *Oral Tradition* 2.1 (1987): 301–22.

——. "Vocal Communication and Technological Society" [Review of Walter J. Ong's *The Barbarian Within*]. *Social Order* 13 (1963): 36–44.

Sussman, Henry. *High Resolution: Critical Theory and the Problem of Literacy*. New York: Oxford University Press, 1989.

Swearingen, C. Jan. "Oral Hermeneutics during the Transition to Literacy: The Contemporary Debate." The Dialectic of Oral and Literary Hermeneutics. *Cultural Anthropology* 1.2 (1986): 138–56.

Tyler, Stephen A. "On Being Out of Words." *Cultural Anthropology* 1.2 (1986): 131–37.

———. *The Said and the Unsaid: Mind, Meaning, and Culture.* New York: Academic Press, 1978.

———. *The Unspeakable: Discourse, Dialogue, and Rhetoric in the Postmodern World.* Madison: University of Wisconsin Press, 1987.

Valesio, Paolo. *Ascoltare il silenzio: La retorica come teoria.* Bologna: Il Mulino, 1986.

van den Berg, Sara. "Current Opportunities in Ong Scholarship." *Communication Research Trends* 33.1 (2014): 4–9.

———, ed. "Centennial Forum on Walter Ong." *Religion and Literature* 44.2 (2012): 152–204. [Essays by Thomas D. Zlatic, Paula McDowell, Twyla Gibson, Jerry Harp, Sheila Nayar, and Sara van den Berg.]

———. "Walter Ong on the Road: Research before the Internet." Centennial Forum on Walter Ong, *Religion and Literature* 44.2 (2014): 152–59.

van den Berg, Sara, and Thomas M. Walsh, eds. *Language, Culture, and Identity: The Legacy of Walter J. Ong, S.J.* New York: Hampton Press, 2011.

Walhout, Clarence. "Christianity, History, and Literary Criticism: Walter Ong's Global Vision." *Journal of the American Academy of Religion* 62.2 (1994): 435–59.

Walsh, Thomas M. "Walter J. Ong, S.J.: A Bibliography 1929–2006." In *Language, Culture, and Identity: The Legacy of Walter J. Ong, S.J.,* ed. Sara van den Berg and Thomas M. Walsh, 185–245. New York: Hampton Press, 2011.

Weeks, Dennis L., and Jane Hoogestraat, eds. *Time, Memory, and the Verbal Arts: Essays on the Thought of Walter Ong.* Selinsgrove, PA: Susquehanna University Press, 1998.

Welch, Kathleen E. *Electric Rhetoric: Classical Rhetoric, Oralism, and a New Literacy.* Cambridge: MIT Press, 1999.

Yates, Frances A. *The Art of Memory.* London: Routledge and Kegan Paul, 1966.

Youngkin, Betty Rogers. *The Contributions of Walter J. Ong to the Study of Rhetoric: History and Metaphor.* Lewiston, ME: Mellen Press, 1995.

Zlatic, Thomas D. "The Articulate Self in a Particulate World: The Ins and Outs of Ong." In *Language, Culture, and Identity: The Legacy of Walter J. Ong, S.J.,* ed. Sara van den Berg and Thomas M. Walsh, 7–30. New York: Hampton Press, 2010.

———. "Faith in Pretext: An Ongian Context for *The Confidence-Man.*" In *Of Ong and Media Ecology: Essays in Communication, Composition, and Literary Studies,* ed. Thomas Farrell and Paul A. Soukup, 239–78. New York: Hampton Press, 2012.

———. "The Persistence of Memory: Picturing Ong's Oral Hermeneutics." *Communication Research Trends* 33.1 (2014): 10–15.

———. "Talking Literature and Religion: Walter Ong." *Religion and Literature* 44.2 (2012): 133–43.

———. "Walter Ong as Teacher: The Conversation Continues." *Explorations in Media Ecology* 1.3–4 (2012): 273–83.

INDEX